THE BUNDY ARCHIVE

*Bernadette Marie Calafell, Marina Levina,
and Kendall R. Phillips, General Editors*

THE BUNDY ARCHIVE

Genealogies of White Masculinity

BRYAN J. McCANN

University Press of Mississippi / Jackson

The University Press of Mississippi is the scholarly publishing agency of
the Mississippi Institutions of Higher Learning: Alcorn State University,
Delta State University, Jackson State University, Mississippi State University,
Mississippi University for Women, Mississippi Valley State University,
University of Mississippi, and University of Southern Mississippi.

www.upress.state.ms.us

The University Press of Mississippi is a member
of the Association of University Presses.

Portions of chapter 1 and chapter 2 originally appeared in
"Duplicity and the Depraved Uncanny in Mediations of Ted Bundy,"
Women's Studies in Communication 44, no. 3 (2021): 340–59.

Portions of chapter 1, chapter 4, and the conclusion originally appeared in
"Serial Murder as Modernist Ritual," *Rhetoric and Public Affairs* 25, no. 3 (2022): 49–74.

Any discriminatory or derogatory language or hate speech regarding race,
ethnicity, religion, sex, gender, class, national origin, age, or disability
that has been retained or appears in elided form is in no way an endorsement
of the use of such language outside a scholarly context.

Copyright © 2026 by University Press of Mississippi
All rights reserved
Manufactured in the United States of America

∞

Publisher: University Press of Mississippi, Jackson, USA
Authorised GPSR Safety Representative: Easy Access System Europe
- Mustamäe tee 50, 10621 Tallinn, Estonia, *gpsr.requests@easproject.com*

Library of Congress Cataloging-in-Publication Data

Names: McCann, Bryan J. author
Title: The Bundy archive : genealogies of white masculinity / Bryan J. McCann.
Other titles: Horror and monstrosity studies series
Description: Jackson : University Press of Mississippi, 2026. | Series:
Horror and monstrosity studies series | Includes bibliographical references and index.
Identifiers: LCCN 2025042009 (print) | LCCN 2025042010 (ebook) | ISBN 9781496860774
hardback | ISBN 9781496860781 trade paperback | ISBN 9781496860798 epub | ISBN 9781496860804
epub | ISBN 9781496860811 pdf | ISBN 9781496860828 pdf
Subjects: LCSH: Bundy, Ted | Serial murderers—United States | Serial
murders—United States | Criminals—United States | Violence in
men—United States | Masculinity—United States | Men, White—United States—Attitudes | BISAC:
TRUE CRIME / Murder / Serial Killers | SOCIAL SCIENCE / Gender Studies
Classification: LCC HV6248.B773 M33 2026 (print) | LCC HV6248.B773 (ebook)
LC record available at https://lccn.loc.gov/2025042009
LC ebook record available at https://lccn.loc.gov/2025042010

British Library Cataloging-in-Publication Data available

CONTENTS

Acknowledgments vii

Introduction: We Are Ted Bundy 3

Chapter 1: Serial Killers as Modern Monsters 23

Chapter 2: Two Teds, One Monster 37

Chapter 3: Ted Bundy, Pornographer 71

Chapter 4: Student Bodies, Campus Rituals 99

Chapter 5: My Art Shall Be My Revenge 125

Conclusion 147

Notes 169

Bibliography 193

Index 217

ACKNOWLEDGMENTS

Although I began this project in earnest during 2019, the idea of writing a book about Ted Bundy had been percolating in my mind for quite some time. It began in the classroom. I owe immense gratitude to students at Louisiana State University who, since 2014, have enrolled in my courses Crime, Communication, and Culture in the Department of Communication Studies and Crime, Popular Culture in the Roger Hadfield Ogden Honors College, and White Masculinity and US Culture in the Women's, Gender, and Sexuality Studies Program. Thank you for indulging my many tangents, laughing at my dumb jokes, and, most importantly, navigating the often unpleasant but always illuminating terrain of crime and gendered violence in US culture. Your collective willingness to embrace discomfort with me on a range of topics, including serial killers, catalyzed the thinking that produced this book. At a time when it is easy to be disillusioned and downright terrified about higher education in the United States, my semesters with you help me rediscover the simple joys of collaboratively working through big ideas.

Equally important to this project's completion have been colleagues who helped me weave the various threads that run through it into something resembling a coherent argument. This includes people who invited me to participate in conference panels where I tried out some of my ideas about Ted Bundy, those who took the time to read early drafts and provide feedback, and many who, in the midst of a conversation about this project or a seemingly unrelated topic, uttered something profound that set my mind on a course that found expression in the following pages. I am surely leaving some people out, but thank you to Bernadette Calafell, Reslie Cortés, Shinsuke Eguchi, Serap Erincin, Josh Gunn, Atilla Hallsby, Leandra Hernández, Matthew Houdek, Jo Hsu, Paul Johnson, Casey Kelly, Amber Kelsie, Jessie Kindig, Stephanie Larson, Marina Levina, Chuck Morris, Tom Nakayama, Kendall Phillips, Erin Rand, Evan Schares, Sarah De Los Santos Upton, and, of course, the two anonymous reviewers who so thoughtfully reviewed this manuscript in its entirety. I am also indebted to Drs. Calafell, Levina, and Phillips in their capacities as editors for the Horror and Monstrosity Studies series. And thank you to the faculty and students of the Rhetoric, Film, and Screen Studies program at Bates College for the opportunity to present some of this work in conjunction with your Foundational Dialogues Program. And many thanks to Jay Childers and Claire Sisco King for your editorial generosity and for publishing earlier iterations of this project in *Rhetoric and Public Affairs* and *Women's Studies in Communication*, respectively. And this project benefited from the financial support of the Department of Communication Studies and College of Humanities and Social Sciences at Louisiana State University.

Working with Emily Bandy at the University Press of Mississippi has been a joy. Thank you for your faith in this strange project. I also benefited from the labor of Amy Atwood, Joey Brown, Corley Longmire, Courtney McCreary, Jai Reaves, and Will Rigby, as well as other staff members at the Press whose names I do not know. Thank you. I am also deeply grateful to Justin Coffman for allowing me to reproduce his artwork in chapter 2. And thank you, Greg Wohead, for entrusting me with access to the video of *The Ted Bundy Project*, which I discuss in this book's conclusion. The value of such generosity from working artists is not lost on me. And my friend and colleague Michael Bibler helped me bring this project to a close when he shared with me the meme I discuss in the book's final pages. I am also indebted to my former barber, Paula Niven, in whose waiting area I discovered the back issue of *Life* dealing with coed dormitories that I reference in chapter 4. At the time, it was a novel bit of nostalgia that helped me pass the time while I awaited my turn in your chair. But, a few years later, I was grateful that such a random dormant memory emerged while I was immersed in this project. And I am grateful for the willingness of the library staff of my alma mater, Homewood-Flossmoor Community High School, to comb through the back issues of the student literary magazine *Edda* so that I might engage with my past writing in this book's fifth chapter.

I am also perpetually indebted to colleagues who aided this project by modeling the kinds of principled criticality, professional integrity, and friendship that I hope I even modestly concretize in this work and beyond. Thank you especially to Karma Chávez, Carmen Kynard, Michelle Massé, Rico Self, and Ersula Ore. And thank you Danielle Bacibianco for your friendship and for inspiring me to live and write openly as a sober academic in recovery.

And then there is family. To my mother, whatever grief and anger I process in these pages, I remain grateful for the parts of my childhood that gave me the space to read, watch, and listen broadly. And thank you for never clearing out my old bedroom, therefore giving me access to a vast teenage archive of journals and embarrassing poetry, which I discuss in this volume's penultimate chapter. And to my sister, Megan, I hope you can receive this book as my attempt to process my own story.

I am also blessed with a strong chosen family. To my Wednesday morning therapy group, you have collectively saved my life more than once. Thank you for hearing me out and allowing me space to grow. And to my fellows in addiction recovery, thank you for teaching me to practice these principles in all my affairs. Thanks to my childhood friends, Clark Bernier and Jim Hatch, for playing key roles in many of the fraught engagements with masculinity I chronicle here. And thank you to the monastic and lay members of the Magnolia Grove Monastery sangha for cultivating what has been an indispensable refuge for me. To Kina Reed, thank you for being a consistent lifeline amid the chaos of everyday life. And to Judith Santano, thank you for inspiring me to live and love in ways that I hope enact the value commitments I espouse in the following pages.

As I wrote this project, I became a parent to two amazing kids. Adrian, your energy, curiosity, and ambition fill me with so much hope for your future. I hope that, as you grow to become a man, you avoid many of the pitfalls I describe in this book. You are a kind and brilliant soul, and I am eager to see those traits blossom. To Stephanie, I adore your emotional intelligence, sense of humor, rebellious disposition, and creativity. To both of you, your presence in my life has introduced me to new parts of myself and, even during the most stressful times, I like this version of me far better than the one preceding our connection.

And thank you to my spouse, nesting partner, coparent, colleague, and collaborator Ashley Mack. You have helped me to flesh out most of the ideas in this book. And you shared the labor of parenting and household maintenance in ways that afforded me time to work on the manuscript. You also bore witness to some of the uglier manifestations of the genealogy I chart throughout these pages. It has not always been easy. I love you—especially today.

Lastly, Ted Bundy kidnapped, raped, and murdered at least thirty young women and girls. In addition to his broader place in the genealogy of white masculinity in the United States, the echoes of Bundy's cruelties reside in the lives of the many families and communities he so violently disrupted. While I have written in the past about the ways rhetorics of victimhood rationalize regimes of domination such as the carceral state, I never want such critique to diminish the overwhelming trauma that men such as Bundy create. For anyone reading this book who experiences the Bundy archive as much more than an abstract concept, I hope you find in these pages a fundamental yearning for a world where Ted Bundy is unfathomable.

# THE BUNDY ARCHIVE

Introduction

WE ARE TED BUNDY

The 2002 film *Ted Bundy* concludes with a montage of young white children, mostly boys, giggling, staring at the camera, and gleefully declaring, "I'm Ted Bundy!"¹ The sole girl in the sequence proudly holds up a dead rodent by its tail, perhaps signaling the role of animal abuse in the evolution of many serial killers.² The montage comes immediately after the film's fictionalized version of Bundy's ex-girlfriend, "Lee," watches television news coverage of his execution with her new romantic partner—a seemingly decent white man who exclaims "Finally!" upon news of the execution, demonstrating his investment in carceral justice and normative masculinity. Lee asks aloud with a shocked, perplexed look on her face as she gazes at the television, "Who *was* Ted Bundy?" With this rhetorical question, that this group of children answer, she reifies the common narrative of Bundy in which the serial killer masqueraded as a normal man even as he kidnapped, raped, and murdered young white women and girls in the Pacific Northwest, Utah, Colorado, and Florida. For those who knew him as a boyfriend, father figure, brother, son, acquaintance, student, and citizen, the question "Who was Ted Bundy?" was common.³ Its implication that the serial killer Florida executed in 1989 was an enigma persists in present-day representations of Bundy.⁴

Concluding a feature film about one of the United States' most ubiquitous serial killers with children yelling, "I'm Ted Bundy!" is provocative, if also tongue-in-cheek and ham-fisted. As one online critic noted, this montage, whether intentionally or not, mimics the final sequence of Spike Lee's 1992 film *Malcolm X*.⁵ Following the scene of the civil rights icon's assassination,

Lee's acclaimed biographical film portrayed a series of children in the African diaspora proclaiming "I am Malcolm X!" to concretize the antiracist radical's genealogy within the ongoing struggle against Black oppression. To be Black, Lee suggests, is to be among Malcolm's kin.[6] Thus, tethering director Matthew Bright's closing sequence to Lee's film frames it as a suggestion that white children are Bundy's progeny—that Ted Bundy is white people's Malcolm X. If Malcolm inspired Black people in the United States to lay claim to their dignity and heritage, perhaps Bundy reveals fundamental truths about whiteness, or at least white masculinity. Maybe he is our champion, our patron saint.

Having viewed every feature film about Ted Bundy multiple times (as I joke with friends, so you don't have to), this 2002 production remains among my favorites. I do not admire it for its quality. *Ted Bundy*'s current rating on the review aggregator site *Rotten Tomatoes* is a tepid 41 percent. The site's "critical consensus" reads, "*Ted Bundy* wastes an impressive performance from Michael Reilly [Burke] on an exploitative film devoid of any social context or depth."[7] Burke indeed commits to a role that requires him to perform numerous onscreen rapes and murders, as well as necrophilic acts. But his portrayal of Bundy as a clumsy sociopath with depraved sexual proclivities disappointed some critics. One complains that Burke plays Bundy "with none of the charm and intelligence that made the real man so creepy and fascinating."[8] Another writer describes this Bundy as "a flabby, slobby pervert . . . with weird sexual deviancies."[9] They add, "Parts of *Ted Bundy* are so gross and exploitative that most viewers will probably feel like taking a shower afterward."[10] Writing for *The Guardian*, Peter Bradshaw writes, "The film just plods blankly along, detailing each slashing and bludgeoning with crude explicitness, and each grisly blow elicits not a gasp of horror but a wince of impatience and distaste."[11]

Although the real Ted Bundy's excesses included performing necrophilia with his victims' corpses until the smells associated with decomposition made doing so impossible, these critics desired a Bundy with more "charm and intelligence" rather than a "pervert" acting on "weird sexual deviancies." They want the thrills of a horror film, rather than the banality of serial sexual violence.[12] In making such demands of the 2002 film, these writers betray sustained public anxieties regarding representations of Bundy. They desire texts about him but prefer to avoid confrontations with the actuality of his sex murders. Prevailing rhetorical norms regarding Bundy characterize him as a killer who employed disingenuous performances of normalcy to conceal his true violent nature. But it is Bundy's violence that I argue resonates with the publics that his archive addresses. To acknowledge such resonance through alternative tellings of the Bundy saga risks disclosing the violence of white masculinity in general. E. Chebrolu writes, "Anxiety emerges when the subject's enjoyment is disturbed because of the breakdown of the symbolic rules that govern the game of fantasy."[13] Critics of Bright's film accuse him of breaking the representational rules regarding Bundy's depravities. It is therefore unsurprising that most mass mediated texts regarding Bundy function in ways that typically obscure the homologies, or structural similarities, between his violent acts and the gendered violence that sustains Western modernity.[14] Of course critics desired a more charming Bundy.

Ted Bundy's production values are terrible, most of its acting is abysmal, and its script is boring and expository. Bright apparently does not care why Bundy did what he did, does not care to accentuate the enduring narrative of a charming and duplicitous killer, and dedicates precious little time to anything approaching social commentary. *Ted Bundy* is a bad and sleazy movie. As such, it is the biographical film that Ted Bundy deserves. And it is the Ted Bundy movie the publics who consume him, of which I am part, deserve. Whereas most other cinematic meditations on Bundy work to contain his story within explanatory frames such as duplicity, trauma, and mental illness, *Ted Bundy* is far more unwieldy. In a negative review of the film for *The New York Times*, Dave Kehr writes, "Bundy is presented as a sympathetic monster whose lack of remorse enables him to act out the impulses that—or so the theory goes, at least—the rest of us are too cowardly and conventional to own up to. He's pure id, running loose in a society that is all repressive superego. And we're supposed to have a sneaky admiration for him."[15]

While Bright would likely dispute that his film sought to induce admiration for Bundy, the script he cowrote with Stephen Johnston is hardly overwrought with explicit condemnations or explanations.[16] He dwells instead at the scene of depravity, to which most cinematic versions of the Bundy story only allude. Bright portrays Bundy slobbering and masturbating outside a woman's window while she undresses. He chronicles in visceral detail Bundy's 1974 kidnapping, rape, and murder of Denise Naslund and Janice Ott after luring them from the beach at Lake Sammamish State Park in Issaquah, Washington. And while mainstream Bundy films have portrayed his attack at the Chi Omega sorority house at Florida State University with minimal detail, Bright characterizes Bundy's attack that evening with gory specificity.[17]

It is possible that some readers will wish to take a shower by the time they are done with this book. Do we really need another book about Ted Bundy? While no academic book, to my knowledge, has a singular focus on Bundy, his ubiquity in popular culture and true crime circles is sufficient to induce eye-rolling rather than interest—or eye-rolling at one's own and/or others' interest. Ted Bundy is a cliché metonym for serial murder in the United States.[18] He is an especially macabre celebrity.[19] But even those among us who wish Bundy would simply disappear from the public scene can recognize that his ubiquity is a site of meaning making and therefore struggle. Although Bundy is a morbid spectacle that fuels some of US civil society's worst collective tendencies, he also, as Claire Sisco King says of celebrity culture in general, creates "space for considering the citational and performative aspects of all forms of self-making."[20] That is, attention toward public obsessions with Bundy and other serial killers informs critical approaches to public culture in general. Bundy's archive discloses the sadistic rot of white masculinity, and, in so doing, offers critical resources for undermining the very investments and practices his cruel legacy concretizes.

While I hope this project will be of greater quality than Bright's film, it will be flabby, slobby, and weird. It may be the book that Ted Bundy deserves, as well as the Ted Bundy book that many of us deserve. In the following pages, I demonstrate how popular and political texts about Bundy, rhetoric from the serial killer himself and others in his orbit, texts with peripheral but nonetheless meaningful linkages to the Bundy saga, and ephemeral embodiments of white masculinity such as Bundy's murders and narratives of my own constitution as a gendered subject are fecund resources for interrogating white masculinity in the United States. Taken in their totality, these texts, fragments, and ephemera coalesce into what I am calling the Bundy archive. By attending to the Bundy archive's rhetorical contours, I explain how it discloses public anxieties about white masculinity and the gendered violence to which rhetorics of white masculinity give expression. The Bundy archive functions as a heuristic for various hegemonic enactments of white masculinity in US public culture. In other words, various "we's" are Ted Bundy and Ted Bundy belongs to various "we's." A libidinal yearning for fungible feminine flesh is what connects them.[21] The Bundy archive is a critical lens that illuminates these linkages.

Ultimately, I am claiming, along with the giggling children at the end of Bright's exploitation film, that we *are* Ted Bundy. But this "we" is not a royal one. Those many bodies and communities who function as raw materials for the sadistic fantasies that characterize white masculinity in Western modernity are not, to be clear, Ted Bundy. Rather, this is a "we" whose affective investments in the violent domination of vulnerable bodies constitute us as subjects and assemble us as publics.[22] Bundy made such a claim in his infamous pre-execution interview with Dr. James Dobson in which he attributed much of his violence to pornography's insidious inducements. According to Bundy, men who succumb to such sadistic temptations are ordinary and everywhere. Said Bundy, "We are your sons, and we are your husbands."[23] As I will make clear in the following pages, I reject Bundy and Dobson's opportunistic crusade against pornography. But Bundy's implicit argument regarding the banality of sexual violence in contemporary US culture is spot on. "We" are your sons. We are the progeny of a sadistic enterprise whose victims' corpses are modernity's foundation. I, to be clear, am part of this "we." My late father is part of this "we." Hence, my use of memoir as a resource for scrutinizing the Bundy archive. And as I document throughout this book, myriad other popular, political, and quotidian enactments of white masculinity constitute this "we." This genealogical approach, which combines the discretely textual and ephemeral experiential, helps map white masculine violence across contexts—especially ones that are less conspicuous than one of Bundy's crime scenes.[24] My hope is that a critical project such as this one is a modest move in the direction of doing gender otherwise.

Serial Killers in US Culture

Since 2019, Ted Bundy has experienced a renaissance. He has again been the topic of numerous films and television series, true crime books, and podcasts. For example, director Joe Berlinger, whose career up to this point had been characterized mainly by documentaries such as the *Paradise Lost* films, directed the Netflix documentary series *Conversations with a Killer: The Ted Bundy Tapes* and the feature film *Extremely Wicked, Shockingly Evil, and Vile*.[25] At year's end, Wikipedia reported that "Ted Bundy" was the online encyclopedia's third most-read entry, outranking topics such as Freddie Mercury and the Chernobyl disaster, which were also foci of major 2019 films and television series, as well as the acclaimed 2019 film *Joker*, which itself dealt with violent white masculinity in controversial ways.[26] The following year, Elizabeth Kendall, Bundy's partner of several years, released an updated edition of her memoir *The Phantom Prince: My Life with Ted Bundy*.[27] Prior to 2020, the book was out of print and demanded triple-digit prices online. Amazon released the documentary series *Ted Bundy: Falling for a Killer* to correspond with the rerelease of Kendall's book.[28] And in 2021, Amber Sealey's *No Man of God* and Daniel Farrands's *Ted Bundy: American Boogeyman* appeared in theaters and via streaming services.[29] Beyond Bundy, mass mediated texts about serial killers and other realms of true crime have proliferated steadily in recent years.[30]

Suffice it to say, US publics remain interested in the Bundy and serial killers in general. While Bundy's recent resurgence in public culture is in large part a function of the thirty-year anniversary of his 1989 execution, the proliferation of texts trading in the Bundy saga did not derive solely from a commemorative impulse nor did such an impulse alone shape the ways these texts have circulated in public life. Rather, Bundy reemerged in a contemporary context characterized by escalating authoritarian and fascist tendencies in mainstream politics and popular culture, other violent expressions of white masculinity, and a mass reckoning with such violence through the #MeToo movement.[31] Rhetorical scholars such as Paul Elliott Johnson and Casey Ryan Kelly have demonstrated the ways Trumpian demagoguery and other rhetorical norms associated with contemporary white masculinity give expression to what sociologist Michael Kimmel calls aggrieved entitlement.[32] Furthermore, Kelly and Joshua Gunn separately claim that the pleasures associated with violating the norms of presidential rhetoric and other closely held rhetorical customs mobilized public investments in Trump.[33]

A key premise of this book is that the enactment and violation of norms are by no means incompatible when it comes to performances of white masculinity. I share Kelly's position that the violation of norms is indeed a hallmark of contemporary white masculinity.[34] But even as Trump and his ilk flout the rhetorical traditions that structure US political and popular culture, such rule breaking rests on a foundation of Western modernity—a foundation that Trumpian politicians and voters, garden-variety liberals, serial killers, and alcoholic fathers enact even as they appear to break sacred rules.[35] Such rule breaking is a function of their power. I agree with Karma R. Chávez who notes that, for historically marginalized communities and their accomplices, it is the structures that mobilize our contemporary political moment that are perverse, not Trump or other white masculine sadists.[36] Many white men are angry because they believe they have experienced the seizure of what was once theirs. Indeed, the injunction to "Make America Great Again" presupposes the once and future possession of that which is now under threat.[37] What links the anxious Trumpian subject and the more assured hegemonic masculine figure is an investment in violently possessing the feminine.[38] Popular representations of Bundy, other serial killers, and gendered violence in general are mutually constitutive with such a political context.

Representations of serial killers are always expressive of their context and therefore function as sites of meaning production. Writing in one of the foundational scholarly texts on serial murder, Philip Jenkins explains that taking stock in the depravities of killers such as Bundy requires coming to terms with the kind of world that produces them: "The question asked is, in effect, What kind of society are we? Or What kind of society have we become? And the various solutions offered have provided great rhetorical opportunities for claims-makers."[39] Mark Seltzer agrees, writing, "The spectacular public representation of violated bodies . . . has come to function as a way of imagining and situating our notions of public, social, and collective identity."[40] Jon Stratton claims the popular figure of the serial killer is "a function of the discursive production of the social."[41] The serial killer, in other words, is a site of hegemonic struggle over various regimes of meaning in civil society, including the very meaning of civil society itself. That is, serial killers are rhetorical.

For example, feminist scholar Jane Caputi has argued that the ubiquity of popular representations of serial killers, the vast majority of whom are cisgender men who murder cisgender women, betrays broader societal investments in misogyny and violence against feminine bodies.[42] Aileen Wuornos, who murdered several men while a sex worker in Florida, on the other hand, figures for some feminist publics as an avenging force against such misogyny.[43] Seltzer situates serial killers in what he calls the United States' "wound culture," in which publics coalesce to consume images and other texts portraying violent rupture.[44] David Schmid makes similar claims when he describes serial killers as contemporary celebrities, or "idols of destruction" who provide audiences with access to the macabre.[45] Brett A. B. Robinson claims that twenty-first-century US representations of serial murder function as media for popular anxieties regarding villainy and vulnerability in the wake of the September 11, 2001, attacks.[46] Others have observed that discourses regarding serial murder characterize killers as entrepreneurial agents or artists whose sadistic deeds function as agency.[47]

Serial killers are thus profoundly nimble in their cultural functions. They can resonate with a range of partisan projects and serve as modalities through which publics reckon with their violent world. Because it is such a flexible category, it is important to emphasize that the meaning of serial murder itself is neither stable nor beholden to criminological frameworks.[48] Most academic definitions of the serial killer characterize him as patterned murderer who kills at least three people over a period and does so for personal gratification.[49] But examining the serial killer as a figure in public culture reveals important inconsistencies vis-à-vis such definitions. For example, Ed Gein is a popular template for fictional serial killers and is himself a prominent figure in the US lexicon of such murderers.[50] However, the State of Wisconsin convicted Gein of "only" two murders following his 1957 arrest. Most of his depravities entailed exhuming women's graves and making clothing, furniture, and other items from their corpses.[51] Gein's notoriety rests largely on what he did to corpses regardless of his role in rendering them as such. Wuornos, on the other hand, murdered seven men who allegedly patronized her for sex. Whereas Wuornos claimed she killed the men in self-defense against rape, the state concluded her primary motive was robbery. Only a small contingent of radical feminists characterized Wuornos's crimes as part of a violent crusade against misogyny. Very little of what we know about her suggests she murdered to satisfy powerful libidinal urges.[52] While Richard Speck murdered eight women in Chicago in 1966, and undoubtedly did so for personal gratification, his mass killing of student nurses occurred during one evening.[53] However, Speck is far more consistent with most popular renderings of serial murder than Wuornos. Whereas a feature film about Wuornos's crimes won critical acclaim and awards, movies about Gein and Speck are usually low-budget exploitation films.[54]

Adopting the words of Michael Calvin McGee, I proceed in this project to understand the serial killer more as process than phenomenon. In his influential work on the figure of "the people" as a rhetorical production rather than empirical fact, McGee wrote, "They are conjured into objective reality, remain so long as the rhetoric which defined them has force, and in the end wilt away, becoming once again merely a collection of individuals."[55] The serial killer's designation is less a function of how many people he murders over a given period of time, or his motives for doing so. Rather, public discourse must constitute a serial killer as such. Bundy's status as one of US history's most consumed serial killers is a symbolic rendering. Therein lies this book's orientation. This is not so much a book about Ted Bundy as it is an engagement with the ways public discourse conjures Bundy vis-à-vis the structures that underlie modernist gender normativity. Bundy functions as a critical, performative, and textual focal point that I situate within various contexts and map onto various structural relations to take stock in how his archive addresses situated publics, and, in so doing, illuminates the sadistic workings of white US masculinity.[56]

The Bundy Archive

The archive, writes Charles E. Morris III, is a "long-standing habitus of the rhetorical critic and theorist."[57] Those of us who attend to the ways discourse addresses, and in so doing constitutes and mobilizes, publics are inherently interested in archives. They are repositories of myriad artifacts the critic might engage, both as focal objects and resources for historical contextualization. While an archive need not necessarily reside in a library or museum, traditional understandings thereof nonetheless characterize it as a discrete collection of artifacts sharing a common frame of historical reference.[58] Based on such criteria, the Bundy archive includes primary documents such as news coverage about Bundy, legal documents, private correspondence between key figures in the case, and popular and political artifacts that help contextualize Bundy and his publics. And for a project such as this, which scrutinizes discourse about Bundy up until and including the present, film and other media presuming to tell the Bundy story in retrospect are also part of the archive.

But this archive is necessarily diffuse. In addition to online journalistic databases, the Bundy archive resides in the state archives of Washington, Utah, Colorado, and Florida.[59] One also finds Bundy artifacts on streaming services and DVDs, and in the form of true crime books written over the past several decades. All these objects are salient parts of the Bundy archive. So too are the scores of raucous fraternity parties occurring on any given weekend in the United States, or the time my father beat me for tracking mud inside the house. Allow me to explain.

Archives are a function of curation. One must build an archive. As such, archives arise as such through rhetorical invention.[60] The archive is never a given. As Jenny Rice argues in her theorization of rhetorical ecologies, "Rhetorical situations involve the amalgamation and mixture of many different events and happenings that are not properly segmented into audience, text, or rhetorician."[61] Similarly, regarding what he calls rhetorical formations, Omedi Ochieng writes, "In this way, the assemblage of a rhetorical formation consists in tracing an itinerary of concrete and spectral formations and their transmutations across time and place."[62] Archives function in similar ways, making it neither easy nor particularly useful to reduce them to location, text, theme, or other constraints. Just as the telling of history is itself a rhetorical undertaking, so too is assembling and marking artifacts that presumably reveal empirical insights into history. A multitude of modalities mediate the archive's every utterance. Cara A. Finnegan explains that one must account for the ways archives "function as terministic screens, simultaneously revealing and concealing 'facts,' at once enabling and constraining interpretation."[63] Archives are the result of selection, categorization, and arrangement that require interpretation by the critic while framing and constraining critical practice itself.

Furthermore, archives are embodied. Emerson Cram explains, "Archival environments *curate* their memorializing context by coordinating visual design, portraiture lining walls, maps, and sculptures with mission statements, and imagine an ideal visitor, their comportment, and capacity to inhabit its spaces."[64] An archive is more than what lies in dusty folders, protective plastic, or microfiche. It is also the rooms and buildings that contain it, the campus or museum that hosts it, and the city or other geographic area it inhabits. Even surveying the Bundy archive on a laptop computer in a college town's local coffeehouse, where young white women and girls who Bundy would have eagerly murdered sip iced coffees, shapes how my white masculine body encounters the historical record. The actuality of their bodies, my speculations about the sexual violence they may experience at a bar or party during the weekend, or coming to and remembering that these women simply want to live their lives without worrying about the fantasies of a serial killer or frat boy, or a professor intellectualizing their vulnerability to sexually violent death all mediate my reading of commentary regarding Zac Efron's portrayal of Bundy eleven years after some of these young women watched him portray Troy Bolton one last time in *High School Musical 3: Senior Year*. These fragments coalesce to produce bodies in feeling whose encounters with the archive will pivot dramatically based on positionality.[65] In this respect, my engagement with the Bundy archive differs significantly from how a young white woman or girl might appraise it. Men such as I need not worry that a man such as Bundy will murder us (although, as a queer kid growing up in the Chicago suburbs, the legacies of Jeffrey Dahmer and John Wayne Gacy loomed large), so regarding him as an intellectually provocative specimen is plausible. Being vulnerable to such violence might make Bundy and his ilk far less "interesting." But even this rendering of the Bundy archive's publics is limited given the number of white women and girls who proclaim interest in or even attraction to Bundy.[66] Bodies concretize infinite specificities that condition subjects' encounters with the Bundy archive.

In her work on cultural memory, Diana Taylor argues that the archive is a limiting heuristic for taking stock in the past and its implications for the present. As a corrective, she posits the repertoire, which "enacts embodied memory: performances, gestures, orality, movement, dance, singing—in short, all those acts usually thought of as ephemeral, nonreproductive knowledge."[67] Attention to ephemera is especially salient for queer and other marginalized histories. Scholars such as José Esteban Muñoz note that the ephemeral is the domain of those who, by virtue of myriad interlocking oppressions, lack access to the dominant written record and other traditionally "archival" means of historicization.[68] Therefore, those fleeting embodied practices whose actualization in the present leaves no written record, but only traces, are themselves media for the dissemination of memory.

For example, Saidiya V. Hartman illustrates that the afterlives of slavery and other modes of oppression manifest through everyday practices of embodiment that are illegible through a mere visit to a place called an archive. Rather, they find expression through the body, and such performances themselves enable critical reappraisals of archives.[69] Such recognition demonstrates that modernist understandings of the archive subordinate antiracist, decolonial, feminist, queer, and other minoritized epistemologies by obscuring the diffuse and ephemeral character of domination and resistance.[70] And as Peggy Phelan argues, refusing the archive or other modalities that may capture and reproduce ephemeral performance is itself a transgressive act against capital's mass-producing logics.[71]

Whereas many scholars of public address privilege the traditional archive as a means of imbuing their scholarship with empirical integrity, insistence on discrete texts and other focal objects presuppose modernist epistemologies.[72] Hartman makes a vital observation in this regard when she writes,

"History pledges to be faithful to the limits of fact, evidence, and archive, even as those dead certainties are produced by terror."[73] The archive's exclusions tend to be the consequence of and alibi for violent erasures. Insisting on a written record is therefore especially limiting for publics whose bodies store their experiences with colonization, genocide, and enslavement.[74] Black and women of color feminists such as Gloria Anzaldúa, Patricia Hill Collins, Audre Lorde, and Cherríe Moraga have demonstrated that the body is a key epistemological resource for theorizing and critique.[75] V. Jo Hsu argues that bodies are repositories for "our experiences and the stories we are given."[76] That is, bodies themselves are archives.[77] Such an orientation toward the archive illuminates the necessarily embodied and therefore contingent ways archival meaning circulates.[78]

Because the archive is never fully anchored and is necessarily embodied, the Bundy archive is more than the sum of texts about the serial killer. It also contains ephemeral gendered performances that precede and follow Bundy. And for that reason, it also contains texts that need never utter Bundy's name.[79] Instead, Bundy himself is a particular instantiation of a historically expansive gender performativity whose grounding logic is violent possession. Ted Bundy is not analogous to other enactments of white masculinity, nor are more quotidian enactments thereof analogous to Bundy. Rather, both give expression to a grounding modernist legacy of racial and gender dominion. Naming the Bundy archive as such is therefore itself a rhetorical maneuver that marks certain objects and genealogies as salient while relegating others to the margins. Naming it the University of Washington (where Bundy stalked and kidnapped many of his victims) archive, the Kimberly Dianne Leach (the twelve-year-old girl who was Bundy's final victim) archive, or the Elizabeth Kendall archive would still lead us to Bundy and his crimes but do so through alternative routes and entail different stops along the way. For example, while Kendall's *Phantom Prince* certainly centers her romantic relationship with Bundy, it is also a narrative of her alcoholism and sobriety that employs many tropes from twelve-step recovery traditions—tropes I can detect due to my own participation in such traditions.[80] Bundy might be a pit stop rather than a destination. His centrality is a function of Kendall's framing, that of her publisher, and the publics who, often already immersed in the Bundy archive, engage her work. And for the purposes of this project, the Bundy archive does not necessarily conclude at the scene of his execution or with the release of the most recent book, movie, or true crime show about him. Its character forms at the point where curatorial and critical invention, as well as embodied knowledge, converge.

Acknowledging the rhetorical character of the archive requires something more of critics than examining the role of curation in the production of archives. It also entails attending to the critic's role in archival practice. In his influential work on fragmentation, McGee challenged the prevailing orthodoxies of public address studies that presumed the centrality of a discrete and finished text as the privileged critical object. Commenting on what he characterized as the inherently fragmented nature of contemporary public discourse, McGee wrote, "I think we can reconcile traditional modes of analysis with the so-called post-modern condition by understanding that our first job as professional consumers of discourse is *inventing a text suitable for criticism*."[81] He also argued that critics should focus "more on the performance of discourse than on the archaeology of discourse."[82] Whereas many scholars in the rhetorical tradition before and since McGee's provocation characterized discourse as an empirical fact upon which the critic directed attention, McGee recast the critic as a rhetor in their own right.[83] For him, the critical object is the progeny of the coalescence of cultural fragments that the critic assembles.

I am advancing the same argument about archives. In other words, the archive as it manifests physically in space and time does not exhaust the boundaries thereof. Rather, the critic plays a central role in creating the archive. Not only does the critic discern what objects warrant archival attention, but they also mark temporal and spatial boundaries. I share Hsu's investment in identifying the "relationships among stories" that an archive contains and mapping them into "constellations" that might illuminate white masculinity's workings.[84] This is not to suggest that the work of archival criticism is purely arbitrary and at the critic's whims. One must make good arguments and justify curatorial choices. Furthermore, McGee's characterization of critical invention carries with it many modernist epistemological entailments. He posits the singular critic as a privileged auditor charged with making coherent a fragmented public culture—one that has been fragmented for colonized and enslaved peoples long before so-called postmodernity.[85] Indeed, ephemera is necessarily fragmentary, as its primary material conduit is the body. Suffice it to say, McGee's categorization of the critic centers Western modernity's individualizing norms of knowledge production.[86]

Critiquing the Archive

Two approaches inform my engagements with the Bundy archive. First, I am a rhetorical critic with investments in critical and cultural communication studies.[87] Rhetoric is both an object of critique and a critical modality itself.[88] Texts such as oratories, important historical documents, advertisements, electoral campaigns, and social movements are usually conspicuously and intentionally rhetorical. That is, they seek to constitute and mobilize audiences in the service of a desired end. But rhetoric is also an approach. In the following pages, I engage many texts that, on face value, may not register as rhetorical. This includes low-budget exploitation films about the Bundy saga, more mainstream cinematic and televisual texts, embodied practices such as Bundy's crimes, and other fragments whose ambitions may appear more popular than persuasive. To approach discourse rhetorically is to attend to their suasive dynamics—that is, their capacity to address, name, and move bodies. A text need not explicitly aim to induce collective action to have rhetorical dynamics. Rhetorical criticism calls attention to such dynamics.

Fundamental to my approach in *The Bundy Archive: Genealogies of White Masculinity* is approaching the Bundy archive itself as a critical object and modality. It is an object in that I attend to the varied rhetorical dynamics therein. Specifically, I examine how fragments of the Bundy archive induce responses to white masculinity. In so doing, I also describe how the Bundy archive functions as a terrain upon which contestations over white masculinity's character occur. But Bundy also serves as a critical modality because I map the patterned, gendered dynamics of white US masculinity he performed onto other cultural artifacts in order to trace the vast and disturbing sadistic logics to which he and so many other artifacts of white masculinity give expression. Specifically, Bundy's *modus operandi* entailed rendering feminine bodies docile and enacting sadistic carnal fantasies upon them. During his death row confessions, Bundy explained that his primary motivation was a desire to possess the women he murdered.[89] By mapping this logic onto other gendered discourses, I illustrate how these impulses that drove Bundy's many cruelties are quite normative in the broader context of white US masculinity. Ted Bundy is no freak.

Second, I employ critical memoir. No critic of the Bundy archive performs critique outside the context of lived experience. Bernadette Marie Calafell invokes McGee when she writes, "In our text construction we may draw on methodologies, such as performance ethnography, which ask us to put our bodies on the line and also be reflexive."[90] For Calafell, situating the body within the archive, not only as a critical modality, but as a fragment in its own right, can serve as a corrective to hegemonic reading practices that devalue the corporeal and experiential. Bodies encounter archives through specific sensory registers that are generative of critical insights.[91] Furthermore, archives exist within networks of power relations that interpellate the critical body in ways that condition its epistemological relationship thereto.[92]

The more I engaged the Bundy archive, the more I saw myself in it. Perhaps it was a moment of recognition that attracted me to Bundy in the first place, as well as so many other true crime artifacts over decades of gendered becoming. I wonder now in hindsight why my middle school library even held a true crime collection, but I devoured it at the time. And while my sustained interest in the cultural politics of crime have always rested in part on investments in social justice, I would be lying if I claimed morbid curiosity was not another salient factor. And more than any of the other sordid characters I encountered in the annals of US criminality, Bundy was consistently among the most captivating.

Taylor writes, "Forms handed down from the past are experienced as present."[93] And form manifests through embodied practices just as surely as the textual fragment. For this reason, I employ reflexive formal criticism as a means of situating myself in the process of identifying and naming structural patterns and homologies in the Bundy archive.[94] My capacity to recognize the gendered repertoire Bundy performed every time he kidnapped, raped, and murdered a young white woman or girl necessarily implicates me in that very repertoire. It suggests a moment of recognition—of identification. Identifying Bundy's many cruelties as expressions of a broader rhetorical ecology of white masculine violence unavoidably implies my complicities in that ecology.[95] To see it, one must know it. If I am going to claim that modernity's gendered economy interpellates other white men in ways homologous to Bundy, then I am in no position to let myself off the hook. If critical insight is in part a function of embodiment and therefore experience, I cannot deny my own yearnings for violent possession that provoke resonance between my desires and popular representations of Bundy's. Nor can I ignore the gendered legacies of which I am progeny. Bundy's archive is also mine. Incorporating memoir and amplifying its homologies with more conspicuously gratuitous expressions of white masculine violence discloses the vast scaffold upon which such violence takes form. That is, memoir helps me better understand Bundy, and Bundy helps me better understand my constitution as a gendered subject. And together, we function heuristically to illuminate the gendered sadism through which Western modernity thrives.

For this reason, I use memoir as a critical framework for engaging the Bundy archive through a rhetorical lens. I employ it as a humanistic mode of inquiry that brings narrative and embodiment, as well as conspicuously aesthetic prose, to bear on public discourse to enable valuable insights and broad social critique.[96] My use of memoir includes visceral recollections of gender performativity, as well as the ways I continue to experience my late father as a gendered subject. I also consider artifacts such as angry high school journals, embarrassing teenage poetry, the sonic and visual landscape of so many gendered memories, and the telling of those memories as salient parts of the Bundy archive.[97] These artifacts are descriptive and evocative in ways that provide experiential critical resources for navigating the Bundy archive.

I also follow the lead of scholars such as Michael Bowman, who writes, "Perhaps what we need now is a method that begins with *pronuntiatio* and *memoria*, that begins with performed memories, and then looks for a style, and arrangement, and a logic of invention that will serve them, rather than vice-versa."[98] What Bowman calls for is an embodied fidelity to memory. But whose memory? And on whose terms? I am mindful that the world does not necessarily need more white men performing their memories and claiming they are a critical apparatus for understanding subjectivity, power, or whatever else critics claim to illuminate through our work. The performance of white memories is canon in Western humanistic inquiry, begging the question of whether I ought to explicitly name what has functioned as an enthymeme for most intellectual work in the Western world.[99] Furthermore, I argue throughout this project that public memory regarding Bundy reifies and rationalizes the gendered violence that sustains Western modernity. If I am right, my use of memoir risks doing the very work I claim to critique. But fidelity to embodiment, at least if one's telos is challenging modernist violence, requires accounting for the individual body's entanglements in popular cultural memory.[100]

This is especially true when the object is gendered violence. While I am a survivor of childhood abuse and an alcoholic home, my wounded flesh is a fraught conduit for critical insights into the Bundy archive. For mine is also a body that has perpetrated harm. I perform modernity's gendered repertoire just as surely as Bundy or other, more conspicuously monstrous exemplars of white masculinity. Returning to Calafell, the work must be vulnerable and reflexive, especially for privileged bodies such as mine.[101] The goal here is not a mea culpa that would only entrench the narcissism already inherent in a project such as this. I do not suggest that my confessional approach in this project absolves me of my complicities within the violent structures I critique.[102] Nor is it a narrow meditation on the ways I, too, have suffered under modernity's heel. Instead, fidelity to memory must not figure it as corporeally or temporally static. Invoking my histories of abuse and alcoholism (as both victim and culprit), as well as misogyny, should not, indeed cannot freeze such memories in the temporal or spatial constraints of my autobiography, nor invest in facile narratives that position me as culprit or victim. As much as I tether murders that occurred in the Pacific Northwest, Utah, Colorado, and Florida during the 1970s to modernity's grander project, I must also situate my performances of gender and sexuality at the scene of Bundy's crimes. And in so doing, my responsibility is not solely to my own story, but also the legacies of gratuitous violence that are Bundy's and mine, and ultimately modernity's. Performing fidelity entails writing in ways that respond to the embodied intellectual traditions of those who endure and resist that of which Bundy and I are progeny and often custodians—and recognizing that, even as I endure and resist, I also perpetrate.[103] My goal regarding white masculinity is, to borrow wording from Louis M. Maraj, to understand and illuminate "how it feels, how it works, how it moves, how it manifests, performs, and churns every day."[104] Dwelling in and writing from such a subject position is how one authors and engages an archive worthy of critique.

Chapter Preview

As I caution above, this is a weird book. In charting a diffuse genealogy of white masculinity through the Bundy archive, its detours will be, by necessity, many. To readers who will at times feel lost, your confusion is largely a function of my own. The proceeding chapters are themselves the result of curation: ways of assembling the Bundy archive that I hope renders its relationship to the broader enterprise of white masculinity and Western modernity legible. Chapter 1 theorizes the serial killer as a distinctly modern monster. In it, I outline a critique of Western modernity that attends closely to its gendered dimensions. Drawing from traditions such as Black studies and decolonial feminism, I argue that white masculinity concretizes modernity's grounding logics of violent possession. In so doing, I also theorize sadistic form as a critical protocol for engaging the Bundy archive.

The book's second chapter takes stock in the most prominent narrative in the Bundy archive; that of a duplicitous killer who masqueraded as a charming man to disguise his true sadistic nature. I critique this characterization of Bundy alongside recollections of my father's often abrupt oscillations between a hard-working man who loved his family and a resentful alcoholic capable of extreme cruelty. Meditating specifically on the work of memorializing my dad after his death, I reflect on how my embodied knowledge of him as a parent makes a clean distinction between his different selves impossible. Similarly, bifurcating the monstrous Bundy from his charming double invests in a normative ideal regarding white masculinity. Such a distinction obscures the myriad ways sadism finds expression in white masculinity's most quotidian iterations.

Chapter 3 examines Bundy's 1989 interview with Dobson the evening before his execution. Dobson, a conservative culture warrior waging a crusade against pornography and other threats to so-called "family values," eagerly circulated Bundy's claim that "violent pornography" motivated him to kidnap, rape, and murder his many victims. Drawing on work by thinkers such as Audre Lorde, I theorize pornography as a modality of sadistic form. Unlike the erotic, which embraces reciprocity, the pornographic is a domain of violent possession whose expressions exceed the generic boundaries of sexually explicit material. As my experiences of becoming a desiring gendered subject through adolescent exposure to pornography reflect, such material concretizes a logic that circulates in myriad contexts. Indeed, Dobson's own investments in possessing and disciplining feminine flesh in the service of his theocratic designs were themselves pornographic. Far from a good-faith meditation on the perils of sexual exploitation and violence, Dobson's interview with Bundy was itself a pornographic text.

Chapter 4 situates the Bundy archive within the cultural politics of higher education. Most of Bundy's victims were college-aged white women, many of whom were pursuing degrees at the time he kidnapped, raped, and murdered them. Chroniclers of the Bundy saga often frame his violence against such women as especially tragic and misogynistic given the normative ideals of feminist futurity his victims embodied. Bundy, as most renderings would have it, was anathema to higher education's lofty ideals. But the university is itself an expression of modernity's designs, making it a purveyor of white supremacist violence. The sadistic form that Bundy made flesh finds expression in beloved cultural artifacts such as the 1978 film *National Lampoon's Animal House* and in the university's hallowed domains where rituals of hazing and sexual violence lay claim to the same kinds of fungible feminine flesh Bundy brutalized. As I note in this chapter, texts such as *Animal House* and the celebratory rituals that occurred during Bundy's 1989 execution reify the same white masculine logics the serial killer enacted at his many crime scenes, even as so many rhetorical norms regarding the university conspire to obscure its myriad cruelties.

In this book's fifth chapter, I discuss shame and vengeance as central themes in the Bundy archive. Numerous versions of the serial killer's story position him as a bitter, pathetic man whose crimes against white women and girls functioned as retaliation against a world that he believed had wronged him. I know something of this rage. Alongside texts that center shame and vengeance as motives that propel the Bundy saga, I revisit journal entries and poetry I composed as a teenager, spying in them the same retributive logics of possession that presumably motivated Bundy, as well as so-called incels such as the mass murderer Elliot Rodger. Also relevant in this domain of the Bundy archive are various popular musical texts, which I situate broadly in the emo genre, that give form and expression to a kind of frustrated yearning searching for vindication. Such artistry does the work of naming and symbolically annihilating the elusive feminine object.

I conclude *The Bundy Archive* with little in the way of satisfying answers. As exhausted as I am with engaging the cultural politics surrounding a white man who kidnapped, raped, and murdered over two dozen white women and girls, I do not anticipate Bundy will go away anytime soon. He will continue to reemerge in the form of a new film, documentary, true crime book, or podcast every few years. And his serial killer brethren such as Dahmer and Richard Ramirez will similarly continue to populate public discourse regarding crime and punishment in the United States. We cannot quit Bundy. But, as I speculate in this final chapter, it may be possible to do Bundy better. Taking stock in several texts that offer explicitly critical engagements with the Bundy archive, I note that the same proximity that is a precondition for sadism potentially manifests as empathy. The fungible feminine flesh that is white masculinity's currency can look and speak back. But even efforts to assemble a more transgressive Bundy archive trade in a relational politics whose emancipatory investments leave others for dead.

Chapter 1

SERIAL KILLERS AS MODERN MONSTERS

Ted Bundy was a creep. Creeps are banal. They are unexceptional. We encounter them daily. In many respects, describing a man who repeatedly performed some variation on the gendered atrocities I catalogue in the following pages as a mere creep is a cruel understatement. Creeps leer at you, make inappropriate comments at work, or ghost you after a one-night stand. They do not do what Bundy did. But to call Bundy a creep is to refuse to categorize his acts as somehow in excess of the more quotidian modes of gendered violence that structure daily life in white Western modernity. To begin with the presumption that Bundy is creep, a mere misogynist, and a garden-variety precursor to more contemporary exemplars of white masculine violence such as the incel movement or Trumpian populism, is to place him among other performances of white Western masculinity and to defy the stark boundaries of monstrosity that distinguish him from his gendered kin.[1]

But to encounter Bundy through the voluminous texts that presume to accurately tell his story or reckon with his relevance in the annals of twentieth-century US history is to meet a monster. Monsters, Calafell explains, are projections of the cruelty that permeates public culture.[2] Rhetorics of monstrosity are modalities of capture that discipline their objects' excesses, even as they accentuate them. Edward J. Ingebretsen writes, "The rhetoric of monstrosity suggests an anxiety that monsters can neither be kept at bay, nor with any certainty confined within the certainties of grammar."[3] Monstrosity is excessive. It is a genre of discourse that betrays the very thing it seeks to subordinate.[4] Thus, the expansive archive of attempts to render Bundy monstrous and therefore anathema to normative gender performativity expresses the anxieties that inspire those renderings in the first place.[5] It is a tell, and therefore discloses a latent and repressed acknowledgment that Bundy is ultimately one of the guys—that we are Ted Bundy. Bundy was famous for his many escapes from state custody, and his public renderings are even more evasive. Thus, in addition to critiquing the rhetorics of monstrosity that conceal Bundy's normativity, this book reads the seams of such discourses to name and engage the more fundamental cruelties public mediations work to obscure.[6]

Sadistic Form

Walter Mignolo explains that custodians of Western modernity employ narratives to conceal the violence of coloniality, or what he calls modernity's darker side.[7] Similarly, the characteristics of the modern masculine ideal function to conceal the monstrosity that structures performativity. The men who occupy the upper echelons of governance wear suits and appeal to the rule of law, even as they serve as stewards of a violent legacy of gendered possession expressed through genocide, colonization, enslavement, incarceration, exploitation, and disposability.[8] The Bundy that meets publics through film, television, and other media offers no such pretense outside his diegetic masquerades as a charming and intelligent man. Whereas those who build empires conceal the structures of sadism that characterize their work, Bundy risks revealing such structures in their totality.[9] If he is a monster, he is modernity's monster. His singularity is a myth.

Rhetorical form describes patterned suasive expressions that exist in the public imaginary. As such, it structures audience encounters with cultural artifacts.[10] Formal criticism is not an empirical taxonomy of discourse, but instead a humanistic, even artistic, approach to scrutinizing texts.[11] In other words, critics bring form to bear on discourse toward critical ends. Sadistic form figures cruelty as pleasurable violence against prone and fungible, or interchangeable, bodies.[12] In so doing, it organizes and mobilizes affective investments in Others' suffering and is therefore constitutive of publicity.[13] The *Oxford English Dictionary* traces *sadism* to 1818 when the poet Thomas Moore wrote, "There is at present a society of Debaucheries in Paris founded upon the principles contained in [Marquis de Sade's novel] *Justine* . . . , which they call Sadism."[14] The *OED*'s main entry reads, "Enthusiasm for inflicting pain, suffering, or humiliation on others," adding, "a psychological disorder characterized by sexual fantasies, urges, or behaviour involving the subjection of another person to pain, humiliation, bondage, etc."[15] Whereas an indifference to others' suffering may characterize garden-variety cruelty, sadism depends on such suffering. That is, it entails the explicit enjoyment of others' pain. But Calum Lister Matheson challenges the *OED*'s notion that sadism is a mental illness. To the contrary, he explains, "When I refer to sadists or sadistic subjects this is not a diagnosis of any individuals because these subjects are conduits for discourses that exceed them and their speech is a contingent, rhetorical manifestation of a larger grammar that carves the channels for the flow of desire."[16] The sadist is not an abnormal pervert, but an ordinary creep who expresses a gleeful cruelty that permeates modern life.

Thus, critical engagements with sadistic texts illuminate cruelties that structure Western modernity in general. To wit, Matheson writes, "If speech reveals more about desire than the speaker intends, we should expect this to be especially true for endlessly verbose sadistic subjects who rely on speech to enact their rituals of enjoyment."[17] But the sadist's rhetoric need not be particularly verbose. Arthur Leonoff explains, "We can further define sadism not by its behavioural expression or degree but by its superordinate aim of achieving self-definition and ultimate narcissistic survival through the psychic or even physical degradation and annihilation of the object."[18] Such cruelties circulate in the formal networks that comprise the necessarily gendered violence of quotidian modernity. Attending to sadistic form reveals homologies between what occurred at Bundy's many crime scenes and other acts of sadism that constitute public belonging in US modernity. Barry Brummett describes homologies as "formal parallels among seemingly disparate things or experiences."[19] Illuminating common formal characteristics between expressions of sadism discloses how a figure such as Bundy gives expression to the same kinds of cruel affects as, for example, a military superpower waging warfare against a poor and colonized part of the world, elected officials characterizing the cruelties of austerity as freedom, or a cismasculine university student or professor pursuing sexual conquests with little regard for consent.

While a serial killer's proclivities might bear little resemblance to the daily workings of normative white Western masculinity in the United States, they adhere to a performativity whose structure characterizes such quotidian gendered expressions. Caputi describes serial murder as nothing less than "a paradigmatic phenomenon of the modern period."[20] Men such as Bundy are not perversions of Western modernity, but actualizations thereof. They give particularly macabre expression to a misogynistic culture in their compulsive enactments of fatal sexual violence against feminized bodies.[21] Furthermore, Caputi claims, their popular ubiquity is also a function of the misogyny that permeates public life. In other words, publics consume that which gives expression to collective misogynistic fantasies.[22]

All violence in US public culture is gendered. Carine M. Mardorossian explains, "Violence does not have to be of an explicitly sexual nature or even entail verbalized gendered invectives to implicate a subject who seeks to occupy the dominant masculine position through the subordination of another (who is in the feminine position)."[23] Klaus Theweleit makes a similar claim when he writes, "The sexuality of the patriarch is less 'male' than it is deadly, just as that of the subjected women is not so much 'female' as suppressed, devivified."[24] In her decolonial feminist work, María Lugones writes, "The colonized became subjects in colonial situations in the first modernity, in the tensions created by the brutal imposition of the modern, colonial, gender system."[25] She adds, "We see the gender dichotomy operating normatively in the construction of the social and in the colonial processes of oppressive subjectification."[26] Sarah Deer similarly observes, "Sexual assault mimics the worst traits of colonization in its attack on the body, invasion of physical boundaries, and disregard for humanity."[27] While a libidinal economy underwrites the gendered violence that characterizes white Western modernity, such violence is not inherently tethered to a specific kind of body—only a specifically gendered and fungible body. Gendered imposition functions to produce dichotomies that naturalize violence downward. It is ultimately the relations between bodies that constitute gender normativity and the violence thereof.[28]

To be white, Western, and masculine is to yearn to possess bodies and land—all of which are always already feminized relative to the performative masculinity that characterizes the sovereign.[29] Aileen Moreton-Robinson explains that "possessive logics" structure white Western notions of sovereignty. She writes, "Possession and nationhood are thus constituted symbiotically."[30] Just as the more traditional colonizer does, the serial killer seeks and exercises sovereignty over feminized fungible flesh.[31] He is therefore an expression of what Achille Mbembe describes as "the slaving logic of capture and predation" that manifests through the containment of Black and other racialized bodies, seizures and occupations of land, the ideological durability of coloniality, and the macabre sexualized desecration of feminine flesh.[32] Thus, the individual serial killer may enact his own distinct monstrosity at the level of narrative, but his deeds are also a variation on a grander form of white masculine performativity whose violent legacy is modernity.[33]

Eduardo Subirats explains, gratuitous violence is "the most privileged spiritual expression" of sovereignty. And Frank B. Wilderson III theorizes such violence as foundational to anti-Blackness, which, for him, is itself fundamental to Western modernity's ontology. He writes, "The violence of slavery is repeatedly checked, subdued into becoming a contingent violence for that entity which is beginning to call itself 'White' at the very same moment that it is being ratcheted up to a gratuitous violence for that entity which is being called (by Whites) 'Black.'"[34] The serial killer is therefore surely a salient expression of the Western modernist enterprise.[35] He is a sadist and a collector, as are so many others who perform white masculinity in Western modernity.[36] And just as the colonizer or capitalist knows no other logic than expansion, the serial killer will always require new bodies to consume.

To Have and Destroy

A core pattern of the serial killer's sadism—indeed a common marker of virtually all serial killers—is a drive to possess. Bundy and his peers, such as Edmund Kemper and Dahmer, attest to the salience of having and controlling the bodies they hunted and destroyed. Some serial killers are collectors in that they retain body parts, or pieces of clothing or jewelry. Others take photographs and some return to the dump site. In a televised interview, Dahmer explained that he murdered and ritualistically mutilated seventeen young men and boys "not because I was angry with them, not because I hated them, but because I wanted to keep them with me."[37] Consistently, serial killers explain to lay and professional audiences that they sought complete control over their victims' bodies to fulfill their desires. They are curators of macabre experiences that, for them, produce actualization. During one of his confessions, Samuel Little, who, by official numbers, is the most prolific serial killer in US history, recalled his strangulation murder of a woman in Arkansas, laughing and explaining, "She is fighting for her life, and I'm fighting for my pleasure."[38]

Several years ago, during a discussion about the cultural politics of serial murder in my course on crime, communication, and culture, a student raised his hand. He said, "You literally cannot describe what Ted Bundy did." For this young white man, the deeds of another white man are so depraved that they exceed the limits of language. Such an assessment holds with most texts about Bundy. Authors, filmmakers, and podcasters rarely dwell at the scene of the crime. They trade instead in implication and vague verbal description. But mapping Bundy's place in the cultural politics of white masculinity requires a confrontation with the crime scene.

I recognize that reproducing atrocities such as Bundy's holds many entailments. In her influential discussion of anti-Black violence in the work of Frederick Douglass, Hartman writes, "I have chosen not to reproduce Douglass's account of the beating of Aunt Hester in order to call attention to the ease with which such scenes are usually reiterated, the casualness with which they are circulated, and the consequences of this routine display of the slave's ravaged body."[39] My goals in critiquing serial murder resemble Hartman's work in that we both chart genealogies of sadism across a range of contexts. But for this project, attending to the specificities of the serial killer's violent acts is necessary to understand how men such as Bundy enacted sadistic form. While Hartman subordinated the grotesque to name the anti-Black violence of the quotidian, I amplify excesses such as Bundy's to map them onto Western modernity's other, more banal, sadistic rituals. Furthermore, while readers may find my descriptions of Bundy's crimes disturbing and problematic, it is such a response to serial murder that I challenge. Disgust toward the serial killer often conceals some audiences' deep affective investments in his sadistic acts. In other words, such responses betray anxiety regarding the actuality of such violent investments.[40] Regarding popular texts about serial murder, Philip L. Simpson writes, "These texts dramatize the fears and lusts of the flesh in a modern world undergoing an intellectual crisis of representation."[41] Texts regarding killers such as Bundy offer publics opportunities to satisfy their lusts, or what Kelly calls "obscene enjoyment," through excessive stories of sadistic form while providing escape routes that allow audiences to disavow serial murder as a modernist enterprise.[42] The result is the benefit of plausible deniability for publics who consume films, television shows, podcasts, fan fiction, meme pages, and other texts about men such as Bundy.

Bundy preferred to identify victims well in advance of kidnapping them, although he would sometimes murder hitchhikers or other young women and girls he encountered by chance.[43] He often self-medicated with alcohol to reduce his inhibitions. In some cases, he feigned injury or falsely identified as an authority figure such as a police officer to earn his targets' trust and lure them to his Volkswagen Bug. There, he would retrieve a tire iron or crowbar he hid in advance and knock the woman unconscious with a blow to the head. Other times, he kidnapped victims as they slept at home or subdued them by surprise. Once he immobilized and secured the woman inside his vehicle, he drove, often several hours, to an isolated area he had selected in advance, although sometimes he brought them to his apartment or a hotel room. Such places were usually heavily wooded parts of the Cascade Mountains or other scenic areas of the places where he operated.

Here he would remove the young white woman from his car. If she was sufficiently lucid, he might demand that she undress and get on her hands and knees. With the woman perhaps seeking to negotiate with the strange man she previously thought needed help carrying books to his car or was working in his official capacity as a state agent, Bundy sometimes began taking photographs. He later disclosed that he kept these mementos in a shoebox in the basement of the Salt Lake City house where he rented an apartment. Although police searched his unit following his first arrest, they did not venture into the basement. Upon making bail, Bundy retrieved and destroyed the shoebox's contents.

Bundy then undid his pants and began raping the young white woman from behind as he strangled her to death with a garrote.[44] This practice of penetrating the young women and girls he murdered as he asphyxiated them was among his most treasured rituals, for their writhing, dying, and prone bodies excited him immensely. In his descriptions of these murders, Bundy expressed what journalists Stephen G. Michaud and Hugh Aynesworth called a "deep, almost mystical, satisfaction" in the act of killing.[45] Bundy explained shortly before his execution that when one person murders another, "You're looking into their eyes and basically, a person in that situation is God! You then possess them and they shall forever be a part of you."[46] Quoting FBI profiler Bill Hagmaier, to whom Bundy likely disclosed the most about his crimes, Michaud and Aynesworth add, "He said that even after twenty or thirty [murders] that it's the same thing, because you're the last one *there*. He said, 'You *feel* the last bit of breath leaving their body.'"[47] Bundy imbued his onanistic assaults with a spiritual character that rendered his cruel acts sacred.

In addition to taking great pains to conceal his crime, Bundy performed many postmortem rituals to satisfy his desire to absolutely dominate the feminine bodies he collected. During the days following a murder, he returned to the victim's corpse to take more photographs. He engaged in necrophilia and decapitated several of his victims, sometimes keeping the heads as totems. Shortly before his execution, he explained to Hagmaier, "If you've got time, they can be anything you want them to be."[48] Regarding the photographs, Bundy said, "When you work hard to do something right, you don't want to forget it."[49] Suffice it to say, acts of murder and necrophilia were sources of boundless imagination, entrepreneurial ambition, and spiritual ecstasy for Bundy.[50] They were rituals whose patterns Bundy savored and repeated. Since his 1989 execution, numerous publics have adopted their own practices of serially reproducing the Bundy archive through film, television, true crime writing, podcasts, and other media. But fundamental to the archive is the scene of the crime, through which the violence the archive enacts and conceals becomes manifest.

Besides the serial killer's violent compulsions, other possessive yearnings that underwrite white Western modernity operate from a place of sadistic libertine lust. One of Western modernity's most enduring thinkers regarding such matters, the Marquis de Sade, spied an intimate connection between eros and sovereignty. He wrote, "There is not a living man who does not wish to play the despot when he is stiff."[51] Seeking and satisfying one's libidinal urges, Sade claimed, was a kind of conquest. Regarding the aroused despot's proclivities, Sade continues, "It seems to him his joy is less when others appear to have as much as he . . . he would like to be the only one in the world capable of experiencing what he feels."[52] Matheson similarly explains that the sadist's pleasure derives from issuing "a threat to a specific object that the sadist imagines the other to enjoy."[53] Dominion is the sadist's province.

Many writers have found in Sade's work a libidinal theory of modernity. In her essay on his legacy, Simone de Beauvoir wrote, "Sade a hundred times insisted upon this point: it is not the other's misfortune that excites the libertine, it is knowing that he authored it."[54] Lisa Downing explains that Sade was part of a broader Western intellectual tradition that especially characterized the murderer as an exceptional subject, whether for his unrelenting individuality, depravity, or both. She writes, "In these aesthetic modes, the murderer paralleled the artist and genius as exceptional and exempt from adherence to ordinary morality."[55] Similarly, Maggie Nelson observes that figures such as Sade who posited cruelty as a modality for self-actualization imbued it with a seemingly mystical quality.[56] For the likes of Sade, the unrepentant sadist is one whose ingenuity and ambition untethered him from social norms and enabled him to embrace pleasure.

During a scene in director Pier Pasolini's controversial 1975 adaptation of Sade's work, *Saló, or the 120 Days of Sodom*, a fascist kidnapper pulls the trigger on an unloaded pistol he pointed at a naked and imprisoned young man's head. When the prisoner flinches as the pistol hammer clicks, the captor scolds his captive, "Fool, how could you believe I'd kill you? Don't you know we'd want to kill you a thousand times to the limits of eternity if eternity has any?"[57] The compulsive drive of the libertine, the sadist, the serial killer, and other embodied expressions of modernity's gendered monstrosity all seek to repetitiously bask in the glory of their invention—a desire that sadistic form renders coherent.[58] The notion of an autonomous agent, or sovereign state, joyfully realizing his cruel desires is expressive of the individualism and administrative politics of Western modernity.[59]

Subirats argues that sadistic acts such as torture, which are always already gendered, are one among many depraved "expressions of human dominance" which take myriad forms in public life.[60] He also notes that "the secret sadist society is a visionary anticipation of the totalitarian organization inherent to contemporary global military and political bureaucracies."[61] In other words, Subirats claims, spectacles of sadism express the same logics that structure sovereign cruelties that persist when publics read them as banal and normative. Scholarly and artistic reckonings with European fascism, Western colonialism, and US American slavery have observed such sadistic libidinal impulses at the heart of sovereign violence. Theodor Adorno and Max Horkheimer wrote, "The less danger to the one on top, the more unhampered the joy in the torments he can now inflict: only through the hopeless despair of the victim can power become pleasure and triumphantly revoke his own principle, discipline."[62]

Regarding the role of anti-Blackness in structuring civil society, Wilderson writes, "This violence which turns a body into flesh, ripped apart literally and imaginatively, destroys the possibility of ontology because it positions the Black in an infinite and indeterminately horrifying and open vulnerability, an object made available (which is to say fungible) for any subject."[63] In other words, the condition of Blackness within Western modernity is to be prone, fungible, and therefore subject to accumulation and exchange.[64] Acts of gratuitous violence that objectify bodies in such a way need not target a body explicitly racialized as Black to operate within the formal economy of anti-Blackness.[65] Anti-Blackness is the condition of possibility for dehumanization in Western modernity.[66] Contextualizing objectifying violence within the anti-Blackness and colonialism that structures modernity illuminates the homologous relationships between seemingly disparate acts of cruelty. Even though Bundy murdered white women and girls, his crimes operated within a civilizational context of anti-Blackness. Sadism against Black bodies structured the power relations in which Bundy participated each time he subordinated some body to his sadistic designs.

The joys of cruelty are also constitutive of publicity. Cristina Beltrán makes this observation regarding the suffering of migrant bodies. She writes, "For those invested in an ideology of whiteness, racial exclusion, violence, and domination *produce* a sense of membership, creating a commonsense understanding of community, opportunity, futurity, and possibility."[67] Whereas some publics coalesce around affective divestments from the suffering of Others, many regard suffering as salient because of the joy it induces.[68] Kumarini Silva explains that cruelty is often an expression of "love of country and family" that therefore figures violence against Others as an affirmation of publicity rather than a solemn remainder thereof.[69] Marina Levina explains, "As intensity, or an emotional force which acts upon the body, cruelty emerges out of an encounter between the self and Other."[70] Matheson echoes Levina, writing, "The critical aspect of sadism is that the sadist can affectively occupy the fantasy of the victim's suffering."[71] Levina adds, "Cruelty therefore makes us consider not only what power is, but also and even more importantly, what power *feels* like."[72] Power, expressed as cruelty, can overwhelm the body that performs or consumes it with ecstasy. In Johnson's wording, cruelty has the capacity to "generate more felt personhood for the antagonist."[73] Regarding texts about serial murder, Annalee Newitz writes, "We might postulate that part of the pleasure an audience gets out of consuming serial killer narratives is in the way serialized homicidal crimes seem so well-adapted to the mass cultural form."[74] Serial murder shares with other kinds of cruelty a common formal sadistic character that finds pleasure in the application of violence to prone and fungible bodies.[75]

Economies of Sadism

While often lacking in conspicuous Sadean excess, the realms of economics and governance also function vis-à-vis sadistic form.[76] In this way, sadistic form need not be the province of gruesome excess alone. Describing it as a "market regime of governance," Robert Asen explains that contemporary advocates for neoliberalism posit the market as "a model for human relationships, politics, and society."[77] By reconstituting individuals from stewards of the public good into autonomous entrepreneurial subjects, neoliberalism names the individual as the historical agent par excellence.[78] Jennifer McClearen explains that neoliberalism constitutes distinctly gendered subjects through regimes of masculinity "emphasizing individualism, competition, and entrepreneurship within the framework of free market capitalism."[79] Furthermore, Asen and Kelly explain that whiteness functions as a cornerstone of neoliberal governance, functioning to entrench the regimes of domination that make logics of exploitation and disposability cohere.[80] Emerging in the late 1970s and early 1980s with the political ascents of Ronald Reagan and Margaret Thatcher, neoliberalism is, by bipartisan consensus, the governance model that structures contemporary capitalism.[81]

Given his investment in the autonomous and ruthless pursuit of individual gratification, the serial killer is a quintessential neoliberal subject.[82] At least one of neoliberalism's intellectual forbears understood this. Early in her career, Ayn Rand, the novelist and self-fashioned philosopher whose works such as *Atlas Shrugged* and *The Fountainhead* anticipated neoliberalism and remain influential among US American conservatives, praised the US murderer William Edward Hickman.[83] In 1927 in Los Angeles, Hickman kidnapped twelve-year-old Marion Parker and demanded ransom from her wealthy parents. However, Hickman never intended to return the child. Instead, he murdered and dismembered her before the scheduled ransom exchange.[84]

Like Bundy, Hickman died for killing a child and public sentiment cheered news of his hanging. But Rand regarded Hickman as an actualized Nietzschean "Superman" who, in the spirit of her own philosophy, expressed no remorse for murdering Parker and regarded others as pawns in the pursuit of his desires. While she claimed that Hickman's crimes represented a distortion of her normative ideal, Rand nonetheless regarded him as an embryonic basis for the kinds of men who populated her later work. Such a character, Rand wrote, was "a Hickman with a purpose. And without the degeneracy."[85] The sadistic drives that mobilized men such as Hickman were, in Rand's estimation, the raw material for building a society rooted in individualism and self-actualization.[86] For this reason, Rand proceeded to rhetorically finesse Hickman's macabre impulses and enact them through her writing.

I am not suggesting that contemporary apologists for neoliberalism privately idolize violent sadists such as Hickman or Bundy. However, some domains of the neoliberal archive suggest otherwise. For example, China Miéville observes a proliferation of discourse in the realms of business and finance characterizing sociopathy as a desirable trait for success.[87] The rise of the sadist as a neoliberal hero also appears in popular critiques of contemporary capitalism. Patrick Bateman, the serial killing main character in Brett Easton Ellis's controversial novel *American Psycho*, and its 2000 cinematic adaptation, functioned as an allegory for neoliberal consumerist ethics taken to their logical ends.[88] Gordon Gekko, from Oliver Stone's *Wall Street*, served a similar, albeit less gruesome role.[89] Of course, Ellis and Stone sought to critique neoliberal greed. The texts Miéville scrutinizes, on the other hand, lack such irony. Ultimately, there is a formal symmetry between the libertarian dogmas that characterize philosophies such as Rand's and serial killers such as Bundy. As Johnson explains, "This need to witness the suffering of others is compensatory for neoliberalism's intolerance of a common good, insofar as there is no shared realm that might provide a point of anchorage and psychological comfort."[90] Rand disclosed such a homology in her praise of Hickman, identifying in his excesses the same myopic investment in personal ambition that she exalted in her writings. And she did so without Ellis or Stone's satirical ambitions. While neoliberalism's legacies include sadistic economic policies and foreign policy adventures masquerading as freedom and liberation, Rand said the quiet parts out loud.[91] The key difference between Rand and Bundy is that the former's intellectual framework for expressing her investments in the ruthless pursuit of self-interest was able to cultivate a philosophy of governance and economics that did not exceed the decorous boundaries of Western civil society. Instead, neoliberalism is decorum.

We Are Ted Bundy, Redux

While the nuances of sadistic fantasies can vary dramatically, the fundamental impulse that underwrites them is remarkably consistent and imbued with almost mystical qualities. Whiteness, which is always gendered in ways that center the masculine, demands constant expansion and therefore possession of Other bodies.[92] And possession must occur by violently emptying the feminine body of agency. Theweleit explains that the masculine sovereign accomplishes this by "robbing the woman of her identity as an object with concrete dimensions and a unique name. Once she has lost all that and is reduced to a pulp, a shapeless, bloody mass, the man can breathe a sigh of relief."[93] Matheson similarly argues, "The sadist's identity ... depends for its enjoyment and therefore coherence on the presence of something that it can negate."[94] And because this demand for possession and incapacitation is antagonistic vis-à-vis the interests of Black, brown, and Indigenous feminized bodies, Wilderson argues that it is "the foundation on which all subsequent conflicts in the Western Hemisphere are possible."[95] The workings of expansion and possession are violent, and the fatal suffering of feminized flesh is the source of sovereign enjoyment.[96]

To conclude that Bundy is an actualization, rather than a monstrous perversion of normative white Western masculinity is to implicate the entire project thereof. It is to understand mediations of Bundy and his depravity as uncanny in their resonance with the quotidian.[97] Such an argument denies the monster's singularity.[98] It resists what Darrel Wanzer-Serrano calls "a perpetrator perspective" that allows publics to lament modernity's cruelties while never reckoning with the ways such evils saturate the normative just as surely as the conspicuously excessive.[99] At times when I discuss this project with others or present it to academic audiences, some express concern that I am painting white men with too broad of a brush. Such critique is curious on its own terms given the Western humanities' investments in positing the specificities of white cismasculine experience as universal heuristics for theorizing the social. Writers in rhetorical studies such as Sarah Baugh-Harris, Andre E. Johnson, Morris, and Wanzer-Serrano explain that the archives of public address and theory are overwhelmingly white, cismasculine, and heterosexual.[100] Nonetheless, they historically function as synecdoche for human symbol use in general. But my suggestion that a man who kidnapped, raped, and murdered over thirty young white women and girls is a representative anecdote for modernity's darker side is, to individuals who hold such canonical investments, an essentialist step too far. Just as those who defend the efficacy of studying minoritized archives and epistemologies perform work that is allegedly too niche, my deep dives into the macabre dare not overstate the explanatory power of what I find.[101] Universals should flatter, not indict.

Recognizing Bundy as unexceptional acknowledges sadism's central role in the performativity of white Western masculinity and therefore functions as a critical heuristic for discourses that attempt to reckon with this centrality.

Texts about Ted Bundy induce consumption from the publics they address. Indeed, Bundy's prominence among US history's other serial killers, many of whom claimed considerably more victims than he, suggests narratives about him address publics in ways those regarding his peers do not. Such consumption, I argue, is a function of Bundy's uncanny resonance with the sadism that structures white Western masculinity in general. In other words, publics consume texts about Bundy because such texts appeal to the libidinal impulses that characterize white Western modernity. But because Bundy also risks disclosing the extent of white Western modernity's depravity, texts trading in his crimes must also render such consumption permissible by enabling publics to disavow Bundy even as they consume him. We name him a monster to conceal our own monstrosity.[102] And in narratives about Bundy, the monster always gets the electric chair in the end.[103] Such just desserts enable the publics who consume the Bundy archive to deny the ways his violence might implicate us.[104] Doing so absolves modernity of its violent gendered legacies. The critical work that follows traces those strategies of disavowal and performs accountability to those legacies.

Chapter 2

TWO TEDS, ONE MONSTER

The founders of Alcoholics Anonymous described the prototypical alcoholic as "a real Dr. Jekyll and Mr. Hyde," explaining, "He may be one of the finest fellows in the world. Yet let him drink for a day, and he frequently becomes disgustingly, and even dangerously anti-social."[1] Invoking the fictional figures of Jekyll and Hyde implies that the alcoholic is a split subject whose nonintoxicated self is a kind and normal person whose Freudian ego keeps them in check. But with sufficient imbibing, the alcoholic descends into destructive chaos. They become all id. But later in the recovery fellowship's canonical text, the authors explain, "Our liquor was but a symptom. So we had to get down to causes and conditions."[2] In other words, the founders of Alcoholics Anonymous and subsequent practitioners of twelve-step recovery understood that an addict's worst excesses were an amplification of what was already there. Drugs and alcohol did not create dangerous impulses but simply loosened the restraints that prevented their actualization. For this reason, twelve-step recovery hinges on the capacity to interrogate one's very essence and not simply blame alcohol and other substances or compulsions for past transgressions.

When my father died from cancer in 2017, I helped my mother and sister prepare the visitation and funeral. Among my responsibilities was preparing a digital photo montage that would play on a large television screen at the funeral home. My family's visual archive was substantial. Decades worth of photo albums eventually gave way to a vast collection of digital pictures. I surveyed smiling images of my father flanked by my sister and me, our mother, other family, and friends. Often, he was holding a beer in his hand, and I remembered the tension and trauma that those smiles often concealed, as well as the authentic joys they conveyed. I also noted that there were no visual artifacts of the many times he was drunk and asleep on the living room couch or, for example, the time he allowed my sister and I—both in elementary school—to drink alcohol at a relative's house only to beat us later that evening for misbehaving.

I was in my ninth month of sobriety during my father's funeral, and I had come to detect echoes of him in my past behavior. Especially pronounced was our tendency to keep secrets. We went to extraordinary lengths to conceal those elements of ourselves we could not shake, even when they caused us considerable shame. My father sloppily hid his drinking from my mother, my sister, and me. I frequently heard clinking glass in the cooler he kept in the back seat of his car. His forced early retirement from the US Postal Service followed decades of stealing mail. The news was not especially shocking since approximately three quarters of my CD collection came as unexpected and unsolicited gifts from him. And his explanations for the occasional appearance of gift cards rarely cohered. But all of us, my dad, my mom, my sister, and I kept quiet. I loved having so many CDs. And my mom loved the gift cards. And I imagine my dad needed desperately to compensate for the myriad disappointments of US working class life in the late twentieth century. His mail theft was a crime hiding in plain sight whose evasiveness was as much a function of our willful ignorance as his craftiness.

For my part, I typically concealed my worst alcoholic excesses by attempting to weave them into daily life. My trusty flask manifested as a tongue-in-cheek homage to a kind of dignified alcoholism rather than the plain fact that I wanted to always have booze available. Over time, I convinced myself that refilling a glass of bourbon before it was empty still only counted as one drink and would escape my spouse's scrutiny. And like most alcoholics I know, I always assumed I was doing a better job of hiding my drunkenness than I truly was. Especially crucial for me was the capacity to maintain a successful career. Most of my published work prior to earning tenure and promotion occurred in the context of active and accelerating alcoholism. As I have written elsewhere, the bright emerging scholar masked the self-loathing drunk.[3]

And so these stories go. Ted Bundy adopted the role of a charming and handsome law student to camouflage his compulsive consumption of young white women and girls' bodies. My father played the loyal working-class dad to serve as an alibi for his alcoholic brokenness. And I named myself a scholar to cultivate an exterior life whose successes I hoped concealed my father's scarred progeny cowering inside. My life's work since sobriety is collapsing the wall between the various versions of myself I invented to obscure what I considered unspeakable. Similarly, the work of mourning my father is reconciling the loyal dad with the exhausted drunk. But decades of popular culture regarding Ted Bundy conspires against tethering the charming man and the sadistic monster. Rather, Bundy's charm functions in most films, books, and other cultural artifacts regarding his crimes as a mask that concealed his authentic depravity. Just as my use of career to conceal my brokenness rationalized the cruelties that structure US higher education, or my father's performances of fatherhood often obscured the bankruptcy of the US American Dream, narratives about Bundy's duplicity provide cover for hegemonic white masculinity. But collapsing the boundaries between the alcoholic and devoted father, the rising academic and clinical depressive, or the charming man and the serial killer disclose the cruelties inherent to white masculinity. Disrupting narratives of duplicity underscores the violence inherent to the enterprise in its totality.

Hiding in Plain Sight

Space can mask the depravity it contains. In her scholarship on slasher films, Carol J. Clover calls locations such as the killer's home or an unfamiliar wooded area the Terrible Place.[4] It is where those fleeing the killer come to terms with the extent of the clear and present danger he poses. Such spaces also curate and display past atrocities, such as victims' corpses, that now stand as concrete monuments or ethereal specters. And the Terrible Place is where the killer does his cruelest work outside of the public gaze.

Whereas Ted Bundy usually murdered women and girls such as Lynda Ann Healy, Donna Gail Manson, Susan Elaine Rancourt, Roberta Kathleen Parks, Brenda Carol Ball, Georgeann Hawkins, Janice Ann Ott, Denise Marie Naslund, Nancy Wilcox, Melissa Anne Smith, Laura Ann Aime, Debra Jean Kent, Caryn Eileen Campbell, Julie Cunningham, Denise Lynn Oliverson, Lynette Dawn Culver, Susan Curtis, and Kimberly Dianne Leach under the cover of wooded mountain areas or other isolated locales in the Pacific Northwest, Colorado, Utah, and Florida to perform depravity in secret and left their corpses there to hide evidence, the park at the end of my childhood street's cul-de-sac was the neighborhood's Terrible Place.[5] Dad would bring beers with him to the park when he walked the dog after work and guzzle them before returning home. My parents told me stories about "the teenagers" who spent weekend nights in the park drinking beers and doing God knows what else. As a high school senior, I became such a teenager when I smoked my first joint in the park. My little league baseball coach, who also attended my family's Catholic church and worked for the local fire department, met his mistress there during weekday lunch breaks. This idyllic local playground and park, while unassuming to the uninformed observer, disclosed considerable transgression and, at times, rot.

That white suburbia conceals unsavory secrets is not a new insight. The oeuvres of directors such as David Lynch and Todd Solondz frequently return to this theme.[6] Acclaimed films such as *American Beauty* or *The Ice Storm* explored the ways white suburban ideals serve as alibis for underlying cruelty and despair.[7] But those invested in the suburban fantasy go to great lengths to protect it, often at the expense of Others. Historically, Black and brown communities serve as scapegoats for white suburban children's drug use, allowing white parents to characterize their addict children as victims rather than delinquents.[8] The majority of my musical tastes as a teenager found me listening to punk, goth, and industrial artists who angrily sought to undo the suburbs' mythologies. Many of my white peers consumed hood fantasies without the accompanying risk through work by artists such as Dr. Dre, Snoop Dogg, and Tupac Shakur.[9] And, following acts of mass violence such as school shootings, publics deliberate regarding causes but ultimately agree that white suburbia's cultural norms need not bear any blame.[10] The notion that suburbia is a duplicitous enterprise whose communal exterior conceals a monstrous core permeates much popular culture and cultural criticism.

Similarly, the most common trope of the Ted Bundy story is his duplicity. The story usually goes like this: Bundy was a handsome, charming, intelligent man. On the outside, he embodied the virtues of white suburban masculinity. He was a young man who a young woman would gladly bring home to meet her parents. But the Bundy of US popular culture used his charm and talents to trick naïve young women into trusting him. He sometimes wore a fake cast or pretended to be on crutches to seek their help and get them back to his car. Other times, he posed as a police officer or other authority figure to get women alone, knock them unconscious, and bring them to his designated Terrible Place so that he could carry out his sadistic proclivities in private. This version of Bundy also used charm to fool his family, friends, and associates into believing he was normal.

Ann Rule, a true crime author who capitalized on her association with Bundy to launch her career, wrote about meeting Bundy in her aptly titled book *The Stranger Beside Me*, "I liked him immediately. It would have been hard not to."[11] She continued, "My memory of Ted Bundy is clear, but bifurcated; I remember *two* Teds. One is the young man who sat beside me two nights a week in Seattle's Crisis Clinic. The other is the voyeur, the rapist, the killer, and the necrophile."[12] Rule then characterizes Bundy as an organism fit for scientific inquiry, explaining, "Try as I might, I still can't bring the images together. Looking at them under an imaginary microscope, I cannot superimpose the murderer over the promising student."[13] She *cannot* reconcile the nice guy with the monster. Bundy's maternal cousin, Edna Cowell Martin, expresses similar recollections in her memoir. Regarding her cousin, Martin writes, "Ted always gave his full attention and interest. He knew how to make a person feel special. I loved him for that."[14] She adds, "Later on, he learned he could use this skill to his terrible advantage."[15] For Rule and Martin, as well as others whose renderings operate within a narrative of duplicity, the Ted Bundy for whom they had come to care so deeply was a myth. Worse, he mobilized such a normative masculine ideal as a ruse while the authentic Bundy raised hell in the Pacific Northwest, Utah, Colorado, and Florida.

In their conversations prior to his execution, Bundy and his death row attorney, Polly Nelson, similarly spoke of "another Ted" who consumed his faculties and drove him to kill.[16] While discussing an internal "voice" that beckoned him to "Give in to me," Bundy told Nelson, "It advises me about women, women that I would see in the streets, in a very hateful manner, in a very angry, in a very malicious manner."[17] Paraphrasing the interior dialogue, Bundy continued, "'Look at that bitch there. Do this and this and this.'"[18] Later he explains that, once the other "Ted" became dominant, "The need, the thought, the feeling, the excitement of harming, of getting some sort of sexual gratification at harming someone, was absolutely paramount."[19] He tells Nelson, "That was coming from some source within me, and yet it was not me. And it was very powerful."[20] This conversation, transcribed in its entirety in Nelson's memoir *Defending the Devil*, was part of the Bundy defense team's final, and doomed, attempt to prove he was incompetent to be executed. Her final move was to save the allegedly normal Bundy from the monster whose sadistic proclivities overtook him. Describing her difficulties coming to terms with her cousin's crimes, Martin frames the Bundy saga similarly when she writes, "The Ted I knew didn't deserve to die."[21] The notion of two Teds has always functioned as a mode of rescue, whether it be saving Bundy from execution, or the many publics who consume him from acknowledging their own investments in gendered violence.

The notion that Bundy's warm and confident exterior was merely a disguise for the monster therein is canon in the archive. Such a characterization also figures significantly in Daniel Farrands's critically panned 2021 film, *Ted Bundy: American Boogeyman*. Following an interrogation sequence after Bundy's initial arrest in Utah, an FBI psychiatrist, in conversation with his law enforcement colleagues, distinguishes "Ted," who he describes as "helpful, personable, articulate, charming," from "the entity" that drives him to kill.[22] Visual artifacts in the Bundy archive also sustain the duplicity narrative. One of the most ubiquitous photographs of Bundy is an image of him inside a courtroom. It appears prominently on the cover of Nelson's memoir and is a fixture in other Bundy texts. The caption under the picture on the last page of the photo insert of *The Stranger Beside Me* reads, "The Ted Bundy who hid behind a charming mask suddenly revealed himself in the Orlando trial for the murder of Kimberly Leach."[23] In the book proper, Rule speculates that the image revealed "the Ted his victims saw." She adds, "I use that slide to end my Bundy seminar, and the audience never fails to gasp."[24] The image shows one of the many times Bundy lost his cool at trial when things did not go his way, which was often (figure 1). In this picture, he stares downward, and his mouth is wide open as if screaming or howling. His entire face contorts. The photograph's lighting is such that Bundy's eyes are barely detectable, appearing instead as vacant black holes in his head. Behind and slightly above his head, his right hand floats as if detached from the rest of the body. Bundy forms the hand in an odd position resembling a claw. It looks unnatural and monstrous. One might expect him to slam the hand on a courtroom table or emit black magic from his fingertips. One artist's rendering of the photograph displays blood dripping from the hand (figure 2).[25] Or, as Rule would have her readers believe, Bundy could be preparing to wrap his hand around the neck of a victim. For Rule, and many others who have told Bundy's story through various media, this image embodies the real Ted.[26]

The existence of a real Ted presumes a fake one behind which the howling monster in the courtroom hid. And the fake Ted has appeared in many

Two Teds, One Monster 43

Figure 1. Ted Bundy screaming in court. Warner Media, 2018.

Figure 2. Artistic rendering of Bundy screaming in court. Justin Coffman, 2011. Courtesy of the artist.

Figure 3. From left to right: Liz Kendall, Molly Kendall, and Bundy. Amazon, 2020.

forms over the decades. The 2020 edition of Kendall's *The Phantom Prince* and its accompanying Amazon Prime documentary series *Ted Bundy: Falling for a Killer* features numerous photographs of the years she and Bundy dated. They include images of the serial killer spending time with Liz and her daughter Molly. The photographs suggest a normal nuclear family participating in suburban rituals such as Bundy teaching Molly to ride a bicycle, Molly sitting on Bundy's shoulders, Bundy and Liz in swimming suits enjoying a beach, and several other images of the three smiling and often draping their arms around each other (figure 3). In many of the photographs, Bundy held a young Molly in his lap. The only image in *The Phantom Prince*'s insert that reflects Bundy's monstrosity is a 1974 composite drawing of the suspect in many women's disappearances in the Seattle area (figure 4).[27] That this is the final image among so many seemingly benign family photos is relevant, for it portrays the specter that haunts those pictures. In *The Phantom Prince*, Kendall describes calling police twice to report that her boyfriend matched their suspect description, but quickly convinced herself that Bundy could not be the man they sought. In 1974, no one in Bundy's social orbit seriously suspected that the man in the widely circulated police sketch was Bundy. But with hindsight, this sketch, coupled with the ubiquitous photograph of Bundy screaming in a courtroom resembles the smiling man in the family photographs, but differs in that his appearance discloses so many sadistic deeds.

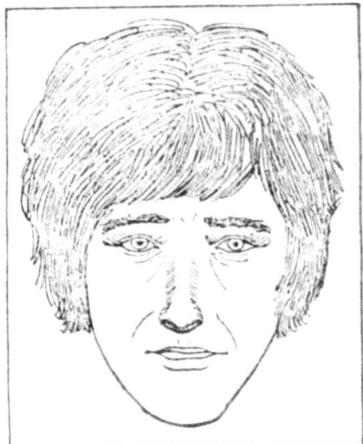

Figure 4. Seattle police sketch of "Ted" killer. *Daily News*, 1974.

Bundy's spectacular monstrosity itself functioned to suppress public acknowledgment of his complicities in more quotidian enactments of white masculine violence. As recently as the 2019 release of *Extremely Wicked*, many popular texts about Bundy characterize his relationship with Liz and Molly Kendall as an elaborate ruse to hide his monstrous essence. For example, during a montage early in *Extremely Wicked*, Berlinger overlays sequences of Bundy performing the role of the perfect boyfriend and patriarch with audio news coverage of what the contemporary audience understands to be his many crimes. In other words, Bundy providing Liz and Molly with a strong and reliable masculine figure functions as a smokescreen for his depravity. But the 2020 publication of an updated edition of Kendall's *The Phantom Prince* and the accompanying Amazon series *Ted Bundy: Falling for a Killer* describe a very different domestic situation. For example, in her contribution to the new edition, an adult Molly recalls a game of hide and seek during which Bundy suddenly removed his clothes. She writes, "Being an only child, a girl, who lived with her mom, I'm not sure if I had ever seen a penis before, let alone an erection."[28] She continues, "Something was very wrong. The pupils of his eyes had become tiny, almost as small as the point of a pencil.... It's as if the person who I loved was now at the end of a long hallway and we could barely see each other. And then he wasn't there anymore."[29]

While this and other examples of sexual abuse Molly recalls in her brief contribution to *The Phantom Prince* still operate within the generic norms of duplicity, they also disclose an element of the Bundy archive that previously received scant attention. While the original edition of *The Phantom Prince* appeared in print in 1981, copies were so difficult to acquire in the interim years that they cost several hundred dollars to purchase. Whereas Rule's *The Stranger Beside Me*, which capitalizes on her decidedly less intimate relationship with Bundy, has been through several reprints and remains among of the most influential true crime books of all time, Liz Kendall's testimony was virtually invisible for nearly forty years.[30] Were it more popular, perhaps the publics who so readily consume narratives about Bundy would know that he emotionally and physically abused Liz and behaved in ways bizarre enough to inspire her to contact law enforcement twice on the suspicion that he might be responsible for women's disappearances in the Seattle area and Utah.[31] Instead, within the vast constellation of texts trading in Bundy's monstrosity, the imperative to characterize him as duplicitous marginalized such inconvenient truths.

Berlinger recalled surveying Liz's collection of photos from her time with Bundy as he developed *Conversations* and *Extremely Wicked*. He told a journalist, "It was what you would expect from family photos—except the man of the family was Ted Bundy."[32] Similarly, the man in the montage during his visitation looked like my loving father—except he was also the cruel drunk who at times tormented and humiliated me. And mine is the name that appears on many scholarly tables of contents—except the mind that produced such published work can also spiral into crises of self-loathing and toxicity. My father and I invested great effort into concealing our Mr. Hydes, as did Bundy in the prevailing narratives that circulate in his archive. In his work, Berlinger amplifies the ironic juxtaposition of Bundy the family man and Bundy the murderer. The killer's sadism prefigures suspicious readings of his visual archive. What we see functions as a substitute for what occurred in the Terrible Place.

For example, in *Conversations*, the director uses frequent montages of stock news footage, such as a television reporter noting Bundy's charm and the fact that he was a law student. Berlinger also displays reproductions of period-specific newspaper headlines including "Charming Killer Seems 'One of Us'" and "Killer's Sketch: Young, Handsome . . . Familiar." Such sequences also include newscasts and photographs showing Bundy during various court proceedings wearing business suits and smiling at cameras. Michaud describes the killer as an "enigma" because he was "Clean-cut, good looking, articulate, very intelligent—just a handsome, young, mild-mannered law student." Later, the journalist adds regarding his interviews with Bundy, "And there was nothing besides his belly chain and his death row clothes to tell you that Ted was anything other than just a regular guy in his early thirties who was there talking over a business deal." He adds, "He didn't look like anybody's notion of someone who would tear apart young girls."

Who looks like someone who would tear apart young girls? In the white Western imaginary, those who would defile and murder "[white] young girls" are racialized—either Black men and others easily read through registers of monstrosity, or less normative white men whose failures in the realm of performative white masculinity rendered them something other than, and therefore "less than," white. The American lynch mob and its progeny, such as the carceral state, express a compulsive preoccupation with protecting white femininity from Black masculinity. The mythos of the Black masculine rapist figures Black men as precisely the kind of person who would tear apart young girls.[33] In fact, murderers such as Charles Stuart, Susan Smith, and Jesse Anderson attempted to avoid carceral justice by blaming their crimes on fictitious Black men. While Stuart and Anderson murdered their wives, and Smith drowned her young children, all three presumably wagered that reporting their deeds as the violent acts of a Black man could persuade law enforcement and the public to abandon any suspicion toward them.[34] Black masculinity functioned as a commonplace. It was their alibi. Blackness was the mask behind which they hid their monstrosity.

Other serial killers such as Dahmer, Gary Ridgway, or Kemper may have been white, but they appeared unnerving. Their faces and bodies did not adhere to normative standards of a handsome white male. Dahmer's aviator glasses sat awkwardly on his face. Ridgway's narrow nose coalesced with other facial features to create something far less than a Casanova capable of seducing women. At six feet and nine inches, Kemper was a towering man whose capacity to subdue and murder women seemed written on his body. Such men are awkward, even creepy. Their appearance as social outsiders render their capacities for depraved violence more plausible for a consuming white US public. As such, they function as modalities for what King calls *abject hegemony*. She writes, "The construction of the abject as the rejected, outside Other against which subjects and cultures define themselves is itself a fiction, or 'cover,' which obscures the extent to which all cultural formations, including subjects, remain abject and may make use of their abjection."[35]

Dahmer, Ridgway, and Kemper are conspicuously creepy, which prefigures their violence. Such renderings absolve normative white masculinity of its own monstrosity.[36]

But in the most visible Bundy texts, there was no mistaking the killer's whiteness nor his capacity to perform proper masculinity. He appeared perfectly ordinary, or what Seltzer calls "something like the mass in person."[37] He was, it seemed, "one of us." Indeed, during *Conversations*, while Michaud explains that Bundy simply did not "look like" a rapist, murderer, and necrophile, Berlinger displays stock footage of Bundy in a full suit, sitting casually on a courtroom table, and engaging in banter with the press pool during the Chi Omega trial—at which a jury convicted him for fatally bludgeoning and strangling two women as they slept in a sorority house at Florida State University, and severely injuring three others. Berlinger reused this footage later in the series while chronicling the trial itself. The juxtaposition of Bundy shooting the shit with reporters while facing a death sentence for a rampage against five college students reifies his duplicity. Viewers understand who Ted Bundy is and why he is in this courtroom. Wendy Lesser explains, "Part of the point of these works about real-life killers . . . is that their reputation precedes them."[38] There is no mystery. This is not a whodunit narrative. The Bundy in this courtroom scene resembles somebody who has not a care in the world. He has swagger. He reads as a perfect gentleman. He is an "All-American Boy." But viewers in 2019 know he is a monster.

Indeed, Bundy's involvement in electoral politics and pursuit of a law degree aligns with prevailing US American masculine archetypes that privilege intelligence, entrepreneurialism, and upward mobility.[39] And while normative iterations of such archetypes are themselves the province of gendered violence, they lack, at least in the US public imagination, the gratuity of a monster such as Bundy.[40] Among the killer's greatest sins as a figure of public discourse was tethering conspicuous sexual sadism to the kinds of white masculinity US publics embrace. Immediately after sentencing Bundy to death in 1979, Dade County Circuit Court Judge Edward Cowart told him, "You're a bright young man. You'd have made a good lawyer, and I would have loved to have you practice in front of me, but you went another way, partner."[41] He added, in a deep US Southern drawl, "I don't feel any animosity toward you. I want you to know that. Take care of yourself."[42] For Cowart, at the culmination of the first nationally televised criminal trial in the United States, during which the defendant served as his own council to disastrous ends, Bundy's wasted potential to realize the promises of normative white Western US masculinity was one of the saga's great tragedies. The judge regarded Bundy's alleged talent and potential as inconsistent with his depraved acts.[43] Similarly, an interviewee during a Biography Channel documentary about Bundy explained, he was like a "young Cary Grant."[44] During an early scene in the 1986 miniseries *The Deliberate Stranger*, Seattle journalist Richard Larsen, whom actor George Grizzard portrayed and on whose book the miniseries is based, stared at Mark Harmon's Bundy with admiration and described him as the equivalent of John F. Kennedy for Washington's Republican Party.[45] Grant and Kennedy remain archetypes of normative white masculinity in the United States. They were handsome, charming, and intelligent men who proceeded through the world with conspicuous confidence. Comparing Bundy to such men in public contexts, either during a televised interview or a miniseries diegesis, underscores the irony inherent in the relationship between Bundy's body and his deeds. They simply do not coalesce for audiences.

Duplicity as Alibi

At one point in *Conversations*, as Michaud speaks about Bundy's apparent normalcy, Berlinger produces an uncanny sense of dramatic irony when the camera zooms in on the image of Bundy at his indictment for the Chi Omega murders. He appears to stare directly and ominously into the camera. Like many such images of public figures, it is likely that Bundy's disposition in the video was perfectly meaningless. He simply stood idly as the Leon County Sheriff and others went about their business of staging an unnecessary, and politically opportunistic, public reading of the indictment (figure 5). But for Berlinger's purposes, Bundy stares ominously toward the viewing public while Michaud testifies to the killer's banality. In so doing, Michaud's words and the image converge to disclose Bundy's duplicitous monstrosity. This Mr. Hyde who stares into the camera mediates Michaud's words and signals to viewers that Bundy was not a remotely "regular guy" and, therefore, that regular white guys do not kidnap, rape, and murder young white women and girls. Michaud explained, "No one unnerved them more than Ted." Frequently during *Conversations*, Berlinger's interviewees appear to plead their case regarding their failure to detect Bundy sooner. In this telling, they are victims,

Figure 5. Bundy during the reading of his indictment for the Chi Omega attack. Netflix, 2019.

too. Bundy exploited their sacred masculine ideals so that he could murder in the shadows. In a nation forged in part by public executions of scores of Black men on allegations of raping or otherwise defiling white women, an All-American Boy such as Bundy facing death for such transgressions was bound to produce dissonance.[46]

In its broadest sense, the uncanny is the affective experience of encountering ghosts—the sensations of haunting. It "derives from what was once familiar and then repressed."[47] Avery Gordon characterizes it as "an enchanted encounter in a disenchanted world between familiarity and strangeness," or "the reality of being haunted by worldly contacts."[48] Sigmund Freud writes that when encountering the uncanny, one "sees a manifestation of forces that he did not suspect in a fellow human being, but whose stirrings he can dimly perceive in remote corners of his own personality."[49] To experience the uncanny is to behold the repressed in the body of the Double.

Piotr Szpunar describes the Double as "a trope that blends the familiar and the unfamiliar by placing within the familiar an amorphous sense of otherness, strangeness, and potential danger."[50] The Double addresses publics as an uncanny and bifurcated figure who "confuses the boundaries that demarcate us from other."[51] Szpunar was interested in the ways domestically born extremists complicate Orientalist notions of non-Western Others. Similarly, the serial killer functions as a Double, for he threatens the fictive boundaries between normative white Western US masculinity and depraved sadism. Simpson writes, "Any given killer has one pleasant or at least nonthreatening face with which to conduct public negotiations and another evil face with which to terrify helpless victims."[52] Prevailing narratives of the Bundy saga epitomize this characterization. They portray Bundy as not merely a normal white man, but an "All-American Boy."[53] One can identify with his nonthreatening, "Kennedyesque" face and find its juxtaposition with his violence unnerving and disturbing.[54] He looks like the normatively gendered public that texts such as *Conversations* address, even as those texts ultimately disavow him.[55] Such disavowal enables viewers to repress that which they sense in the "remote corners" of their personalities.

Just as documentary texts characterized Bundy as a Double in relation to his true sadistic self, many feature films in the Bundy archive enlisted celebrity bodies to advance the same polarity. Since 1986, three mainstream feature films or televised miniseries cast popular white cis male celebrities as Bundy. Through ironic juxtaposition with Bundy's monstrosity, these famous men concretized the duplicity narrative that characterizes predominant Bundy discourse in general by wielding celebrity to underscore the killer's uncanniness. Mark Harmon starred in *The Deliberate Stranger* in 1986, the same year *People* named him the Sexiest Man Alive.[56] During the mid-1980s, Harmon's professional ascent made him a ubiquitous presence on television and in entertainment media. In addition to starring in the popular television series *St. Elsewhere* and the film *Prince of Bel Air*, Harmon performed a mythical rugged masculinity in Coors beer commercials.[57] Such celebrity status and exemplary sexiness made Harmon's portrayal of Bundy even more captivating, ironic, and ultimately uncanny. One journalist explained, "The irony lies in the fact that Bundy, outwardly, is much like Harmon—handsome, bright, charming and smooth, the sort of fellow women want to take home to meet the family."[58] I wrote in the margin of an adoring *People* profile, "EVERYONE WANTS TO SUCK THIS GUY'S DICK."[59]

I suspect that the producers of *The Deliberate Stranger* banked on an audience wanting to suck Harmon's dick and, therefore, Bundy's. Harmon was, after all, the Sexiest Man Alive. As such, he functioned as an ideal metonym for white masculinity.[60] The dissonance between Harmon's normative performance and Bundy's monstrosity mobilized the film's story and attracted an audience. And since Bundy himself attracted a conspicuous following of young women who sent him love letters and nude photos of themselves, and attended his trials, selecting a hot young thing making waves on television was a natural choice.[61]

Decades later, Joe Berlinger made *Extremely Wicked* with a similar hypothesis. Zac Efron made a name for himself in the *High School Musical* franchise, as well as several romantic films and comedies (including *The Greatest Showman, The Lucky One, Neighbors,* and *Baywatch*). And Efron is also a hottie.[62] Whereas Berlinger's *Conversations* operates within the generic norms of contemporary documentary film, *Extremely Wicked* chronicles Bundy's murders and trials largely from Liz Kendall's perspective. The film begins with actress Lily Collins's Liz visiting Bundy on death row. She tells him firmly, "I didn't come to catch up, Ted." The opening sequence alternates between Liz and Ted's no-contact prison visit and the night they met at a Seattle bar in 1969, creating a firm distinction between the grim, monochromatic scene of death row and the joyful, vibrant space of the bar—the consequence of Bundy's depravity juxtaposed with the feigned normalcy he employed to trick some of the women he murdered and the one he claimed to love. The film then proceeds to chronicle the development of their romantic relationship while Ted was committing murders in the Pacific Northwest, Utah, and Colorado. Berlinger portrays Bundy's many arrests, escapes, and trials alongside Liz's descent into alcoholic paranoia, denial, and guilt. But, as I describe above, the director omits Bundy's emotional and physical abuse of Liz, or his sexual abuse of her daughter, Molly, opting instead to characterize the romance as an idyllic and familial façade concealing sadism.[63] In so doing, although the film is quite sparing in its representation of Bundy's violence, Berlinger subordinates the serial killer's more intimate acts of sadistic form—the kinds that are more typical of quotidian white masculinity—to the spectacularly monstrous ones that exceed the permissible norms of performativity.

While promoting the film, Berlinger often explained that a core message he wished to convey with *Extremely Wicked* was that one cannot always trust those we hold nearest. During an interview with the *Los Angeles Times*, Berlinger said, "And as a father of daughters in the prototypical Bundy victim age, that's a lesson I want my children to have, and a lesson I want to impart with people about the nature of evil—that it's often done by the people you least expect and most want to trust. And therefore, people really need to deserve your trust."[64] Berlinger invokes the normative family, and especially the futurity his daughters embody, to name the moral of his Ted Bundy story: There may be a Bundy out there waiting to kidnap, rape, murder, and desecrate the audience's daughters. Omitting Liz and Molly's violent experiences with Bundy helped amplify Berlinger's morality play, which relies on the family's affective resonance in US public culture. While writers such as Sophie Lewis describe the Western heteronormative family as a white supremacist enterprise that produces gender and sexual violence, Berlinger characterizes family, and therefore Liz and Molly, as a disguise Bundy used to hide his monstrosity.[65] The family as such therefore functions as a virtuous formation whose only flaws lie underneath the surface within the bodies of those who would wear it as a cloak. Framing Bundy's duplicity in this way is fundamentally conservative. By the end of the film, Liz has stopped drinking, entered a relationship with a kind, new man, and surrendered the guilt she felt for failing to recognize Bundy's monstrosity. The only thing standing between her and the promises of family was the serial killer who used her love as an alibi.

In addition to using narrative to constitute Bundy's duplicity, Berlinger's casting of Efron to portray the killer further accentuates the film's uncanniness. Just as the broader narrative of Bundy and his crimes posits the killer as employing a charming exterior to hide his monstrous deeds, Efron functions as an unnerving presence who recalls his past performances and status as a normatively handsome young man while playing another man, who, at the film's conclusion, admits to decapitating a young white woman with a hacksaw. Promotional media for *Extremely Wicked* employed visual representations of Efron's body to underscore Bundy's duality. Many posters and Netflix menu icons for the film feature an image of Liz and Ted visiting on death row (figure 6). Liz sits on one side of the glass staring toward Efron's Ted, who sits on the other side in an orange prison jumpsuit. The back of his head faces the camera, and the viewer sees a partial profile of his face. The separation glass in the visiting booth reflects a different image of Ted. This man appears far more ominous, staring toward Liz with his mouth slightly ajar almost forming a smile. It is as if he is violently lusting after that which he sees. The image floats between the in-the-flesh Liz and Ted, haunting their relationship and functioning as a specter who betrays the monstrosity lingering underneath the body with which Liz fell in love, as well as the celebrity body with whom many viewers will be familiar. But crucially, Liz fell in love with the charming Ted—the Zac Efron Ted. This is the Ted who mediates her and the public's affective investments in the sadistic Ted presumably lingering under the surface.

Figure 6. Promotional image for *Extremely Wicked, Shockingly Evil, and Vile*. Netflix, 2019.

Neither *The Deliberate Stranger* nor *Extremely Wicked* show much onscreen violence. The Harmon version of the Bundy story includes a relatively mild reenactment of the Chi Omega massacre and, earlier, shows Bundy carrying an unconscious woman through the snow. Otherwise, the miniseries only shows the serial killer stalking or suavely manipulating his victims, leaving the offscreen violence to viewers' imaginations. *Extremely Wicked*'s Bundy performs an on-screen kidnapping and murder in the film's final moments, but with minimal detail. The film's most graphic violent imagery is a crime scene photograph of a woman's headless and shirtless corpse, with which Liz confronts Ted to coax his admission that he killed the anonymous victim and scores of other women and girls. But viewers do not see

Efron's Bundy raping and strangling the woman, only a brief, low-lit shot of him dragging her unconscious body into the woods. And they surely do not see him decapitating her, just a closeup of his hand seizing a hacksaw from upon the night's fallen snow.

Similarly, the 2002 television movie *The Stranger Beside Me*, based on Rule's book, stars the handsome actor Billy Campbell. While he was never as high profile as Harmon or Efron, Campbell nonetheless played beloved television characters during the 1980s and 1990s on *Dallas* and *Once and Again* and played the titular role in the action film *The Rocketeer*.[66] While the televised adaptation of Rule's famous book included more on-screen killings, they were sufficiently mild to appear on network television. Notably, films such as Bright's *Ted Bundy* (2002), Michael Feifer's *Bundy: A Legacy of Evil* (2008), or Farrands's *Ted Bundy: American Boogeyman* (2021) dwelled much longer at the crime scene, showing far more graphic violence. And these three movies, besides being poorly made, did not cast men of Harmon or Efron's stature to play Bundy. Whereas Michael Reilly Burke, who starred as Bundy in Bright's film, remains a relatively low-profile character actor, Corin Nemec and Chad Michael Murray, who starred in Feifer and Farrands's films respectively, are once-popular actors past their career primes.[67] The apparent contradiction between their bodies raping and murdering young women was not nearly as conspicuous as the prospect of beloved and handsome superstars such as Harmon and Efron doing the same. Ultimately, celebrity is fundamental to the duplicity frame in the Bundy saga. Monsters such as Bundy manipulate the ideals of normative white masculinity to which charming celebrity men give expression so they might impersonate them and undermine the presumably wholesome values they embody.[68] Just as Bundy's own celebrity and charm rendered his depravities even more disturbing, films such as *The Deliberate Stranger* and *Extremely Wicked* left audiences to imagine the disturbing murders performed by the smiling onscreen hunk.[69]

A presumption that sustains the distinction between Bundy's Dr. Jekyll and Mr. Hyde is that the charming and intelligent man he embodied to hide his monstrosity was virtuous when not concealing a monster. That is, if part of Bundy's cruel legacy is fooling his victims, his family and friends, and the public, a core element of his transgression is sullying the daily masculine performances of so many decent men. Bundy functions as something akin to what Pat J. Gehrke describes as rhetorical studies' "Hitler problem." That is, Hitler, in his capacity to mobilize publics in the service of his genocidal and imperial designs, challenged rhetoric's moral pretenses.[70] Similarly, Bundy's performance of normative white masculinity suggested that the ethical character of such performatives is never guaranteed. White masculinity has a "Ted Bundy problem."

Yet so many custodians of white masculinity engage the Bundy archive in hopes of salvaging the racialized gender norms that help mobilize modernity. In addition to beloved stars such as Harmon and Efron, these men include journalists such as Michaud and Aynesworth, attorneys such as prosecutor Bob Deckle, and law enforcement figures such as Hagmaier and Bob Keppel. Such men figure far more prominently in documentary and narrative texts about Bundy than women involved with the case. Even texts in the Bundy archive that center women's experiences, such as *Falling for a Killer*, *Defending the Devil*, *American Boogeyman*, *No Man of God*, or *The Stranger Beside Me*, do so in ways that invest in the carceral state. In her work, Rule, who worked in law enforcement before becoming a true crime author, writes as a devotee of police and other state agents. Prominent in documentary texts such as *Conversations* and *Falling for a Killer*, as well as the feature film *American Boogeyman*, Kathleen McChesney is a conspicuously feminist figure. She is the first woman to serve as an officer in Seattle's police department. After navigating institutional sexism, McChesney became a lead detective on the Bundy case. Later in her career, she ascended to high ranks in the FBI.[71] Since Bundy's execution, news media, television, and film have speculated that a woman served as executioner, therefore delivering to Bundy an especially satisfying kind of retribution.[72] To the extent that women's voices figure significantly in the Bundy archive, it is often in the service of an explicitly carceral logic.

But in the Bundy archive, Bundy's most fitting foes are usually men, especially those in law enforcement.[73] Thus, many versions of the narrative employ a chivalrous logic that figures women as actual or potential Bundy victims, and strong men, especially law enforcement, as masculine exemplars who deliver justice. In the final episode of *Conversations*, Berlinger portrays such men as avatars of normative masculinity who perform core civic responsibilities. For example, in a portion of archival news footage from the day of Bundy's execution, Aynesworth describes the condemned killer to reporters as a "wimp," explaining that "people who sneak up on women and kill them and—what else can you say?" To inflict gratuitous violence on the weaker sex, Aynesworth claims, is beneath contempt and betrays failed masculinity. Kathy Kleiner Rubin, who Bundy severely injured during his attack at the

Chi Omega house, similarly demeans Bundy, writing in her memoir, "Bundy didn't pick bar fights with hefty men. He didn't box or study martial arts. He attacked women while they were sleeping or he hit them so hard they became unconscious."[74] In *The Stranger Beside Me*, Rule frequently praises law and order performances of masculinity. Commenting on Florida police's contempt for Bundy, Rule writes, "'Good ole boys'—policemen and laymen alike—didn't hold with women-killers, with despoilers and rapists."[75] Such men, by these representations, appreciated the sanctity of a woman's chastity and loathed anyone who would inflict sexual violence. Unlike Bundy, they were not wimps.

Many texts in the Bundy archive prominently feature the killer's tactic of impersonating law enforcement to gain women's trust before kidnapping them. For example, his attempted kidnapping of Carol DaRonch in Utah, which led to Bundy's first conviction, appears in most feature and television films about the serial killer. DaRonch herself is a regular interviewee for documentary texts such as *Conversations*.[76] Thus, in numerous tellings of the Bundy saga, one of the normative modes of white masculinity he frequently employed to hide in plain sight was the figure of the police officer. Implicit in repetitions of this aspect of the Bundy case, especially in the broader context of other men of the law appearing virtuous, is the conviction that law enforcement as such is the province of the gentleman. To trust a police officer, within such a rendering, is the most natural thing in the world. Thus, Bundy wielding that trust to kidnap, rape, and murder women reads as especially despicable.

During his interview segments in *Conversations*, Deckle, who prosecuted Bundy for the Kimberly Leach murder, appears especially sincere and humble. A tall, well-built man with a deep southern accent, he is surely the kind of "good ole boy" Rule praised. He describes sobbing upon seeing Leach's mummified remains in an abandoned Florida hog shed. He admits feeling "elated" while witnessing Bundy's execution, but also confesses shame regarding his joy, explaining that he hopes he never again feels so happy about another person's death. Deckle, perhaps more than any other masculine figure in the Bundy archive, solemnly embodies the ideal of a dedicated man of the law who sought and secured retribution for so many murdered women and girls. That he oversaw the conviction for one of Bundy's most notorious murders, that of a twelve-year-old girl, makes his gender performance even more salient. In documentary interviews and Sealey's *No Man of God*, Hagmaier, who extracted crucial confessions from Bundy in his final days, also appears as a fundamentally decent man who affirms the legitimacy of Bundy's execution while acknowledging the killer's humanity. In this narrative tapestry, such men are humble and heroic archetypes for the masculine ideal Bundy mocked through his duplicity.

I confess to finding Deckle and Hagmaier likeable and sympathetic. In the context of a serial murder saga laden with cheap sensationalism, they consistently appear as thoughtful men with strong moral cores. But crucially, they, and most of the men who figure prominently in the Bundy archive, are agents of the carceral state. As such, they engage in state-sanctioned forms of gendered violence that are inherent to their professions. The violence they enact is immanent to their professional subjectivity. They perform a duplicity all their own by enacting normative white masculinity while functioning as always already violent penal proxies. However, while most texts in the Bundy archive amplify the contradictions between the serial killer and the gentleman, the hegemonic suturing of law enforcement and chivalry diminishes uncanny possibilities.

Indeed, police, prosecutors, and other carceral agents function as heroes in most popular narratives about sexual violence. They rarely register as sadists. Moreton-Robinson explains, "The values and virtues associated with overcoming an oppressive landscape are not easily recuperated when there is evidence of white inhumanity."[77] Elizabeth Bernstein names feminist discourses that "adopt carceral paradigms of social, and in particular gender, justice" carceral feminism.[78] And as anticarceral feminists demonstrate in their work, procarceral modes of feminism center white women's experiences by empowering a carceral apparatus that does disproportionate harm to women and femmes at the margins.[79] Thus, to presuppose affinity between law enforcement and women such as Bundy's actual and potential victims is to adopt an ideal of justice invested in the erasure of BIPOC women and femme's experiences. And in his controversial work on Black manhood, Tommy J. Curry argues that incarceration also inflicts gendered violence against Black masculine bodies. The criminalization of Black men, he explains, with its origins in enslavement and lynching, is always grounded in a desire to control Black sexuality.[80]

While I know little about these men's careers beyond their work on the Bundy case, men such as Deckle and Hagmaier are custodians of a state apparatus whose legacy is brutality against vulnerable bodies and communities.[81] It is a system whose work, although rarely recognizable as such, operates in the same formal registers as Bundy's. Such men are participants in a sadistic enterprise for which violence against fungible bodies serves an indispensable sustaining function.[82] But because Bundy donned decency as a mask while he murdered scores of women and girls, these other men figure as authentic exemplars of masculine integrity. Most of us are above suspicion when a monster such as Ted Bundy is in the room. Thus, the work of naming Bundy duplicitous, and thereby affirming the legitimacy of carcerality and normative masculinity, obscures the myriad forms of gendered violence that enact sadistic form.

Peace at All Costs

The montage from my father's visitation still sits on my computer in a cloud drive folder I share with my mother and sister. While I recall how the images coalesced to produce a narrative of masculine normativity that resonated with the kind Bundy exploited to sickening ends, I encounter them quite like I imagine Liz Kendall, or others with great personal proximity to the Bundy saga, might. I experience the ambivalence of knowing my father was capable of the kindness and care embodied in the photographs, as well as the alcoholic cruelties whose very potentiality still, even years after his death, inspires anxiety in me. But my father is not as famous as Ted Bundy, nor are his more monstrous tendencies. Whereas popular accounts of Bundy's story accentuate his cruelty and distinguish it from his charming persona, familial memories of my father are mostly wholesome. Like many alcoholic families, mine closely guards evidence of our unflattering traits. To this day, members of my family retell idyllic stories of my father that, to my recollection, were far more disturbing than the version they tell implies.

In one of the montage's images, I, wearing glasses and a Marvin the Martian T-shirt, stand next to my father, who, wearing a Chicago Bulls T-shirt and sunglasses, drapes his arm around my shoulder. Both of us are smiling. My father's smile in the photograph is a familiar one. He lightly bites his lower lip with his two front teeth (figure 7).[83] It resembles Bundy's smile in a frequently reprinted photograph of him washing dishes with a smiling woman in a Salt Lake City home (figure 8). By this time, Bundy had left Seattle to attend law school at the University of Utah. He proceeded to murder women. He also joined the Mormon Church.

Figure 7. Childhood photograph of the author (right) and his father. McCann Family, c. 1992.

This was how my father smiled when he was a few drinks in. The scene in this photo is during daylight, so I cannot say what time it was and if it was an appropriate cocktail hour. I do not know if his sunglasses hid bloodshot eyes. Nor do I recall if his breath smelled of beer. I was certainly close enough to detect it. And I cannot remember if he drove the family back to the rental cottage that evening. He probably did. I am confident that my mother took this photo in Door County, Wisconsin, a site of many family vacations. While wealthier friends frequently travelled to California or Florida to attend Disney parks or even went overseas, my frugal working-class family rarely ventured outside the Midwest. It was a source of some insecurity for me and probably my father. Much like Bundy, my family's financial struggles haunt me.[84]

If this image was from a vacation to Door County, then this could be the trip during which, one evening at the cottage, my mother began complaining to my sister and I about the number of beers my dad consumed that evening. She thought he was out of hearing range, but she was wrong. This would not be the first or last time she made such a mistake. Ours was a classically alcoholic household in that my mother often turned to her children for the emotional support my father did not provide, especially regarding his drinking. In hindsight, so much of what I remember about my father

Figure 8. Bundy washing dishes with a friend and biting his tongue as he smiles. Netflix, 2019.

flows through my mother's complaints. And given my alcoholic father's frequent emotional unavailability, her renderings typically took precedent. Her propensity to disclose adult truths to her adolescent son produced an inappropriate intimacy whose legacies remain capable of inducing overpowering resentments in me.[85] Suffice it to say, I have daddy and mommy issues. And with Bundy, my narrative aligns with many others of white masculinity that amplify genealogy's role in future destructive behaviors.[86]

After saying her piece, my mother paused from washing the dishes and went to the restroom. Dad entered the cottage and hovered before the bathroom door, a snarl on his face and his fists clenched. He stood as if waiting to pounce. Maybe this is how Bundy lingered in the shadows awaiting his chance to subdue Caryn Campbell during her ski trip to Snowmass Village, Colorado. Of course, Bundy did not know Campbell and therefore had no reason to resent her personally. But she was an attractive white woman, and that was sufficient cause for Bundy to bludgeon and murder her. Perhaps he was responding to the inner voice that said, "'Look at that bitch there. Do this and this and this.'"[87] I did not know what awaited my mother when she left the bathroom, but it would not be good. In this familial scene, she was, to my dad, "that bitch." And what unfolded was not a gendered catastrophe worthy of Ted Bundy, but it was sufficiently terrifying for a middle-school boy for whom such situations felt like existential threats.

Mom exited, startled, and my father let loose. If she had something to say, she should say it to him and not the kids. When we get back home, she'd better call a divorce lawyer. She's a cunt. And he hit her. By the time that happened, my sister and I had retired to our respective bedrooms, but I remained awake and listened. I heard the pause before he hit her and my mother's soft sobs after he did so. During such moments, my entire sense of stability felt on the verge of collapse. Whatever miseries membership in my family produced, they were a known quantity. Anything else, such as divorce, was a terrifying mystery. Even as so much of my childhood disclosed the fictive nature of the nuclear familial ideal, its mythologies provided a scaffold on which my expectations for safety rested. And my dad's rage betrayed his own investments, despite much available evidence to the contrary, in such an ideal. In my dad's view, my mother had committed the unpardonable sin of sharing adult concerns with children. I am not sure if my father had the presence of mind to worry about the long-term mental health consequences of her behavior, or his violence, although they are considerable. My hunch is that his primary concern was that her complaints risked tarnishing his children's image of their dad.

My sense of my father as an alcoholic was taking form at this time. This was indeed a function of my mother's many inappropriate conversations with me, but I was also savvy enough to associate his unpredictable moods with the quantity and circumstances of his drinking. While the jig was not fully up, it was slouching in that direction. And this is what I suspect horrified my father. I recall the last few years of my drinking when my spouse would confront me about it, or some reckless behavior associated with booze. I felt trapped in a corner and lashed out. During our worst fights, I threatened divorce and self-harm, or deployed insults I knew would hurt them deeply. Sometimes, I still behave this way. Describing her final phone conversation with Bundy following his arrest in Florida, Liz Kendall asked him if he was "sick." He replied, "Back off!" Those of us living in states of surrender to addiction are a defensive bunch. We invest in maintaining duplicity just as surely as some of our chroniclers revel in disclosing it. But such storytellers invest in duplicity just as deeply, responding sharply when outside forces threaten to reveal the fiction that is the boundary between the public charmer and private monster.

I cannot remember how the fight wound down that evening in Door County. The next morning, as was so often the case, it was as if nothing had happened. I felt relief, which is the impulse I have carried into adulthood—peace at all costs. That is the mantra, I believe, of most alcoholic households.[88]

And I suspect it is the same principle that drove Liz, herself an alcoholic presently in recovery, to remain with Bundy even when his bizarre and abusive behavior tempted her to do otherwise. The embrace of normalcy, even in its most toxic forms, is still a known quantity compared to its potentially emancipatory alternatives.

Peace at all costs is surely the ideal for an Irish Catholic patriarch's funeral in the south Chicago suburbs. He was a good man. He loved his family. He was a hard worker. And all of this is true. My sense of my deceased father is not bifurcated, as Rule, Kendall, and others describe their memories of Bundy. The man who dutifully purchased me US savings bonds throughout my childhood and the man who once threw the new family dog down a flight of stairs after it pissed on the carpet one time too many are, to me, the same man. I can bring those images together. That is the problem. Dwelling at their intersection is the essence of my grief. My father's death would likely be easier to process if I could manifest a clear line between my kind and loyal working-class father and the man whose bloodshot eyes, directed at me just so, induced me to flinch automatically—even as an adult. He was a good man who loved his family. He was also a cruel drunk. Watching my dad gradually wither and die from cancer and its toxic treatments may have been simpler if I could see him exclusively as a good father or cruel monster.

The nearly three-minute prelude to the credit sequence in the first episode of *Conversations* deals with various interviewees explaining Bundy's charm and normalcy. Berlinger intersplices photographs of Bundy as a child or during his trials with stock images of prison cellblocks. Over the images, anonymous narrators make comments such as "I considered him a friend, he was a very nice person," "I felt a connection with him," "He was a very normal, active boy," "His mom and dad took him to church every Sunday," and "He wanted to be successful as an attorney or as a politician." Berlinger then interrupts these testaments to familiarity with escalating music. With the sonic shift comes a textual and visual one, as anonymous voices begin saying things such as "Suspected of dozens of sex killings," "The discovery of the skeletal remains of six women," "More than twenty young women in five states," "Beaten and strangled," "Abduction, nude body," "Sexually molested," "Bludgeoned, raped," "Sexually mutilated by mouth, by teeth," and "He had sex with them after they were dead." Many of the grisliest comments come as the camera pans across what were likely yearbook photos of the attractive young white women Bundy murdered. Berlinger requires viewers to

Figure 9. Still from *Conversations with a Killer: The Ted Bundy Tapes*. Netflix, 2019.

reconcile the macabre descriptions of what Bundy did to these women with smiling pictures of them before they encountered him (figure 9). The macabre world Bundy occupied and the wholesome ones he invaded function in a duplicitous dynamic as well. The ruses he used made him legible to the decent people who occupied the normative familial sphere. Like so many narratives of racialized invasions of white suburban space, Bundy's monstrosity ruptured these women's future trajectories by briefly securing a space therein.[89] He brought the Terrible Place to them, their families, and their communities. These young faces, evidently full of the optimism and promise that characterize the futurity that the normative white nuclear family embodies, were subjected to bludgeoning, mutilation, molestation, rape, and necrophilia. And all from this smiling man so many people saw as a "very nice person." Juxtaposing Bundy's sadism with their visualized futures rendered him anathema to normative white masculinity, therefore ameliorating the dissonance of the uncanny. Recalling his monstrosity offered peace and obscured the sadism of white masculinity itself.

If the rituals that culminated with my father's interment at a military cemetery obscured the myriad kinds of intimate and state violence that saturated his biography, even photographs of Bundy's young victims cannot escape their contextualization within the monstrosity of the man who murdered them. There were no interruptions of the voices that contextualized the visual archive displayed at my father's visitation. Statements such as "He was such a hard worker," "He loved you so much," or "He always put family first" did not collide with "I can't imagine what it was like for you to watch him smash a casserole dish on the kitchen floor during that fight with your mother," "You must have been mortified the times he called your Black friends the n-word" or, "It must have felt like such a betrayal when he drove drunk and nearly ran directly into a tree." But while the nuances of these memory texts differ, both reify the normative ideals of white masculinity. Bundy's monstrosity produces alibis for more quotidian norms of white masculine violence, whereas my father's excesses remain unspoken so that the figure of the loyal father affirms the familial unit.

I do not know if my father's appearance resonated with anyone's prefigured image of an abusive, alcoholic father. In his lifetime, there were certainly class-based clues such as his always-shitty cars or frequent disregard for presentable attire. Such an appearance, coupled with what at least I recognized as nonverbal cues for drunkenness, could certainly signal to others the man's capacity for violence. And he did occasionally explode outside the privacy of our home. But his posthumous visual archive offered no explicit clues of monstrosity, at least not for viewers invested in the normative familial enthymemes these solemn rituals reified. The photograph we selected for the visitation program was a close-up of my father staring into the camera during a Chicago White Sox home game tailgate (figure 10). It was the same picture that appeared with his obituary. In it, he wears a Sox hat and T-shirt, as well as a large smile. The image is wholesome and reflects the broader narrative our family's cultivated mourning process sought to build. He was a humble, loving guy with simple pleasures. This narrative is both true and profoundly dishonest.

Figure 10. Image of the author's father featured in his obituary. McCann family, ca. 2012.

Conclusion

My family instructed the funeral home to dress my father's corpse in his favorite suit and tie. We also surrounded his embalmed body with artifacts that conjured positive memories of a normative fatherly figure. These included a box of his favorite chocolate covered cherries, a stuffed teddy bear wearing Chicago White Sox paraphernalia, and a can of Guinness beer. While the Irish stout certainly facilitated memories, at least for the deceased's newly sober alcoholic son, of various traumas scattered throughout the years, that was not what this can of beer signified in this solemn moment. Rather, my Irish American postal worker father wore a suit and was surrounded by signifiers of heterosexual familial belonging because the rituals following his death from a disease that annihilated a body that was once strong enough to inflict pain on his children and wife exalted the normative ideals of white Western masculinity. So too have most renderings of the Bundy saga. But if my father donned signifiers of a humble, white working class, and masculine life, Bundy's adornments accentuated his monstrosity in US public discourse, either through fleeting glimpses at his monstrous essence, such as the famous photograph of him screaming in a courtroom, beloved celebrity actors portraying him in mainstream entertainment media, or ironic circulations of more banal or charming images whose performances of normative white masculinity merely concealed monstrosity.

Central to every iteration of Bundy's sustained circulation in US public culture is a moment, no matter how brief, of recognition for publics invested in normative white masculinity. Following recognition is the question of what such publics must do to prevent it from sullying the very gendered enterprise whose monstrosity it reveals. In her work about haunting and colonization, Renée L. Bergland characterizes the uncanny as an unconquered excess.[90] It is those repressed parts of the collective psyche that still push against the boundaries of the symbolic processes publics deploy to silence those specters that haunt and threaten anxiety. But as Richard Tithecott explains in his writing about serial killers, attempts to suppress the uncanny, by definition, threaten publics with their undoing.[91] Bundy's refusal to disappear discloses that the excess sadism he embodies has not yet fallen under the discipline of the normative. It cannot hide behind or within proper performances of white masculinity. Thus, publics respond to Bundy in ways that seek to silence his status as an echo of white masculinity's cruel legacies. Peace at all costs.

Chief among these responses are narratives of duplicity and the constitution of an ignorant and gullible public. Authors and interview subjects commenting on Bundy's crimes repeatedly rationalize the failure to know. Similarly, films and miniseries such as *The Deliberate Stranger*, *The Stranger Beside Me*, and *Extremely Wicked* fixate on the difficult processes through which Bundy's family and friends went as they came to accept the truth of his monstrosity. And as Rubin laments in her memoir, most portrayals of Bundy's victims characterize them as naïve and gullible women who the suave serial killer disarmed and subdued. She notes that Bundy kidnapped most women and girls by brute force rather than manipulation.[92] Yet, the figure of the monster masquerading as a gentleman endures. And his victims function as soft targets requiring rescue by more authentic white masculine bodies. In his work on US horror cinema, Kendall Phillips describes the American Uncanny as the ability to see the ruse behind mystification.[93] This, he claims, describes the ways early US horror films represented supernatural forces. The shared understanding that the monster was not real was central to the circulation of horrific texts in the early twentieth century. But tales of Bundy's duplicity gesture toward a different kind of US American uncanny. Such texts invite an incredulity that allows another kind of credulity to persist. In revealing the monster behind the mystification of a gentleman, popular discourses about Bundy sustain the more fundamental mystification that obscures the sadism that structures normative white Western US masculinity. In revealing the ravenous serial killer, texts about Bundy conceal his homologies with the quotidian. The public's ability to peek behind one curtain further conceals what lies behind another. Narratives of duplicity therefore allow publics to disavow conspicuous enactments of gendered violence by enabling them to claim ignorance regarding sadistic acts that precede and portend their more visible counterparts.

But not all duplicities follow the same patterns, even as they collectively work to foreclose reckoning with the cruelties inherent to white Western masculinity. Whereas public reckonings with Bundy work to ensure that his monstrosity overshadows his feigned normalcy, my father's status as a loving and dutiful father marginalized and silenced disclosures of his many cruelties—hence my immense discomfort at including them in this book. If Bundy was an authentic Mr. Hyde whose monstrosity renders his kinder moments duplicitous, my father, in the last instance, was an authentic Dr. Jekyll whose frequent surrenders to his more monstrous tendencies need not taint his memory. And because representations of normative white masculinity serve to envelope the violence that underwrites the domestic sphere over which the white masculine claims dominion, the far less spectacular violence that occurs after too many drinks following a bad day at work remain secrets that modernity's custodians would prefer we not disclose.

During the final episode of *Falling for a Killer*, Molly Kendall exclaims, "I don't give a fuck whether he loved us or not. It makes no difference." Unlike her mother, who confesses still-complicated memories of Bundy, Molly understands him firmly as a monster. I envy her clarity. I mean this sincerely. She has earned such clarity, while I yearn for it. This is not to say that I believe my father was an unmitigated monster any more than I was or am. He loved me. And I give a fuck (figure 11). He and I both surrendered to our cruelest capacities, often in response to overwhelming insecurities. I instead wish for clarity at the intersection of Dr. Jekyll and Mr. Hyde. But as Robert Louis Stevenson's novella made clear, the boundary between Jekyll and Hyde is largely fictive. Hyde gives expression to Jekyll's desires. Hyde is Jekyll sans inhibition.[94] Like Bundy, Dr. Jekyll was a monster masquerading as a decent man. But Stevenson's work suggests that the voice urging Bundy

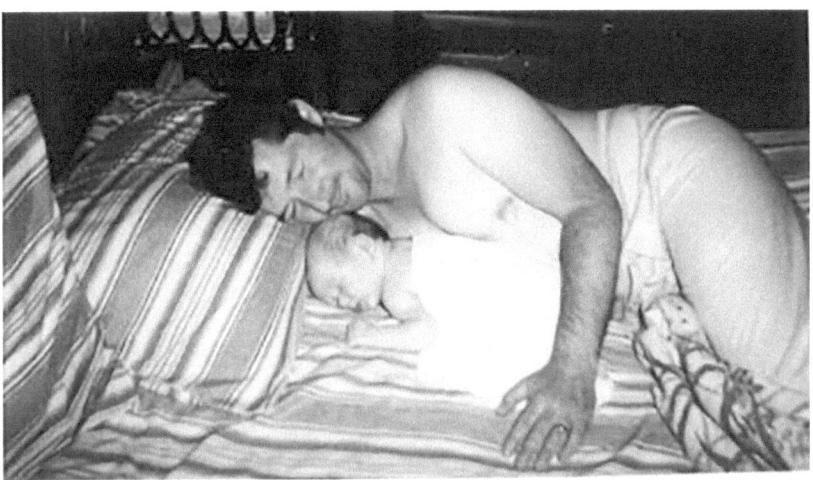

Figure 11. Author and his father. McCann family, 1980.

to commit so many atrocities was merely an amplification of the "bright young man's" desires.

I am too close to my father and myself to dwell anywhere but at the very point where the fictive threshold between the gentleman and the monster materializes. I have feared and loved my father deeply, often simultaneously. And the radical reflexivity of therapy and recovery convince me that my own capacity for cruelty does not negate the better angels of my nature—it only complicates them. But for most US Americans, Bundy is larger than life. Even for Molly Kendall, I suspect the monumental nature of his crimes enables, and perhaps requires, her to settle on the side of monstrosity where Bundy is concerned. More importantly for this project's aims, Molly's testimony buttresses the duplicity narrative that characterizes most Bundy discourse. In so doing, Bundy continues to function as a kind of Frankenstein's monster while the mad scientists who continue resuscitating his corpse breathe life into his legacy in ways that obscure the cruelties of our own.[95]

Chapter 3

TED BUNDY, PORNOGRAPHER

The night before his execution, Ted Bundy granted his final interview to Dr. James Dobson. The founder of the Christian fundamentalist group Focus on the Family, Dobson was a psychologist and conservative activist. Prior to the Bundy interview, he served on the Reagan Administration's so-called Meese Commission, which produced a nearly 2,000-page report describing pornography's impact on US civil society. To virtually nobody's surprise, the report claimed to have found a strong causal relationship between pornography and sexually violent behavior.[1] Because of his participation in the Meese Commission, Dobson was among the most visible antipornography activists in the United States. During their conversation, Bundy, with ample encouragement from Dobson, pontificated on the capacity of "violent pornography" to inspire horrifying acts of sexual sadism such as his. Bundy claimed he became addicted to pornography as a child, which cultivated depraved fantasies he decided to make flesh as an adult.[2]

Few people familiar with Bundy took these claims seriously. Many skeptics characterized the interview as a mutually beneficial performance that Bundy and Dobson curated. Bundy could cast the blame for his many murders elsewhere and possibly delay his execution, while Dobson could enlist Bundy in his years-long campaign against pornography.[3] Others, especially men who were close to the Bundy case, observed that most US American men encounter pornography over the course of their lives and do not murder scores of people.[4] Hagmaier claims during the final episode of *Conversations* that Bundy admitted to him that the Dobson interview was a self-serving charade, that Bundy kidnapped, raped, and murdered women and girls because he wanted to and not because of pornography's insidious inducements.[5]

While pornography's capacity to motivate Bundy and other men to commit acts of sexual sadism against feminine bodies is beyond this project's scope, pornography is nonetheless an enduring theme in the Bundy archive. The Bundy saga unfolded during US feminism's so-called second wave, which included impassioned debates regarding sexuality in general and pornography in particular. These "sex wars" balkanized many feminist coalitions, while constituting surprising new ones between some radical feminists and cultural conservatives. They also functioned as incubators for queer studies as a formal area of inquiry and catalyzed litigious confrontations regarding free speech and obscenity.[6] Feminist thinkers such as Caputi, who characterized Bundy as an embodiment of US civil society's misogynistic investments in sexual violence against women, claimed, "Pornography functions as advertisement, school and fuel for sex crime."[7]

During Bundy's years on death row, cultural conservatives such as Dobson, Pat Buchanan, Jerry Falwell, and Pat Robertson enjoyed significant political influence by leveraging the Republican Party's growing reliance on conservative Christian voters to win elections. Bundy's imprisonment coincided with a culture war that named sexual permissiveness as one of the chief factors hastening civilizational collapse.[8] Joel Black writes, "As was customary during Reagan's presidency, the regulation of representations . . . took precedence over the prior and tougher task of combatting actual social problems."[9] Regarding letters that ordinary citizens wrote in favor of the Meese Commission, Stephanie R. Larson similarly writes, "Instead of uncovering the underlying causes of repeated instances of sexual violence, letter writers collectively sought to intervene in the debate by rehabilitating an alternative subjectivity: heteronormative, white, male bodies who presumably had 'fallen off track' and been wrongly seduced by the evils of female sexuality."[10] Indeed, as Laura Kipnis and Lawrence W. Rosenfield separately observe, pornography functions for such activists as an empty signifier that names and seeks to eliminate what they characterize as "heretical messages."[11] While Dobson and his ilk were certainly not feminists, their ambitions and connections to political power made an alliance with some antiporn feminists mutually beneficial.

Public discourse regarding pornography and Bundy's crimes rests on disagreements about the capacity of sexually explicit materials to motivate sexually sadistic behavior. Debate regarding such a causal relationship locates pornography within the confines of its most traditional commercial manifestations, such as pornographic films or magazines, dirty novels, or strip clubs.[12] Lisa Duggan explains that such a myopic view of pornography characterizes it as "a condensed metaphor for female degradation."[13] Such renderings, she argues, do not account for the diffuse character of sexual violence in US civil society.[14] Pornography's many opponents have little difficulty explaining how visual representations of bukkake, gang bangs, anal sex, blow jobs, asphyxiation, and money shots reduce women's bodies to objects that legions of horny men can consume function as "advertisement, school and fuel for sex crime."[15] But their critiques are often ill equipped to describe how quotidian enactments of gender normativity also function pornographically, or how subjects come to experience as pornographic those texts whose authors never envisioned such uses.

A more fecund manner of theorizing pornography is as a structuring logic of white masculinity in modernity, or as a rhetorical form.[16] Such an approach understands pornography as a mode of mass mediated public address, embodiment, and reception. As such, it gives expression and form to modernity's core gendered logics. It is an iteration of sadistic form. If pornography's key characteristic is its mobilization of the nonreciprocal libidinal impulses of modernist gender norms, Ted Bundy is not a product of pornography, nor is such a question particularly useful in reckoning with his archive. Instead, Bundy was and is a pornographer in that he performed pornographic impulses in his sexual sadism. And texts about Bundy are themselves pornographic, for they enable and induce public consumption of his many depravities. Reading the Bundy archive through a pornographic lens illuminates the barely latent enjoyments that arise for many publics that consume it, as well as the rhetorical practices that seek to figure Bundy as monstrous and therefore inconsistent with modernity's carnal norms. Pornographic reading discloses the yearnings that mobilize those norms.

Pornographic Form

Defining what is and is not a pornographic text is a notoriously difficult and contentious enterprise, prompting Catherine Helen Palczewski to note that public debates about pornography fundamentally trade in definitional argument.[17] In his concurring opinion in *Jacobellis v. Ohio*, US Supreme Court Justice Potter Stewart penned the now-infamous phrase "I know it when I see it" regarding what constitutes obscene hardcore pornography. With this succinct comment, Stewart conceded the difficulty of defining pornography in a universally satisfactory way.[18] Such definitional slippage creates conditions under which rhetors can mobilize stigma regarding pornography to discredit myriad gender performances and sexual proclivities.[19] Writes Kipnis, "Pornography seems to live on perpetual standby to represent the nadir of culture, on call to provide the necessary opposition to culture's apex, which is, of course, the canon."[20]

Fundamental to public discourse about pornography is that public anxieties regarding, for example, VHS tapes portraying vaginal penetration, are inescapably about something else.[21] Gunn writes, "At the affective level of bodily excitation, pornography concerns the formal arousal of appetites as well as a fundamental failure to satisfy them."[22] For him, pornographic texts induce audience participation by promising the libidinal apotheosis they cannot deliver. Rosenfield characterizes pornography as "a surrogate for freedom."[23] In ways that resonate with Norman Mailer's controversial writing regarding white consumption of jazz, Rosenfield claims that the forbidden territory pornography presumes to disclose offers spectators fleeting moments of emancipation from the banal and prudish constraints of everyday life.[24] Gunn also claims that "pornography is watched because one does not want or cannot have 'the real thing.'"[25] For these thinkers, the pornographic entails projecting fantasy onto the pornographic action onscreen.[26] One can approach fantasy with minimal risk. For this reason, Kipnis theorizes pornography as a repository for fantasies that such texts mobilize as "dangerous and socially destabilizing incendiary devices."[27] This, Kipnis argues, is fundamental to pornography's capacity to provoke the ire of so many publics. Its economy of fantasy, she claims, is too unwieldy to warrant anything besides sanction.[28]

Also fundamental to pornography's rhetorical character is form. Structuring logics, rather than sexually explicit materials themselves, render pornographic texts as such.[29] Attention to form also reveals that, despite its capacity to mimic transgression, pornography is thoroughly normative. Audre Lorde describes pornography's formal character when she distinguishes it from the erotic. She writes, "To share the power of each other's feelings is different from using another's feelings as we would use a kleenex.

When we look the other way from our experience, erotic or otherwise, we use rather than share the feelings of those others who participate in the experience with us. And use without consent of the used is abuse."[30] Pornography, in other words, entails the nonreciprocal enjoyment of other fungible bodies. Pornographic form is a variation on sadistic form.

Describing what they call *pornification* in electoral politics, Ignacio Moreno Segarra and Karrin Vasby Anderson write, "When pornified, women are treated not as individuals with political agency but as interchangeable objects which may be manipulated for political and commercial gain."[31] Such a claim resonates with Dennis Giles, who writes, "Once he projects the 'bad' in himself into the pornographic woman, the spectator is free to *desire* those very qualities he has expelled."[32] The penetrated feminine object of the pornographic text functions to concretize the viewer's fantasies. And such form can structure discourse with no apparent sexual content just as surely as explicit online materials or other "hardcore" texts.[33] Pornography possesses a formal logic that manifests in contexts devoid of explicit sexual content, but nonetheless trade in the subordination and use of fungible feminine bodies. Pornography need not be that freaky.

Indeed, even the most risqué material is quite normative vis-à-vis the logics that structure white masculinity. Consider the following from Susan Brownmiller: "The staple of porn will always be the naked female body, breasts and genitals exposed, because as man devised it, her naked body is the female's 'shame,' her private parts the private property of man, while his are the ancient, holy, universal, patriarchal instrument of his power, his rule by force over her."[34] Similarly, Andrea Dworkin writes, "The power of men in pornography is imperial power, the power of the sovereigns who are cruel and arrogant, who keep taking and conquering for the pleasure of power and the power of pleasure."[35] For Brownmiller and Dworkin, pornography expresses the same patriarchal logics as rape. That is, pornography concretizes rape's rhetorical form. In theorizing pornography in such a way, scholars such as Dworkin and Brownmiller, as well as Segarra and Anderson, build outward from the concrete brutalities of rape to name a gendered logic that manifests in myriad contexts.

What these critiques of pornography and gendered violence provide is the makings of a heuristic that refuses to take the nature of a sexually explicit text, or a fully nonsexual text, for granted. Yes, texts that carry the commercial and legal marker of pornography are usually misogynistic. But misogyny is not inherent to the visual representation of copulating bodies as such. Regarding antiporn activism, Linda Williams cautions, "As long as we emphasize woman's role as the absolute victim of male sadism, we only perpetuate the supposedly essential nature of woman's powerlessness."[36] As Jennifer C. Nash illustrates in her study of Black women in pornography, such texts possess transgressive potential realized through oppositional readings and subversive production.[37] Thus, to categorically critique pornography through white feminist heuristics risks negating Black women's agency.[38] In his work on so-called "torture porn," Dean Lockwood claims that such seemingly exploitative films potentially dismantle "the normal limitations and accepted self-definitions of the subject."[39] Furthermore, pornography historically plays a deeply salient role for queer intimacies and therefore the constitution of queer publics.[40] This is where a distinction between the pornographic and the erotic, such as Lorde's, becomes especially useful.[41] Such an approach underscores the salience of the relations that frame and contextualize a sexual text's circulation, rather than the presence or absence of specific sex acts. In her work on heterosexual desire, Jane Ward writes, "I call upon the wisdom of the dyke experience to illuminate for straight men the human capacity to desire, to fuck, and to be feminist comrades at the same time."[42] Thus, while many antiporn feminists would characterize the visual representation of a sex act such as fellatio or bondage as irredeemably degrading and therefore misogynistic, Ward's work suggests that the gendered character of such acts is contingent on the structuring logics that govern their representation and circulation.[43] Fucking can be erotic. Pornography is a rhetorical form that makes claims regarding whose desires matter and whose bodies should serve as surfaces for actualizing fantasies of dominion. And such form is neither exclusively nor necessarily the domain of sexually explicit material.

Wandering Boys

In his interview with Dobson, Bundy narrativized his evolving proclivities. While his imminent execution was for the 1978 kidnapping, rape, and murder of a middle school girl, Bundy contends the foundations for his crimes began forming during childhood. He tells Dobson, "As I think I explained to you last night, Dr. Dobson, in an anecdote, that, as young boys do, we explored the back roads and sideways and byways of our neighborhood, and oftentimes people would dump the garbage and whatever they're cleaning out of their house and from time to time, we'd come across pornographic books of a harder nature than . . . a more graphic, you might say, a more explicit nature of what we would encounter, let's say, in your local grocery store."[44]

Much like conservative antiporn crusades during the late twentieth century, Bundy casts himself as a victim of women's bodies.[45] That is, pornography destroyed his youthful innocence. It caused him to fall off track. Liz Kendall recalls her phone conversation with Bundy following his final arrest in Florida. As he essentially confesses to Liz, although he would proceed to publicly declare his innocence until shortly before his execution, Bundy explains, "I have a sickness . . . a disease like your alcoholism . . . you can't take another drink and with my . . . sickness . . . there is something . . . that I just can't be around . . . and I know it now."[46] That "something" is presumably white girls and young women walking across or around colleges and universities, hitchhiking, shopping at a local mall, watching a high school play, sleeping, or, in Leach's case, rushing to her homeroom to retrieve the purse she left behind.[47] In ways that resonate with former Vice President Mike Pence's refusal to be alone in a room with women besides his wife, Bundy suggests that if only he could avoid proximity to these women and girls, his sickness would go into remission.[48] They are the problem. In casting pornographic material and feminine bodies this way, Bundy diminishes his own culpability. As he explains it, his actual and potential victims trigger his Mr. Hyde.

Noting that he too grew up in Tacoma during the postwar period, Michaud told the interviewer for the 2006 documentary *Ted Bundy: Natural Porn Killer* that the Seattle suburb of his and Bundy's youths did not overflow with pornographic materials in family trashcans or dumpsters.[49] But Bundy's account rings true for me in salient ways. At least, I understand how pornography is something many of us find and that each subsequent encounter can reconstitute our relations with our bodies and Others'. For example, as a Cub Scout during the late 1980s, my den volunteered at a local recycling location. While climbing across the piles of old magazines and newspapers that filled semi-truck trailers, the other Scouts and I discovered discarded porn magazines such as *Playboy* and *Penthouse*. On more than one occasion, I stole away with a few copies that became my inaugural collection of adult materials. As a prepubescent Scout, I did little but stare at the various centerfolds, surveying the women's nude bodies with little sense of what I might do with one of them if they suddenly materialized from the page. But the pornographic logic of "what I might do with one of them" was itself taking hold, as was my ocular scanning of their every curvature.

But later discoveries awaited. While Bundy hid bodies in the woods, my father hid them in the garage. I was sixteen when I found them in a brown paper bag hidden among various tools, dusty holiday decorations, and six packs of beer. Here was another discovery whose aura of mystery and danger made it addictive. If Bundy returned to his victim's corpses to relive their first visceral encounter, I initially returned to my family's musty one-car garage to simply stand in the presence of these mysterious VHS cassettes. After several days of contemplating, I brought one of the tapes inside when no one was home. I slipped it into the VCR. I recall the immense tension filling the space between my throat and abdomen, both worrying that a parent or my sister would return home and feeling anxiously enticed by what was about to appear on the television screen. I suspect this is what young people feel when they are about the lose their virginity. While I had intercourse for the first time about four years later, I was too drunk to register much of what was taking place. So, this time in the basement of my childhood home was to be my deflowering.

The video began playing in medias res. On the television screen, the same I used to play video games or watch pretentious art films, appeared a closeup of an erect, large, white phallus. It was much bigger than mine. Having never had "the talk" with my father or any other elder outside a handful of K–12 health classes, I assumed this was a deficiency on my part.[50] A woman with a curly blonde bob and tacky earrings fellated the penis whose accompanying body parts were mostly offscreen. Precisely the kind of music one would expect in a 1990s porno played in the background.

I watched the video for less than sixty seconds before returning it to its hiding place in the garage. From the garage, I went to my basement bedroom. By this stage of my life, I had already begun touching myself, but not in a way that induced orgasm. The sex acts of my imagination were all rubbing, no tugging or penetrating. But amid the haze of my inaugural porno viewing, I noticed the logistics of fellatio well enough to detect a kind of neck and mouth motion I could duplicate with my hands. And so, I did. I proceeded to make a mess. I rested in my childhood twin bed in my basement bedroom where I spent so many hours keeping family, school, and the rest of the world at bay. I felt sticky. I felt disgusting. And I was alone. And in my loneliness, I began orchestrating my carnal being through pornographic form. My desires would often be messy, sticky, and disgusting.

After later viewings of my father's pornos, I was sure to rewind the tape to the exact spot where I found it when I first inserted it into the VCR. On this Bundy and I agreed: one must painstakingly orchestrate onanistic exploits to avoid detection. And such orchestration itself becomes ritualistic. Watching my father's pornos was never solely about naked bodies copulating. The garage's musty smell, the VHS tapes' cold feel during winter months, the care of returning the tape to its original spot, and even the prospect of someone returning home heightened the newfound pleasures of gazing pornographically. For me, sex would always be about secrecy, and under secrecy always lingers shame.

These tactics were also an early foray into adopting my father's sneaky habits of hiding things such as his porn use, drinking, or theft. But I often wondered if my rewinding scheme worked. Maybe my father knew I was watching his pornos. This inspired obvious fear toward the man who, I knew by now, could find reasons to violently lash out against me. But I also felt a degree of confidence in what I thought was mutually assured destruction. Punishing me for watching the tapes would require him to acknowledge their existence. I imagined his pornography use as a lonely pursuit alongside his heavy drinking that functioned to build walls in lieu of intimacy. It was decidedly nonerotic. Ted Bundy hid bodies in the woods so he could return to them and exercise dominion. So too, I suspect, did my father keep the bodies inside a paper bag in the garage so that he might view and fantasize on his own terms—terms he perhaps found lacking in his life's other aspects.

The only time I recall telling my father as an adult that I loved him was when he lay dead, his body ravaged by cancer, on an emergency room gurney. His inability to reciprocate then was typical, for I have no lucid memories of him saying he loved me. But we bonded through prone feminine bodies, a practice Ward explains is fundamental to homosociality in the United States.[51] My father and I cocreated ways of being white and masculine that found expression through pornographic form.[52]

Like an Addiction

Traditionally, enclaves are the domain of the marginalized. In her work on the Black public sphere, Catherine Squires explains that Black publics oscillate between different modes of publicity. Among these are enclaves where the exploited and oppressed assemble as a means of protection and relatively uninterrupted becoming. Enclaves are where *les damned* find space to breathe.[53] But other enclaves are the domain of privilege when it sheds pretense. For example, Jeffrey Epstein orchestrated a complex underworld of powerful men who raped teenage girls.[54] David Peace's *Red Riding* novels chronicle the workings of a similar network of powerful pedophiles who stole away to enact their fantasies.[55] The first season of Nic Pizzolatto's *True Detective* likewise features antagonists whose access to economic and political power enable them to kidnap, torture, and murder children and young women with impunity.[56] Suffice it to say, the figure of the powerful white man whose most sadistic proclivities only find expression in private endures in Western culture.

Such renderings figure the enclave as a space where the desiring subject performs sovereignty in excess of the power he enjoys in public. Authors such as Georges Bataille claimed secrecy is inherent to the erotic, for the latter presupposes a transgressed taboo.[57] Thus, there comes a point where even the most privileged among us must conceal our desires. Hence, male accountants and lawyers dispense with dollar bills at strip clubs while the normative responsibilities of family wait at home. But both spaces, the strip club and the domicile, function as concretizations of normative white masculinity, even if the former masquerades as transgression. Blue-collar alcoholics hide booze and porn tapes in the garage. There were surely powerful, violent linkages between the fantasy world my father built with pornographic videos and his sometimes cruel and frequently feeble attempts to retain control over his daily life. The bodies that gyrated and moaned for him, and his son, on the television screen were far more compliant and fungible than those, such as my mother, my sister, and myself, whose recalcitrance likely convinced him of his many failures. And serial murderers such as Ted Bundy find private spaces where they can rape and murder young women and girls. It is on these sacred grounds, these Terrible Places, that authentic desire reaches its apotheosis.[58] And for Bataille, the domain of the sacred is where desiring subjects shatter taboos.[59]

While Bataille is correct that all subjects reckon with taboo in salient ways, he ignores the ways even the most shocking transgressions can reify the normative. What he calls the erotic is the province of domination.[60] Fundamental to Bataille's work is an autonomous agent in defiance of social norms. Such a subject, for the French philosopher, is necessarily counterhegemonic.[61] But Bataille's landscape of desire possesses no theory of power outside a

Nietzschean individualism.⁶² Such a characterization of libidinal yearnings against taboo is quite resonant with modernity's core impulses. Giving oneself over to taboo feels like freedom.⁶³ In a way, it is. But such indulgence also occurs upon a field of social relations. For this reason, the libertine's freedom claims possession over the objects that concretize the rush of transgressing. Conquerors seek dominion over their conquests.⁶⁴ As I have noted earlier, such individualism is consistent with the white Western masculine subject. It is especially resonant with neoliberal capitalism. Thus, while Bataille's libertine appears as a heroic iconoclast whose activated pleasures disavow social orthodoxies, critics such as Hortense Spillers, Hartman, Alexander G. Weheliye, and Lugones understand that freakiness among the powerful is ultimately quite vanilla. It actualizes the very norms it presumes to disavow.⁶⁵

Crucial to understanding the ultimate banality of what passes for taboo in white Western modernity is the ways quotidian acts of gendered violence do the same work. In their writing about pornotroping, Spillers and Weheliye explain that reducing bodies to fungible flesh for violent and sexual enjoyment is fundamental to anti-Blackness and, therefore, modernity. Pornotroping functions as a representational logic that materializes Black bodies as less-than-human.⁶⁶ Such an understanding of pornographic desire is why Hartman's attention to quotidian, rather than spectacular, forms of anti-Black violence is so essential for critiquing modernity.⁶⁷ Similarly, Sayak Valencia writes regarding gruesome drug violence in México, "We are talking about practices that are transgressive solely because their forcefulness makes the vulnerability of the human body clear, in how it is mutilated and desecrated."⁶⁸ To make manifest the violence that characterizes Western modernity is taboo. The violence itself is not.

The distinctions between differently rendered kinds of violence are ultimately a matter of amplification, not form. Bundy's crimes, as well as Epstein and his brethren's pedophilic cruelty, confront US publics invested in normative ideals of gender and sexuality with their own logics taken to their most monstrous ends. And such confrontation risks catalyzing anxiety. The violence itself is normative because it enacts gendered relationalities that structure civil society. Enjoying prone, fungible, and feminized bodies, whether as serial murder or videos on PornHub, is the province of modernity's white masculine subject.⁶⁹ As Mardorossian insists, "We need to understand that the will to dominate is not an expression of free will or of a subject exercising agency so much as it is the expression of a subject bound to gendered expectations that have turned the will to dominate into identity itself."[70] Bundy's transgression was not acting on his desire to possess and enjoy feminine bodies, but inflicting cruelty in ways that were so undeniable. He went too far. His acts therefore required a kind of rhetorical finessing that would subordinate the incisive critique of modernity that acknowledging his normativity might enable. The forms of depravity sadists such as Bundy enact give expression to the logics of violent possession that underwrite Western civil society in general. They ultimately reify relations of dominance through their carnal excesses.

For example, the sadistic spectacles that dominate Pasolini's *Salò* seem to defy Western civilization's espoused mores.[71] Writers such as Gunn and Kelly would observe that the pleasure the fascist kidnappers experienced while humiliating and brutalizing their young captives stemmed from a perverse enjoyment of boundaries transgressed.[72] And it is likely that the sadist experiences enjoyment in such a way. That is, he believes he is breaking the rules and it feels good. But film scholar Roberto Chiesi explains that, in *Salò*, "Once these norms are codified and imposed as law, they cease being what they were and become instead the norms of a new and sinister conformity that assimilates and wipes out any variation."[73] In other words, the affects of transgression often circulate within a structural context of actual domination.[74] The joys of breaking the rules function ideologically to sustain them. When one of Pasolini's fascists demands that a naked young woman captive urinate on his face, he is by no means submitting nor engaging in a queer sex act. Rather, because the golden shower he enjoys occurs within the normative grip of the law as he and his fascist brethren have named it, it is, within the film's diegesis, a most missionary and sadistic sex act against the young woman. And it is this relationship between the joys of perversion and enforcement of dominion that confronts publics through Pasolini's cinematic text. The director expressed as much at the time of the film's release, telling an interviewer, "In this new film, sex is nothing but an allegory of the commodification of bodies at the hands of power."[75] For this reason, *Salò* remains a salient commentary on the relationship between sadistic lust and sovereign power.

I have strayed considerably from Bundy and Dobson, my father, and my pubescent self absorbing pornography's pedagogies. But doing so illuminates the ways even the freakiest, filthiest pornographic excesses are remarkably conservative and ubiquitous. Throughout his interview with Dobson, Bundy distinguished mainstream pornography from what he called "violent pornography," or "pornography that deals on a violent level with sexuality."[76] This, Bundy claimed, was the kind of material that led him astray. It was a gateway drug to serial murder. Said Bundy, "Like an addiction, you keep craving something which is harder, harder, something which . . . which . . . gives you a greater sense of excitement, until you reach that jumping off point where you begin to wonder if . . . if maybe actually doing it will give you that which is just beyond reading about it and looking at it."

In ways that resonate with Bataille's and René Girard's writings on ritual, Bundy characterized the act of raping and killing as an encounter with the sacred.[77] In her capacity as his death row attorney, Nelson observed Bundy experiencing something like religious ecstasy when he finally began confessing days before his 1989 execution. As she listened to his detailed description of murdering a hitchhiker in the Pacific Northwest, Nelson recalls, "I looked at his face. Ted's skin was darkening as he spoke. He was on a roll now, in a sort of trance, recalling every detail as he reviewed the fifteen-some-year-old film in his head, frame by frame."[78] She added, "No detail was too small to recall, everything was important, everything had meaning. He was like a reverent disciple describing a spiritual revelation."[79] Reflecting on the way Bundy's palpable misogyny made her feel vulnerable in her notorious client's presence, Nelson wrote, "His murders were his life's accomplishments."[80] They were his "just beyond."

The sacred's opposite is the profane. It is the tepid day-to-day that monopolizes most lives. Carl Olson explains, "Within the profane world, excessive action is limited and desire is repressed because of its inherent tendency to exceed social limits."[81] My first engagement with pornography surely felt sacred. And the pleasures of excess undoubtedly played a role therein. The feeling of transgression is what makes the fantasy hold. The libertines of *Salò* understood their kidnapping, sexual torture, and murder of eighteen teenagers as a performative critique of morality, even as their status as powerful fascists enabled their deeds. And situating Bundy outside the profane imbues his archive with a pornographic character that ultimately reifies the very monstrosity such situating presumes to condemn. In a searing indictment of Sade's work, Roger Shattuck writes, "Shall we receive among our literary classics the works of an author who desecrates and inverts every principle of human justice and decency developed over four thousand years of civilized life?"[82] Shattuck's exasperation that Sade's work "desecrates and inverts" Western modernist (that is, "civilized") notions of decency betrays, as does Dobson's moralizing, and so many other espoused anxieties about carnal excess, the monsters modernity conceals. In so doing, they mark for exclusion that which amplifies far more profane sadistic acts.[83]

Where Were You, Ted?

In the 1986 miniseries *The Deliberate Stranger*, director Marvin J. Chomsky typically portrays Harmon's Bundy's modus operandi as one of confidence, even cockiness, as he stalked college-aged women throughout the film. But during a sequence chronicling his final murder spree in Florida, Bundy sits inside a parked car and stares stoically at a group of young girls playing jump rope on a suburban street. Aged much younger than Bundy's final known victim, twelve-year-old Leach, these girls embody an innocence lacking in the smoky college bars or busy campuses where Bundy traditionally stalked victims. Harmon's Bundy struggles to sit still, seemingly managing conflicting thoughts. It appears as if a latent decent man lingers far in the recesses of this Bundy's person, but he cannot resist the overwhelming urge to kidnap, rape, and murder one of these little girls.

Similarly, near the end of the Dobson interview, Leach's murder functions as a shocking, if also somewhat inevitable, culmination of Bundy's "fatal addiction." She is the serial killer's rock bottom. Dobson asked, "One of the final murders that you committed, of course, was apparently little Kimberly Leach, 12 years of age. I think the public outcry is greater there because an innocent child was taken from a playground. What did you feel after that? Were there normal emotions three days later? Where were you Ted?" As Dobson speaks, Bundy slowly shifts from the confident learned man pontificating on the wages of pornography (which are death) to a meeker, less assured man. He appears broken, as if the man who knows he will die in less than twenty-four hours has finally penetrated the façade Bundy orchestrated for various audiences. His response is barely coherent. Bundy tells Dobson, "I can't really talk about that right now. That's . . ." Bundy trails off and Dobson finishes the sentence for him, asking, "That's too painful?" It is possible that, contrary to many popular and clinical characterizations of Bundy as an unfeeling narcissist, a serial killer who murdered over thirty young women and girls carried an especially potent morsel of guilt regarding the preteen girl whose mummified corpse police found in a pig shed several weeks after Bundy killed her.[84] At least this is Dobson's implication, as well as cinematic texts such as *Ted Bundy*, *The Deliberate Stranger*, *Extremely Wicked*, and *No Man of God* that characterize Leach's killing as Bundy's most depraved act. Even Bundy himself seemed speechless in the face of such sadism.

And the notion that Leach was especially "innocent" compared to the scores of college students, young professionals, and runaways Bundy murdered resonates strongly with the cultural politics Dobson mobilized through the Meese Commission and other culturally conservative endeavors. Describing the relative absence of rape victims' voices in the Commission report and other texts associated with the Reagan-era antiporn crusade, Larson writes, "In short, to recognize victims would require dealing with histories of misogyny, white supremacy, and violent masculinity, making the move to reaffirm normativity and blame society far easier."[85] For Dobson and his allies, the culprit that mobilized sexual violence in US society was an increasingly permissive culture, and its most concrete manifestation was the adult entertainment industry. It was images of naked women with curly bobs and tacky earrings giving blow jobs to anonymous men that would turn impressionable teenage boys from Tacoma or the Chicago suburbs into predators. Such logic makes suggesting that a condemned killer's memories of raping and murdering a twelve-year-old girl are "too painful" for him quite reasonable.

But centering Leach as the sole named victim in the Dobson interview functions to reaffirm normativity by centering the conservative futurity inherent to the child.[86] Larson explains that many of Dobson's fellow antiporn crusaders "grieved what they believed to be the most worthwhile members of society—children, men, and mothers—and in the process, sought to regulate certain forms of embodiment."[87] While US college and university campuses were and remain key fronts in many culture wars regarding gender equity and sexuality, a virginal figure such as Leach provided Dobson a solemn embodiment of pornography's war on the normative family.[88] In this way, Dobson's conscription of Leach in his broader effort to frame the Bundy saga as a testament to pornography's evils is itself a pornographic claim. Not only did pornography lead Bundy down a path that would waste his own life, but it also induced him to destroy the world of a young girl who might grow to be a devoted wife, mother, and Christian. Bundy's other, nameless victims barely register as salient in comparison.

In her critique of legal renderings of children as pure subjects in need of protection, Erin J. Rand writes, "Of course, it is precisely the impression of purity, wholesomeness, and virginal artlessness that makes children so titillating to adult fantasy, so the 'sacred' child figure both entangles children in circuits of adult desire while also denying childhood's own queerness."[89] While I do not presume to know whether Dr. Dobson harbored secretive carnal fantasies about children in any literal sense of the word, the fantasy that structures his invocation of Leach is downright filthy. His is a ritual that sacrifices young flesh in the service of a theocratic enterprise whose objective is a profane sexuality no less pornographic than what it seeks to supplant.[90] Leach's young, metonymic body remains in a state of rigor mortis for Dobson to use. Black feminists such as Rachel Alicia Griffin, Spillers, and Weheliye, as well as decolonial feminists such as Deer, Ashley Noel Mack, and Tiara R. Na'puti illustrate that centering the body in critical practice regarding sexual violence is essential, for it reveals how violated bodies function as sites for cultural production.[91] Specifically, centering embodiment reveals how much public discourse about rape reifies the logics of sexual violence itself.[92] Dobson's collaboration with Bundy has little regard for women's bodies beyond their rhetorical function in service of a Christian fundamentalist discourse. Like the serial killer he interviewed, as well as so many other men, young and old, who gaze at mass mediated sex acts, Dobson's was an onanistic moral crusade that sacrificed women's bodies to the cause of masculine sovereignty. The interview he recorded and continues to distribute via DVD and streaming video is itself pornographic. It stages Bundy's encounters with docile feminine subjects through which Dobson could exalt the very gendered norms that prefigure men such as his interview subject.

Another Man's Pornography

Opportunities to view my father's pornos could not keep pace with my exploding and unrequited teenage libido. I would retrieve and watch the tapes when I could. I became creative when I could not. At this time, I was also enamored with idealized notions of Bohemia. I read writers such as Allen Ginsberg and William S. Burroughs. I idolized directors such as Stanley Kubrick, Martin Scorsese, and Gus Van Sant. I curated a CD collection and devoured my parents' vinyl collection in ways I hoped broadcast my sophisticated sensibilities. And I read various punk zines and artsy pop periodicals such as *Interview*. *Interview*, which another teenage hero, Andy Warhol, cofounded in 1969, frequently included images of nude bodies, including celebrities. For *Interview*'s purposes, nudes in advertisements, art show reviews, or celebrity interviews signaled its broader pop art sensibilities. For my purposes, such photos sufficed perfectly for my onanistic needs. So too did the dusty copy of George Downing's *The Massage Book*, which my parents kept in plain sight on a bookshelf. An artifact of the period when texts such as *The Joy of Sex* and *Our Bodies, Our Selves* circulated heavily in US public life, this instruction manual included photographs and drawings of naked adult bodies that were both clinical and sensual. I also extracted nude scenes from my favorite films, fast forwarding through unnecessary plot to arrive at the moment I required to accommodate my fantasizing. Suffice it to say, I could find pornography in numerous contexts.

I am unaware of any police investigation into Bundy that discovered the kinds of texts most US Americans would characterize as pornography in his possession. Following his final arrest in Florida, after he kidnapped, raped, and murdered a twelve-year-old girl, law enforcement found several "well-thumbed pamphlets for cheerleader training schools" in his possession.[93] While Bundy was on the lam after escaping from a Colorado jail, and had committed three murders before his arrest, it is unlikely that he was so hard-pressed that the cheerleader pamphlets were a substitute for "actual" pornography. He could have purchased or stolen a *Playboy* or *Hustler*. Given the significant limitations of criminal investigation methods circa 1978, Bundy likely could have sat in a dark booth in a small Florida town strip club or adult movie theater. But he chose photographs of fully clothed adolescent cheerleaders and majorettes.

What was it about the pamphlets that so attracted Bundy? Was it the prospect of enjoying young flesh for its own sake? Maybe he lusted the same way other men do when they search "barely legal" on a site such as PornHub or wander drunkenly into a Hustler Barely Legal strip club. Bundy's desire likely resonated with the more permissible, if still pedophilic, impulses that mobilize mainstream pornographic tastes. Or was his desire located less in exposed legs or perky breasts poking through spandex, and more in the wholesome smiles that captured so many promises of Western futurity? Was it the sadistic drive to destroy such optimism that led him to take those magazines from the drug store rack instead of *Playboy* or *Hustler*?[94] And was that what enticed him about Kimberly Dianne Leach? Was that voice telling him "Look at that bitch there"?[95] Innocence and futurity are surely what catalyzed Dobson's yearning for her preteen corpse.

Also central to Bundy's pornographic tastes were detective and so-called "men's adventure" magazines of the postwar era. Historian Peter Vronsky notes that many late twentieth-century serial killers, all of whom grew up during the postwar baby boom, identified these pulp periodicals as favorites during their childhood and adolescence.[96] Publications such as *Exposé Detective, Crime SuspenStories, Man's Story,* and *Escape to Adventure* were ubiquitous from the 1950s until the early 1970s. The average postwar pulp featured an illustrated cover with sensationalistic fonts and violent scenes. Most covers centered images of scantily clad women in distress. Usually bound, she helplessly awaited some sort of violent end, whether it be rape at the hands of a primitive tribe, cruel experimentation from Nazis, some form of medieval torture, or attack at the hands of a sexual sadist lurking in the shadows. Her cleavage was usually conspicuous, and her legs spread open just so (figure 12). Vronsky remarks, "It all harkened back to the gynocidal dungeons of the Great Witch Hunt of 1450 to 1650 at its most sadistic fantastic."[97]

Whereas contemporary pornographic magazines typically appear at the very top of newsstands wrapped in plastic and obscured from plain view, these postwar periodicals shared space with *Life* and other mainstream magazines. Indeed, they were themselves mainstream. As such, Adam Parfrey argues that these pulps served a postwar pedagogical function. Regarding men's magazines, he writes, "All of them had, among the lures of woman flesh and vicious bad guys, a lot of warnings, how-to's, and comforting memories of wartime, when decisions were black and white, the villains darker and victories sweeter."[98] He also notes that such publications functioned to replace the crude and heavily racialized caricatures of Axis villains such as Hitler and Japanese Emperor Hirohito through their visual representations of spectacular and equally racialized sadism. Such displays of depravity served a postwar constitutive function that presumed to remind white men what it meant to be men.

Furthermore, Vronsky contextualizes these publications within the sexual politics of World War II itself. While contemporary mythos regarding the "Greatest Generation" regards World War II as a Manichean conflict between good and evil to which future generations owe perpetual fealty, the "good guys" engaged in their share of sexual sadism.[99] Vronsky notes

Figure 12. A typical detective magazine cover. *Crime SuspenStories*, 1954.

that US soldiers raped scores of German, Japanese, and other women and collected necrophilic war totems such as skulls and other body parts from the battlefield.[100] During a postconviction interview, Kemper, a white serial killer who decapitated the young women he murdered, compared himself to European paintings of "Viking heroes" who severed their enemies' heads. He explained that he understood his violent acts as "part of our heritage."[101]

Kemper might have also observed macabre parallels with veterans of the war in which his father fought, as well as other ritual performances of white masculine violence.[102] For example, Ersula J. Ore observes that lynching photographs operated within the same formal register as aristocratic hunting portraits. She writes, "Scenes of the hunt were a common subject of portraiture that figured white men as proper providers and protectors."[103] Whether the slain body is that of a hunted animal placed before the hunting party, a Black person hanging from a tree, an enemy's wife or daughter during wartime, a college student heading home after a night of studying at the library, or the affect emanating from a raped and murdered twelve-year-old girl's corpse, dominion over the fungible feminine body reifies white masculine sovereignty. All such displays express pornographic form. For Kemper, possessing a young woman's severed head placed him in the esteemed company of his brethren. He was not wrong.

When Bundy returned to his dump sites following a murder, he often posed his victims in ways that mimicked the covers of his beloved pulp magazines. In addition to applying makeup to the women's faces, he put them in new clothes and styled their hair in ways that recalled a postwar pulp aesthetic. He then took pictures and engaged in necrophilia. Such pornographic proclivities reflect Downing's claim that "necrophilic excesses" complete "the process of feminization which death has begun."[104] Within the white Western US masculine imagination, the enslaved or otherwise captured body functions as a tabula rasa upon which despots can project their monstrous fantasies.[105] Such bodies have "myriad uses."[106] Regarding the sexual fantasies of serial killers, Maria Tatar writes, "The female body in its death throes becomes the site of a transcendent experience that negates sexuality even as it uses it as a vehicle for a privileged moment of insight."[107] Sex as such is not the variable that links the serial killer with the fascist or the slaveowner or the colonist or the neoliberal. Rather, sex is one expression of a pornographic logic whose telos is possession.[108]

Onanism and Projection

Most narratives about Bundy presume that he began as a masturbator who moved on to the "real thing." This is of course true of the Dobson interview. In Bundy's telling, he began jerking off to pornography and eventually, even inevitably, began murdering women and girls. The pornography *led to* the murders. Farrands's *Ted Bundy: American Boogeyman* is rare in the Bundy cinematic archive in that it uncritically affirms this causal relationship. In his postinterrogation exposition, the FBI psychiatrist tells investigators, "In my sixteen years as a clinical psychiatrist, I can honestly say Theodore Bundy is the most dangerous individual I've ever observed." He speculates that Bundy's sadistic proclivities began with "an unnatural obsession with pornography from a very young age." He adds, "And I don't mean the blue magazines that

Figure 13. Bundy looking at pornography in *Ted Bundy: American Boogeyman*. Fathom Events/Voltage Pictures, 2021.

teenage boys hide from their parents, but rather, he became obsessed with sexually explicit images of violence, with human pain and suffering." That is, Farrands's Bundy was indeed the product of the "violent pornography" of which the killer warned Dr. Dobson. Later in the film, Farrands includes an especially bizarre scene in which Bundy, saturated in red lights worthy of a sleazy strip club, ritualistically masturbates to BDSM magazines while wielding a knife and fondling mannequins (figure 13).[109] Following this sequence, Bundy proceeds to attack the young women of the Chi Omega house. Masturbation preceded murder. Farrands's film is, in my view, overwhelmingly the worst feature film in the Bundy archive. It distorts the historical record in baffling ways, is poorly written, and extracts cringe-inducing performances from even seasoned actors. But it represents the most explicit cinematic mimicry of the claims Bundy and Dobson cultivated in 1989.

While other narratives in the Bundy archive do not adhere to the Dobson narrative of pornography's sinister effects on young men, they nonetheless characterize Bundy's murders as the culmination of a depraved evolutionary process. Describing the years just preceding his first murders, true crime writer Kevin M. Sullivan writes, "By this time Bundy was a veteran Peeping Tom, who sought sexual gratification by spying on women at night. These nocturnal and sexually driven forays were an incubator for his fantasies, increasingly demanding more than merely staring into basement windows, masturbating, or dreaming of the day he could actually abduct a pretty young coed."[110]

During their final death row conversation, Bundy and his attorney, Nelson, similarly discussed pornography and voyeurism's roles in amplifying the "voice" that urged him toward rape, homicide, and necrophilia.[111] While assessing the clinical efficacy of such explanations regarding Bundy's crimes falls far outside my realm of expertise, the cultural implications of the framework are salient. It posits a firm distinction between the pornographic pleasures of watching mass mediated sex, or even masturbating in the bushes while a young coed undresses on the other side of a window, and subduing the same woman in order to concretize such pornographic fantasies.

But Bundy never stopped masturbating. He simply found new ways to do so. The "real thing" changed. In its multiagency report on Bundy following his execution, the FBI wrote, "Being voyeuristic, it was important that Bundy be able to see what he was doing. He selected sites where the moon shone brightly, or he would 'operate' in front of the headlights of his vehicle."[112] The show, in other words, went on. Drawing on Jean-Paul Sartre's reading of Jean Genet, author and musician Peter Sotos characterizes the masturbator as both spectator and subject.[113] The pleasure he experiences derives from what he surveils. Bundy raping and murdering a white woman or girl is every bit as onanistic as his younger self jerking off to the cover of a detective magazine in hopes that his mother would not barge into the bedroom. And as writers such as Anderson and Ward illustrate, pornography's formal logic, which is the subordination of fungible bodies for libidinal enjoyment (that is, sadistic form), finds expression in contexts including electoral politics and the dating industry.[114] It surely lingers in the carnal fumblings of bisexual white boys raised in suburban alcoholic homes whose pornographic pedagogy prefigured so many toxic sexual and romantic conquests. Those of us who enact white masculinity author pornography and project it onto available surfaces, whether they be massage books or live flesh. Onanism is the orientation that structures the libidinal impulses that structure white masculinity.

And the Bundy archive itself is pornographic, for it enables and induces public consumption of his many depravities. It is a surface for pornographic projection. Characterizing the Bundy archive in such a way illuminates the barely latent enjoyments that arise for many publics that consume Bundy.[115] In the second issue of his controversial 1980s zine, *Pure*, Sotos characterized Bundy as "the greatest living American example of genius."[116] Such praise is consistent with Sotos's ethos, as he vocally performs admiration for murderers, pedophiles, sexual sadists, and Nazis for their unapologetic pursuits of self-fulfillment. Sotos envisions his work in Sadean and Nietzschean terms, seeing Bundy as one among "those who view and understand their instincts completely and correctly and then go about satisfying them."[117] The enthymeme that saturates Sotos's catalogue of his own writing, police reports, pornographic stills, crime scene and autopsy photographs, and other macabre artifacts is that they are tributes to those sadists who possessed the courage to pursue self-gratification.

If one takes Sotos's work on face value, its primary public is one whose members would immediately grasp the warrant that linked newspaper clippings about pedophilia and genocide to their carnal fantasies. But it is difficult to discern Sotos's sincerity. He is, in this respect, an Andy Kaufman among sexual sadists. It is possible his performance amounts to an ironic cultural critique. Either way, Sotos claims that he is simply saying the quiet parts aloud.[118] He rejects the notion that the more conventional proclivities of desiring men are a function of them "merely wanting to wild away every night away from their noisy daughters and wives."[119] For Sotos, or at least his persona, these men are dupes who deny themselves the fulfillment of their own desires. They choose PornHub or the strip club over the crueler fantasies he claims so many of them suppress. Hence, Bundy is a "genius" for abandoning pretense and taking what he wanted.[120] Sotos exalts Bundy for creating his own pornography. For such claims, Sotos is a creep. Or he feigns creepiness remarkably well. He insists on marking the pornographic function of depraved artifacts such as recorded confessions from pedophiles, or autopsy and crime scene photographs. He names enthymemes that most texts about Bundy and his ilk ignore or suppress. His is a way of marking the sadism that underwrites white masculine desire and the possibilities for finding pornographic form in unexpected places.

A Queer Coda

Although I have not drunk alcohol since summer 2016, I frequent some bars. Among my favorites is a small gay dive bar in the US South. It features hot young men in G-strings performing erotic dances atop an oval bar for dollar bills. The clientele is mostly older queens, but some younger gay and bisexual men frequent the joint. The doorman will not admit women and femmes unless a cisgender man accompanies them. Mandating a one-to-one ratio ensures that the straight boys dancing on the bar remain focused on entertaining the men.

In the past, my spouse and I have visited this bar with queer friends. Unlike many gay go-go bars, most dancers here allow attendees, provided they have ample dollar bills in hand, to grab their ass, fondle their cock, or otherwise grope at them. Frequently, dancers pull down their G-strings to expose their phallus in all its glory. On one occasion, our friends, my spouse, and I watched in disbelief as a chain-smoking woman, probably in her fifties or sixties, lunged forward to wrap her lips around a dancer's erect penis. My spouse, a genderqueer femme, and I are illegible in such a place, which is part of the fun. Sometimes, reading them as a cisgender woman, the straight dancers ask my spouse how they could "let" me enjoy myself in this gay bar. Or they will simply ask, as if in shock, "You two are married?"

This bar is an ambivalent space. The gender normativity of its admissions policies is problematic. Spontaneous fellatio from clientele violates consent. And I doubt that the dancers, who management centers in all its advertising, make a dime beyond tips. As Pamela VanHaitsma explains, the erotic is ultimately a politically variable category that, even as it mobilizes reciprocal intimacies, also relegates its remainders to the margins.[121] The bar has issues. But it is also queer. And many of its queer elements are erotic rather than pornographic. It affords opportunities for queer worldmaking and libidinal abandon.[122] At its best, the bar operates in a framework of nonnormative relationality. This is fundamental to Lorde's theorizing of the erotic, as well as Kipnis's, Williams's, and other feminists' critiques of the sex wars.[123]

Of course, Dobson would make little distinction between this gay bar and the pornography he and Bundy claimed led to rape and homicide. Both, he would claim, are depraved results of a fallen culture. Dobson's investment, expressed consistently in the archive of his career, was in the pornographic, as well as warfare against the erotic.[124] The carnality of his fundamentalist telos was a nonreciprocal relation in which the masculine subdues the feminine for the former's pleasure. The futurity he and his brethren protect requires that they consistently name and excise the queer from the enclave they maintain against a culture they name pornographic, violent, and predatory.[125] Such a culture, for them, permits sex work, sexual violence, gender affirmation, and drag queen story times.[126] Marking Bundy as queer, and pornography as an inducement rather than a relation, sustains the normativity Dobson jealously protects.

But the exposed cocks and handsy queens of my favorite gay bar beckon otherwise. Lee Edelman and Jasbir K. Puar theorize the queer as an exile whose vulnerability to premature death is a precondition for normative civil society to remain legible.[127] In other words, queers such as Bundy provide ideological cover for the quotidian gendered violence of Western modernity.[128] But the queer can also be a site of radical possibility. In work that was largely a response to Edelman's antifuturity, Muñoz theorizes queerness as a utopian horizon.[129] Scores of other thinkers describe queer embodiment and relationality as world-making endeavors capable of imagining desire and belonging otherwise.[130] Similarly, Chávez characterizes coalitional struggle as a queer relation.[131]

Imagining queer in such ways names the erotic as the domain of the antinormative. Ward underscores this conceptualization in her critical work on heterosexuality, explaining that theory emanating from queer carnal contact mobilizes a broader ethic of relationality in defiance of the sadistic masculine dominion whose foundation is Western modernity.[132] In other words, queerness is a disavowal of white masculinity. Bundy, therefore, is no queer. And while they raped and murdered men and boys, serial killers such as Dahmer and Gacy are similarly normative.[133] They were gay, but they were not queer. On the other hand, queerness can thrive in the adult bookstore and the Grindr hookup.[134] Its utopian gestures can unfold via intimate contact through a gloryhole or in a backroom. It is the domain of sex toys, the smells of post-coital lube and dental dams, and the illegibility of so many queer subjects.[135]

And crucially, queerness names the normative relations that prefigured Bundy and Dobson's 1989 collaboration. While neither man spoke explicitly of homosexual desire, both presupposed the efficacy of the heterosexual nuclear family. And they understood pornography as a mortal threat to such ideals. Early in the interview, Bundy characterized his childhood as "normal," claiming that he was the progeny of a "fine, solid, Christian home."[136] Responding to Dobson's probes, he denied experiencing any physical or sexual abuse. For Bundy, his family's normalcy was "part of the tragedy of this whole situation." The dutiful parents who raised him to be an upstanding Christian citizen, just as surely as those who might have made Kimberly Dianne Leach an obedient bride for Christ, were victims, too. Bundy's collaboration with Dobson named pornography as the pollutant that transformed the gentle child into a violent man. It provided an explanation that left the efficacy of the family form intact.

But the idyllic family life Bundy described to Dobson was a myth. It is of course mythical in that the normative white familial form is itself a mythos that rationalizes so many regimes of gendered, sexual, racial, and colonial domination.[137] But it is also mythical because Bundy excluded many inconvenient details regarding his childhood. In *Natural Porn Killer*, Michaud described "the question of Ted's illegitimacy" as "topic A" for individuals seeking answers regarding the serial killer's motives. It is a pervasive topic of Bundy lore. If each of Bundy's murders were part of a war waged against women, many commentators speculate that such misogynistic resentment's true origins were the shame of his family background.

Bundy's mother, Louise Bundy (née Cowell), was in her early twenties when she gave birth to Ted at the Elizabeth Lund Home for Unwed Mothers in Burlington, Vermont. While she claimed Ted's father was an US Air Force veteran who abandoned her, no clear account of paternity exists.[138] In a *Vanity Fair* feature shortly after Bundy's execution, Myra MacPherson wrote of Louise Bundy, "There is evidence that she was made to feel deep shame and had ample motivation to abhor this unborn, unwanted child."[139] Indeed, narrators of the Bundy saga characterize Louise's late-1940s context as suffocatingly judgmental—especially within the conservative Christian networks where the Cowells found community.[140] Ted Bundy was conceived and born into a world that deemed his very being humiliating and immoral. And the normative ideals of family to which the Cowells and their community claimed allegiance furnished the scaffold for the family's shame to take form.

Because of Louise's status as an unwed mother, the Cowells conspired to provide an alternative story regarding Ted's birth. The future serial killer spent his early childhood believing Louise was his sister and his maternal grandparents were his parents.[141] Some figures close to the Bundy saga speculated that Louise's alcoholic and abusive father, Samuel Cowell, impregnated her. The Louise that actress Lin Shaye portrays in Farrand's *Ted Bundy: American Boogeyman* endorses this claim when, during an almost comically expository monologue, she tells a pair of special agents that her father claimed, "Teddy was conceived in hell." She then angrily says, "I suppose that would make my father the Devil!" But while the incest narrative appeals to prurient interests among true crime fans, there is no definitive evidence of its accuracy. Far better established is Samuel Cowell's status as a cruel and abusive alcoholic, despite Bundy's frequent public claims that his grandfather was "a mythic figure he adored as a little boy."[142] And while, during her courtroom testimony at one of Ted's sentencing hearings, Louise described the decision to move to Tacoma as voluntary and based on other relatives' positive experiences in the Pacific Northwest, it is likely she and Ted left the Cowells' Philadelphia home to escape his grandfather's abuse.[143]

Rule's *The Stranger Beside Me* and its television adaptation, as well as Feifer's *Bundy: A Legacy of Evil*, dwell on matters of Bundy's genealogy for considerably longer than other texts in the archive. In Feifer's film, Bundy's visit to the state archives in Burlington precedes his first murder. In the television miniseries based on Rule's popular book, actor Barbara Hershey's Rule discovers disturbing truths when she interviews an old Bundy family friend. In her memoir, Liz Kendall recalls that Bundy's discovery regarding his lineage was a source of overwhelming shame.[144] Virtually all chroniclers of the saga argue either explicitly or implicitly that Bundy's confused sense of his genealogy inspired, even if indirectly, his murders. Says MacPherson, "Bundy could not stop his terrible killing, and like most serial killers, he was desperate to keep it hidden."[145] She adds, "But in his case there was an additional deep compulsion for subterfuge, a consummate need to keep up appearances learned with his first breath in that household of denial, repression, and secrecy."[146] Bundy's capacity to kill with impunity, as well as his insistence that he experienced a happy and normal childhood, were therefore, in MacPherson's telling, the progeny of so many founding deceptions.

Thus, the normative familial form to which Bundy professed devotion to earn Dobson's affection and possibly advocacy likely played a far more salient role in his monstrous deeds than pornography. In the narrative he and Dobson curated, pornography "snatched" him from the home, and threatened to do the same to other families. On what would be Bundy's last full day on Earth, the condemned killer fashioned himself as a doomed prophetic voice intent on using "the minutes and hours I have left as fruitfully as possible." His professed conviction was salvation for the normative familial ideal and, therefore, white masculinity. His moralizing functioned to rationalize the sadistic gendered enterprise he inflicted on several dozen young women and girls, the cruelties he experienced as a child, and Dobson's puritanical yearnings. So too do myriad artifacts in the Bundy archive sanction the family's violent impositions when they posit it as a potential corrective to Bundy's depravities, rather than a mutually constitutive nodal point within a broader rhetorical formation of white masculinity.[147] The queer alternative is a theory of the erotic that names Bundy and Dobson brethren and endeavors to constitute new kindships in which neither man is imaginable.

Chapter 4

STUDENT BODIES, CAMPUS RITUALS

My contempt for Ted Bundy is most concrete when I project it upon the bodies of young, attractive, white college women. During my university's 2019 commencement ceremony, I sat in full regalia surrounded by hundreds of young white women celebrating their college graduation. Some of them had long brown hair parted down the middle, which many true crime writers speculate was an essential part of Bundy's victim profile.[1] Several of these women were former students in my classes. They were women I cared about, and women Ted Bundy would have eagerly knocked unconscious with a crowbar, driven to an isolated wooded area, raped, strangled, and quite possibly decapitated or defiled before the smell of rotting flesh made it so not even a necrophile could get hard. Whatever that description just did to you may be similar to what was happening to me as so many smiling white women walked across stage to take their diploma cover and pose for a picture with the dean.[2] Fascination with figures such as Bundy traditionally flees the materiality of their crimes in favor of more abstract contemplations of what makes them tick.[3] It was during this graduation ceremony that Bundy became invasively corporeal.

To watch attractive young white women walk across a stage to claim their diplomas is to gaze just as Bundy did. Asking their bodies to carry my hatred for Bundy, as if knowledge of what he did was not reason enough, similarly rendered them docile surfaces for masculine projection. This was a pornographic moment. And in this context, I began to recall colleagues who gazed too long and, like Bundy, further concretized their fantasies. For

Lauren Mulvey, the gaze's logic is possession, and the figure of the cis male professor who claims the feminized student body is practically an archetype in US public culture.⁴ Donald Sutherland's professor in *Animal House* slept with Karen Allen's budding bohemian coed. In an early scene of *Indiana Jones and the Raiders of the Lost Arc*, a young woman in Jones's classroom blinks to reveal "Love You" written on her eyelids while the handsome archaeology professor lectures. Sadly, for her, Karen Allen would again be the one to win the professor's attention.⁵ Professors in the Department of Communication at University of Pittsburgh, some of whose pioneering work in rhetorical and cultural studies shaped the intellectual traditions this book engages, rationalized their predations of graduate students with appeals to the "erotics of the classroom."⁶ And administrators at Pittsburgh and so many other institutions chose not to act, ensuring that the figure of the promiscuous masculine professor remained canon.⁷ The university that employs me earned national infamy for repeated failures to address sexual violence in its massive athletics program and elsewhere on campus.⁸ I am myself an intellectual product of competitive collegiate forensics, an activity whose boundaries between coach and competitor sometimes seemed nonexistent. Coaches drank and did drugs with students. Some slept with, dated, and occasionally married them. Directors of nationally prestigious programs mobilized their reputations, as well as students' vulnerabilities and commitments to their programs' "legacy," to groom, harass, and assault them while hiding in plain sight.⁹ And many alums of this activity carried these lessons into academic careers in rhetorical studies and cognate fields. And so, the cycle goes. Suffice it to say, Bundy was not the only man who wandered college and university campuses to find and use vulnerable bodies.

Even norms associated with pedagogy and mentorship that do not take conspicuous carnal turns still express a libidinal logic of possession. One need not perform such logics in the bedroom.¹⁰ After this graduation ceremony, some of these young white women approached me to say, "Thank you," to take pictures, and to give a hug. I recall that at least one told me that my teaching changed her life. On several occasions while writing this chapter, I replaced "my student(s)" with "the(se) student(s)." My instinct is to claim them.¹¹ It feels good when attractive young people appreciate my work. It allows me to part ways with the knowledge that there may be some permanence to the impression I made on them—to believe that, as Bundy did after each murder he committed, "they shall forever be a part of you."¹²

These graduating white women are young and they are attractive and they are participating in a ritual that affirms the futurity to which they are heirs, and Bundy could have killed any of them.[13] I had intellectually known that Bundy murdered college students and I spend most of my days surrounded by such students. But somehow this was a new realization. Any young white woman in this arena who fit Bundy's profile could have been Lynda Ann Healy, Roberta Kathleen Parks, Brenda Carol Ball, Margaret Elizabeth Bowman, Lisa Levy, or others. Bundy's victims, save Kimberly Leach, always looked, at least to me, slightly older than their age in their black-and-white pictures. They seemed older than me if only because they were of college age at a time when I was not even alive. Any of them could have appeared in one of my parents' dusty high school yearbooks, and my parents are obviously older than me. Some of these women were old enough to eventually be my mother. But, to me, the women at this graduation ceremony were children, even if not legally. Recalling that the cultural form of the child is itself contingent and mobilized to various, often deeply racialized, gendered, and other problematic ends, I nonetheless see children claiming their degrees while families cheer on—families including parents who are only ten or so years older than me.[14] Such a ritual infantilizes the adult woman so that she might again manifest the fantasies so many others conjure for her. Some of those parents were alive and self-aware when Bundy stalked the University of Washington campus in Seattle or entered the Chi Omega sorority house in Tallahassee. And we celebrate these children in part precisely because the figure of the child and the futurity it embodies induces identifications with whiteness, heteronormativity, nationalism, and other regimes of hegemonic belonging.[15] Bundy not only destroyed such futures. He desecrated them.

My gazing and fantasies did not lead to the same places as Bundy's or those of colleagues who named their carnal yearnings pedagogy and mentoring. Rather, pedagogy and mentoring are often themselves the fantasy—a way to lay claim and take credit. Gendered violence overdetermines the US American university. In other words, reckoning with Bundy, a serial killer who targeted young white women on US college campuses, also requires an accounting for how the sadistic logics of white masculinity underwrite the various economies that mobilize the university's enterprise. When I refer to the university, I do not only mean the campuses that Bundy stalked and on which my colleagues and I labor, but also the bars and parties that young men surveil for sufficiently drunk conquests, the ways whiteness shapes the benefit of the doubt for survivors and perpetrators in campus settings, cinematic and other mass mediated representations of higher education, the intersectional violence of graduate school and the tenure track, the objectifying toxicity of academic celebrity, and the colonial and anti-Black legacies that are immanent to the project of US American higher education as a whole. The Bundy archive obscures and discloses such violence. It reveals that his violence was an amplification of the university's gendered foundations. Such revelation threatens anxiety, which either demands management or invites critical appraisal.

The Gendered University

Bundy kidnapped and murdered Georgeann Hawkins sometime between June 10 and 11, 1974. Rule describes Hawkins as "one of those golden girls for whom luck or fate had dealt a perfect hand."[16] Such was Rule and others' descriptions of many of Bundy's victims. Authors and commentators universally described most of these white women as laden with promise, unlike the sex workers Ridgway or Little murdered, or the queer men of color Dahmer mutilated.[17] Unlike Bundy, these men murdered people whose futures were illegible to the norms of white civil society.[18] They did not warrant public grief.[19]

The creators of the 2020 Amazon documentary series *Ted Bundy: Falling for a Killer* intentionally centered the stories of Bundy's many victims in the service of an espoused feminist ethic. They often juxtaposed smiling photographs with family members' tearful recollections of the women's kindness and potential. The latter frequently manifested as collegiate success.[20] In a searing critique of Judge Cowart's comments at the conclusion of the Chi Omega trial, when he characterized the man he sentenced to death for murdering two sorority sisters as a "bright young man," Rubin writes, "It wasn't a tragedy that Bundy never fulfilled his greatness, because he was never destined for greatness. His victims, however, had wonderful lives in front of them."[21] A man with no future had extinguished those of so many bright young women and girls. Feminist scholars such as Caputi characterize Bundy and other sexual sadists who target women as expressions of a broader patriarchal retaliation against women's liberation. And the US American university has come to function in public discourse as a prominent space for feminist actualization. That Bundy targeted such women and the futures they pursued was not, for writers such as Caputi, an accident. Rather, they claim that Bundy's misogyny and many insecurities ran so deep that he sought to humiliate and destroy such exemplary women.[22]

But the feminist politics Caputi and many of her colleagues espoused is itself rooted in a fidelity to whiteness and, especially in US university settings, functions to entrench the marginalization of Black and other women of color. As Black and women of color feminists such as Lorde and Lugones argue, white feminist critiques of sexual violence, pornography, and other vectors of women's oppression presuppose white women's experiences.[23] These writers disclose the myriad ways they experience violence at the hands of white women in professional settings.[24] No critique is immune from the possibilities of gendered violence, and the university's gendered violence operates upon many layers.

The university figures significantly in the Bundy archive. Of course, Bundy frequently surveyed campuses for potential and actual victims. In a moment of dramatic irony during the 1986 television movie *The Deliberate Stranger*, Harmon's Bundy tells his brother, "I wouldn't know how to live without a campus nearby."[25] While the miniseries' characters had not yet concluded Bundy was a serial killer, the viewing audience was sufficiently aware to detect the macabre reference. Reliable access to fungible feminine flesh provided him with sustenance. Rule also explained, "He felt at ease in a campus atmosphere, at home."[26] Bundy was himself a student who, by biographical accounts, tethered his worth to academic excellence and upward mobility. He desired futurity.

A graduate of the University of Washington, Bundy was enrolled in law school at the University of Utah at the time of his first arrest. Much Bundy mythology characterizes him as a charismatic criminal genius who used his intellectual talents to manipulate victims, family, and acquaintances.[27] While he was certainly more eloquent and attractive than many other famous serial killers, Bundy suffered frequent educational false starts, struggled to achieve financial stability, and was deeply insecure about his educational and class status. A brilliant mind he was not. But for him, education was a means of upward mobility and a status symbol itself. And, by most accounts, he believed becoming a lawyer would diminish the shame that overpowered his subjectivity.[28]

Equally salient when considering the university's ubiquity in the Bundy archive is the gendered violence that underwrites Western intellectual production and higher education in general. Downing explains that Western modernity constitutes the murderer, especially the serial killer, as distinctly intelligent and creative.[29] Thomas de Quincey parodied this tendency in his 1827 tract *On Murder Considered as One of the Fine Arts*. But whereas de Quincey offered a Swiftian critique of high society's artistic pretenses, other representations of serial murder possess less apparent ironic self-awareness.[30] Fictional murderers such as Thomas Harris's Hannibal Lecter, Lars von Trier's Jack, or Joe Carroll from *The Following*, although they still engage in horrific acts, remain charismatic largely due to their and their creator's ability to articulate their violence to a broader pursuit of creative genius.[31] The contemporary serial killer therefore functions within a broader historical association with the masculine intellect and the macabre.

Although it is true that the university can function as a refuge from the violence that modernity inflicts on its subjects, such functioning is only the result of what Stefano Harney and Fred Moten call fugitive planning.[32] The modernist university itself has no authentic claim to criticality or liberation. It is an inherently colonial and anti-Black project.[33] Julietta Singh explains that the language of mastery on which so much of the university's enterprise rests is the progeny of modernist yearnings for possession. It is a mastery whose origins are colonization, enslavement, and genocide.[34] As such, gendered violence is immanent to the university.[35] Intellectualization is not only a justification or alibi for gendered violence, but, in its modernist iterations, is an enactment thereof.

This is certainly the case regarding instances of campus rape. Consistently, the US university demonstrates its unwillingness to address interpersonal sexual violence in substantive ways.[36] Advocacy from and for campus rape survivors such as Chanel Miller, Emma Sulkowitz, and others has helped galvanize the broader #MeToo zeitgeist against sexual violence.[37] Furthermore, Griffin explains that the experiences of other rape survivors, especially Black women, reveal the racialized boundaries of legibility when it comes to claiming solidarity with survivors.[38] Suffice it to say, the dormitories, Greek houses, nearby bars, and other spaces that officially and unofficially comprise US American campuses nurture sexual violence. And crucially, individuals who occupy positions of power, such as tenured professors, inflict their own carnal sadism on students, as well as junior or contingent faculty.[39]

While the prevalence of rape in US higher education contexts is a desperately salient problem warranting sustained and organized action, Mack and their coauthors explain that the boundaries of what constitutes gendered violence, and therefore sexual violence, are necessarily more diffuse than the scene of the rape itself. They write, "To interrogate the reproduction of colonial epistemologies of gender, scholarship must address other forms of gendered violence on U.S. college campuses (beyond just the sexual assault of cis White women) as a way of revealing the complex rhetorics of modernity that reify logics of coloniality."[40] They contend that because the project of modernity is predicated on gendered violence, such violence is immanent to the university.[41]

Of course, Black women and other women of color have been proclaiming this truth for decades. In my fields of rhetorical and communication studies, scholars such as Calafell, Olga Idriss Davis, and Carmen Kynard write extensively about the myriad indignities they experience in quotidian academic contexts such as the graduate advising session, faculty meeting, promotion and tenure process, classroom, or conference panel.[42] While sexual violence against young white women warrants the construction of an ideal victim in hegemonic discourses regarding rape, Black, Indigenous, and nonblack women of color remain among the university's most disposable bodies. In all instances, docile feminine bodies, whether as tropes mobilized in the service of a politics of victimhood or as objects of erasure absent from such conversations, figure significantly in university discourses about sexual violence.

To characterize Bundy as especially contemptible for his transgressions prefigures not only the privileged futurity of white femininity relative to other gendered bodies, but also the university as a sanctified space where gendered violence is anathema to its mission. Missions are metaphysical, whereas the university is violently material. Administrators historically exert considerable effort to shield athletic and, to a lesser extent, academic programs from the popular and litigious fallout of sexual violence.[43] This often entails protecting rapists and revictimizing survivors.[44] US American campuses rest on occupied Indigenous lands whose acquisition relied on genocidal gendered violence.[45] Moreover, Black women and nonblack women of color experience the university in profoundly degrading ways.[46] To characterize Bundy as an anomaly risks obscuring the degree to which gendered violence overdetermines the university. Engaging the Bundy archive induces reckonings with such violence, and reckonings entail the choice of disavowing or acknowledging shared complicities therein.

Prone Bodies on Campus

National Lampoon's Animal House premiered on July 28, 1978, several months after Ted Bundy entered the Chi Omega house at Florida State University with a log in his hand and bludgeoned four sorority sisters, killing two.[47] In fact, the 1970s were watersheds for cinematic and other mass mediated representations of coed campus life and women who fit Bundy's victim profile.[48] And many of these texts traded in portrayals of gendered violence. For example, the events of the 1974 horror film *Black Christmas* occurred in a sorority house where an anonymous figure stalked the residents with threatening phone calls before murdering most of them.[49] The genre of the US slasher film, whose renaissance occurred during the late 1970s and 1980s, overwhelmingly entails narratives of men murdering scores of college women or teenagers.[50] If one accepts Jean Baudrillard's claim that Western disaster films prior to September 2001 were symptoms of collective fantasies about a 9/11-style event, then the ample representation of young and attractive college-aged women meeting violent ends during the 1970s and 1980s surely prefigured and reified Bundy.[51]

Such portrayals of the US college or university campus occurred in a broader context of public preoccupations with gender in higher education. Amid feminism's so-called second wave, more women sought undergraduate or graduate degrees, and many technologies of gender discipline adapted in ways that brought college-aged men and women into closer proximity with each other.[52] In a 1970 cover story, *Life* characterized coed dormitories as a cultural revolution that radically upended an earlier generation's investments in gender normativity (figure 14). Journalist Karen Thorsen wrote, "Parents sometimes anxiously conclude that sex in its most urgent physical manifestations will overwhelm the rest of college life. The morals of their children will be under constant assault. The good clean fun of the good old days—dating for proms, football games, fraternity beer parties—will be replaced by pleasures more ominously orgiastic."[53]

To the extent that the campus served as synecdoche for fluctuations in gender and sexual normativity, *Life* speculated that students' parents preferred fictive "good old days" over the permissive abandon that characterized their children's college experiences. Of course, the university's gendered violence did not begin with coed dormitories. The previous generation's beloved formals, football games, and beer parties facilitated scores of rapes and other

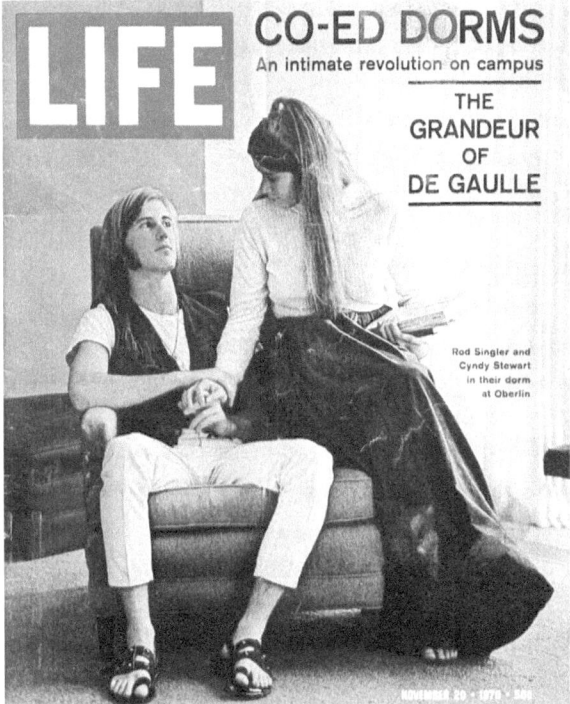

Figure 14. Cover for *Life* magazine story about coed college dormitories. Time, Inc., 1970.

kinds of gendered violence. Just as public responses to Bundy's massacre at Chi Omega performed nostalgia for a safer campus that never existed, so too did the Greatest Generation's longings for a bygone era of carnal innocence.[54]

It was in this context that *Animal House* appeared in theaters. Based largely on stories published in the comedy magazine *National Lampoon*, which themselves recalled writers Harold Ramis, Douglas Kenney, and Chris Miller's fraternity experiences, the film chronicles the conflict between the bacchanalian Delta Tau Chi fraternity and Dean Vernon Wormer of the fictional Faber College.[55] Wormer, a strict disciplinarian, as well as the more traditional Omega fraternity, embody the same idyllic collegiate past that *Life* recalled in its coverage of coed dorms. Meanwhile, the Deltas drink to excess, neglect their academic responsibilities, and pursue young women with little regard for consent. They embody the very nightmares many students' parents disclosed to *Life*. But the Deltas are *Animal House*'s unambiguous heroes.

The film is a comedic meditation on the shifting meanings of the university and takes the side of excess amid the resulting cleavages.[56] The conflict that propels its narrative largely unfolds upon the bodies of young women.

After Dean Wormer places the Deltas on "double-secret probation" for their many transgressions, the men choose nihilism over restraint and host a toga party at their fraternity house. So popular was this portion of *Animal House* that it inspired what many journalists and commentators characterized as a national campus toga party trend.[57] Larry "Pinto" Kroger, a new Delta pledge and one of the film's primary protagonists, brings, unbeknownst to him, the mayor's thirteen-year-old daughter, Clorette, to the party as his date. After she rapidly drinks multiple cups of potent jungle juice, Clorette, who, in the film, is one year older than Kimberly Dianne Leach, and Pinto journey upstairs to fellow Delta "Flounder's" room to hook up. They begin making out and clumsily disrobing. Clorette eventually passes out from her binge drinking. She collapses, prone and naked on the bed (figure 15). An anxious Pinto panics as he holds the tissues Clorette used to accentuate her young breasts in his hands. At this point, a devil and an angel appear on each side of Pinto. The devil, speaking in a deep, raspy voice encourages Pinto to "Fuck her! Fuck her brains out! Suck her tits! Squeeze her buns! You know she wants it!" The angel, holding a small harp and speaking in a high-pitched tone reminiscent of one of the Chipmunks, counters by warning Pinto, "If you lay one hand on that poor, sweet, helpless girl, you'll despise yourself forever." Pinto sides with the better angel of his nature and brings Clorette home in a grocery store cart, leaving her at her parents' doorstep, therefore returning her prone feminine body, if only temporarily, to her mayoral patriarch. The disappointed devil simply says, "You homo!"

Pinto did not rape the unconscious child at the frat party. Later in the film, they would have sex, during which Clorette discloses her true age, and, in the movie's final sequence, she gleefully introduces Pinto to her parents as "the boy who molested me." By legal standards, Pinto was a rapist, but he did not rape the passed-out thirteen-year-old lying on his fraternity brother's bed. Such restraint induces further audience identification with Pinto, who was already among the film's most sympathetic characters as a naïve Delta pledge who only reluctantly engaged in many of his fraternity brother's hijinks in response to considerable peer pressure. Mack and their collaborators explain that the university's gendered violence does not act exclusively on bodies gendered as normatively female. Rather, the gender normativity that renders

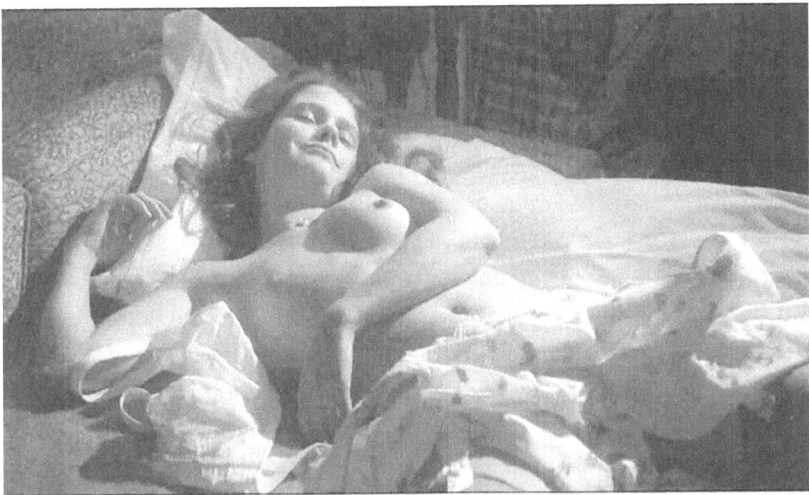

Figure 15. Clorette's prone body in *National Lampoon's Animal House*. Universal Pictures, 1978.

Clorette vulnerable to rape and Pinto subject to degrading masculine rituals that demand his conquest of feminine bodies is "a violence whose genesis is the constitution of gender itself and the social hierarchies that phenomenon sutures in modernity."[58] Such an observation need not, indeed must not, function to absolve sexual predators of their violence, but rather contextualize such acts in ways that amplify the performative foundations thereof. To the extent that theirs are both bodies immersed in others' gendered decadence, Pinto and Clorette were a perfect match.

While Pinto did not rape the unconscious Clorette, the masculine gaze that *Animal House* enabled did. Throughout the battle raging in Pinto's conscience, the camera repeatedly cuts to the unconscious and topless child. Her exposed breasts are visible, and she lies in a state resembling a nude oil painting. She is there for audience gazing even as Pinto declines the opportunity to consume her prone body. Stephen Bishop sang in the song "Animal House," which he wrote for the film, "That Pinto he's a real swell guy / Clorette is jailbait but he gave her a try."[59] He would eventually "give her a try," but director John Landis gave his audience first right far sooner.

A scene such as this is likely unimaginable in our current zeitgeist—at least for a movie filmed and released today. As the norms of consent and campus rape culture have become intense topics of public deliberation, there is nothing funny about a college freshman kissing, let alone contemplating raping, an unconscious underage girl at a frat party—right? It still happens but joking about such things is indecorous. The only ethical move in the face of campus rape, or Ted Bundy, is disavowal. But in 1978, the joke landed. And it still lands by way of streaming services, star John Belushi posters in dorm rooms, and campus cultures of excess that find their most popularized, but by no means only, expressions at the site of the frat house. Krista M. Tucciarone writes, "Still considered as one of the top five college-themed films, [*Animal House*] has durable staying power and has the ability to communicate the workings of higher education institutions . . . and in general, the college experience."[60] For Tucciarone, Landis's film is no mere parody of US college life, but functions pedagogically to cultivate contemporary audience notions of what occurs on campuses.

As of 2001, the US Library of Congress preserves *Animal House* in its National Film Registry, meaning that Clorette's prone and naked body remains entombed as part of a "culturally, historically, or aesthetically significant" film about men in college who drink too much, fail miserably at academics, and concoct ways to manipulate women for carnal ends—men who invite thirteen-year-old girls to toga parties, who sleep with Dean Wormer's intoxicated wife, and professors who have sex and do drugs with their students.[61] One is hard pressed to identify a sexual encounter during *Animal House*'s 109 minutes that would satisfy the standards for consent. And whereas Bundy sometimes donned a sling or a pair of crutches to earn young women's trust before he kidnapped, raped, and murdered them, the men of the Delta House feigned a girlfriend's death to persuade a group of students at a women's college to join them for a night out.[62] Performing masculine vulnerability also functioned as a means of entrapping the feminine.

In fact, Pinto's elder Delta brother, Eric "Otter" Stratton, who pursued the Dean's drunk wife and orchestrated the charade at the women's college, bears a striking resemblance to Bundy (figure 16). The character performs masculinity in ways that read as self-assured even when utterly incompetent. For example, when Faber requires the Deltas to go before a student disciplinary committee, Otter speaks in the fraternity's defense. Although his delivery is soaring and confident, the speech's argumentative content is incoherent and in no way contributes to the defense's cause. Similarly, although Bundy eagerly embodied what he understood to be the role of a brilliant litigator during his Florida trials, his decision to serve as his own attorney likely helped guarantee his convictions and death sentences.[63]

Student Bodies, Campus Rituals

Figure 16. Eric "Otter" Stratton in *National Lampoon's Animal House*. Universal Pictures, 1978.

There is no reason to believe the character of Otter is in any way based on Bundy, which itself suggests that the trope of the charming young white man manipulating women to secure carnal ends was already an overdetermined dimension of public discourse about US colleges and universities. Whereas the Bundy of so much serial killer lore posed as law enforcement or a kind young man in need to murder women and desecrate their corpses, Otter surveyed the local obituaries to lay claim to a recently deceased sorority sister to win sympathy from her friends, therefore inducing them to join him and his Delta brothers for a night on the town. The night that unfolded occurred at a low-lit nightclub where the majority-Black masculine clientele performed the figure of the buck in ways that rendered the Deltas harmless, if mischievous, pranksters in comparison.[64] Bundy and Otter ultimately operated within the same gendered register that performed white masculine charm and derived pleasure from women's corpses.

I want to leave open the possibility that I am being too hard on *Animal House*. In his work on crime novels, Greg Forter argues that such texts demand that the masculine gaze reckon with the desires it projects on the novel's narrative.[65] King and Gunn explain that the gaze, at least as Lacan originally theorized it, is not the province of domination, but rather masculine mastery's foil. They write, "For Lacan, the gaze is something that the spectator encounters as the *failure of* or *limit to* a sense of mastery—it comes from the object and a place beyond the visible field."[66] In other words, the relationship between the text and the reader, as well as the broader vexed politics of white masculinity both perform, is dialogic and capable of unsettling the drive to possess even as it appears to satiate and affirm it. By directing viewers' gaze toward what we are told is a nude thirteen-year-old body (the actress, Sarah Holcomb, was nineteen at the time), Landis invites *Animal House*'s public to reckon with its own internal dialogue between the better angel of its nature and the sadistic devil who wants to consume feminine flesh—between normative ideals of being a good citizen on one hand, and Ted Bundy on the other. Perhaps the joke is on the audience and, as such, the joke works.

The university continues to inflict violence on feminine bodies that attend parties, go to bars, or agree to dates with young men who often belong to organizations whose members at times march past women's dorms chanting "No means yes! Yes means anal!" or "My name is Jack, I'm a necrophiliac; I fuck dead women, and fill them with my semen!"[67] The prone feminine body remains central in this broad constellation of white masculinity. Frat boys joke about fucking dead women, Pinto contemplates the prone body of a naked child, and, on January 15, 1978, Ted Bundy strangled, bludgeoned, raped, and bit four sleeping sorority sisters and another woman, killing two. The docile feminine, sometimes cloaked in humor, sometimes quite serious, is the object mobilizing the fantasies that make some jokes land and others unimaginable. And to the extent that colonized, enslaved, and otherwise subjugated bodies are always already feminized relative to the sovereign, such docile bodies are immanent to the university.

For Florida State

Bundy's Chi Omega attack dominated news coverage in the city of Tallahassee and saturated the Florida State University campus with anxiety. One of the most widely circulated journalistic photographs from the Chi Omega saga is black and white and shows a young white woman with long dark hair pulling back a curtain and staring out a second-story window of the very sorority house where Bundy's massacre unfolded. She wears a turtleneck, and her eyes are wide open and signal fear. The photograph appeared on the cover of the *Tallahassee Democrat* the day following the Chi Omega attack and remains ubiquitous in the Bundy archive (figure 17). Above the image are photographs of Levy, Bowman, as well as their injured sorority sisters Karen Chandler and Rubin (née Kleiner), and Cheryl Thomas, a dancing student

Student Bodies, Campus Rituals 113

Figure 17. Cover of the *Tallahassee Democrat* following the Chi Omega attack. Knight Ridder, 1978.

who lived down the street, smiling and embodying the kind of collegiate promise that Bundy cruelly extinguished. The juxtaposition of the five dead or gravely injured women with that of a terrified sorority sister invites the understanding that, if Bundy had chosen different bedrooms to enter, the woman behind the curtains may have been pictured above. At the time of this photograph, law enforcement had made no arrests and did not know who committed the assault. And few if any people in Tallahassee knew who Ted Bundy was. Although he had escaped from jail in Colorado and was on the FBI's Most Wanted List, there was no reason to anticipate he was in Florida.[68] A specter had attacked Chi Omega. The campus and its city remained in a state of suspended fear. Describing the scene inside one sorority house, James Cramer and Deanna Thompson wrote for the *Tallahassee Democrat*, "Inside 40 women pace, bite nails, and pretend to listen to a radio."[69]

Law enforcement eventually captured Bundy and the state convicted him for the Chi Omega attack and for kidnapping, raping, and murdering Kimberly Leach. The occasion of Bundy's 1989 execution proved deeply important for those invested in seeing him receive his just desserts for the violence he inflicted on the State of Florida, as well as Colorado, Utah, and the Pacific Northwest. When Bundy, who continued insisting he was innocent for most of his conviction, began confessing in a vain attempt to postpone the execution, law enforcement officials from these other areas traveled to Florida in hopes that Bundy would help them resolve many open kidnapping and murder cases.[70]

Officially, Bundy died for the Leach murder. Whereas his Chi Omega convictions remained entangled in various appeals processes, Bundy's legal prospects in the Leach case had reached their limit. But an execution's public work always exceeds its legal boundaries. Dwight Conquergood described executions as rituals that the state performs to legitimize its monopoly on violence. Even though contemporary executions occur behind prison walls to only a select audience of witnesses, Conquergood explained, "The central performance challenge of execution rituals is to differentiate between judicial killing and murder."[71] Thus, if the State of Florida intended to kill Bundy, it would need to do so in ways that distinguished electrocuting a man to death from, for example, entering a sorority house in the dead of night to fatally bludgeon and strangle two women. To this end, Bundy's execution was to be a highly orchestrated affair that was legally and procedurally unimpeachable.

Many of the approximately 300 individuals who gathered outside Florida State Prison to cheer while the state electrocuted Bundy to death invoked his crimes in Tallahassee. The *Tallahassee Democrat*'s front page featured a large photograph of two white men flanking a masked effigy in a mock electric chair. The men, who the photograph's caption identifies as Butch Pierce and Bob Reeves, light several tall candles they had placed in the metallic ring that signified the electric chair's skull cap—in other words, they were "lighting him up." At the base of the effigy is a placard that reads, "TED . . . your turn" (figure 18).[72] In its story reporting the execution, the *Miami Herald* wrote, "The scene was a grim parody of a tailgate party before a big game."[73] Of course, the people of Florida know how to throw a tailgate. Only a few weeks earlier, the Florida State Seminoles defeated Auburn University at the Sugar Bowl.[74] The campus where Bundy attacked five women was indeed having a good month. And while the crowd outside Florida State Prison was geographically and generationally diverse, the Florida State attacks loomed large. One sign at the festivities read, "Chi O, Chi O, It's Off to Hell We Go."[75] Commenting on a group of University of Florida students in attendance, *Newsweek* wrote, "Presumably they were seeking retribution for the 1978 deaths of two Florida State University sorority sisters."[76] If the solemn affair unfolding inside the prison was legally a response to the murder of a preteen girl, many outside the facility gathered to claim some of the 2,000 volts that pulsated through Bundy's body for his other victims.

Crucially, this deep identification with the Chi Omega victims and the collective campus identities they came to embody did not stem from an investment in the US university as an intellectual enterprise. In fact, Bundy's status as a college graduate and aspiring lawyer who confidently, if incompetently, defended himself in court, cemented some revelers' contempt for him. Speaking with a *Newsweek* reporter, a woman in attendance at the execution festivities explained that Bundy "brings out the worst in people because he was so smug" and that he "just thought he was too good."[77] As much as the US college or university campus was conspicuously a site of Bundy's monstrosity, a clear current of anti-intellectualism also inspired some who celebrated his electrocution. Whereas the intellectual promise of the white women Bundy murdered rendered his crimes especially despicable in the public imagination, his own credentials, such as they were, only inspired further resentment. As any faculty member of a university deeply invested in athletics or other nonacademic elements of its mission can attest, fidelity to the university need not be an investment in its intellectual identity.

Figure 18. Cover of the *Tallahassee Democrat* following Bundy's execution. Knight Ridder, 1989.

While the atmosphere outside the prison was, by all accounts, one of joyful and righteous communion, few with greater degrees of proximity to Bundy's crimes had kind words for the revelers. Even the first officer on the scene of the Chi Omega attack, who witnessed the execution, told *Newsweek*, "We were carrying out a serious, concerted effort to bring a hideous case to a close."[78] Rubin echoes this sentiment in her memoir, writing, "There was nothing to celebrate for those of us close to the case."[79] Rule similarly condemned the celebration, writing, "They all seemed quite mad. They had no more humanity than Ted."[80] For those entrenched within the technocratic and bureaucratic machinery of state killing, even Ted Bundy deserved a dignified execution, or at least the families of his victims did. The scenes inside and outside the prison functioned as competing rituals seeking to inscribe different kinds of meaning upon Bundy's electrocuted body. For the state, the imperative was to guarantee that the execution was seamless and clinical. Disruptions of protocol compromise the state's prerogative to kill. Conquergood wrote, "The illusion of nonviolent decency is torn away."[81] The revelry outside the prison threatened to disclose the execution's sadism and therefore its homologies with Bundy's crimes. To the state and its allies, the people outside the prison were an embarrassment to the dignified servants of the law who arrived at the prison to bear proper witness to the ritual of electricity pulsating through Bundy's once (and always) charming and brilliant, now constrained and (never quite) lifeless body.

But decency was not what the group outside Florida State Prison sought. If the official ritual of state killing was, as Conquergood argued, a particular juncture on a broader historical evolution of legitimation rituals, the celebration outside recalled times when the sanctioned taking of a life was a spectacular public sacrament. Indeed, private executions are a relatively recent innovation within the broader historical arc of capital punishment in the West. Earlier executions would include public displays of religious piety and various other practices designed to enhance the likelihood that the viewing public would absorb the pedagogy of punishment and invest in the state's monopoly on violence.[82] The lynch mob also employed rituals in ways that projected white supremacist logics onto slain Black bodies.[83] The condemned body functioned as a spectacle upon which a sovereign would inscribe meaning and a people would materialize.

But in 1989, the state was no longer interested in performing its macabre rituals in the open. Nor did approximately 300 people gather on the morning of January 24 to send a message to would-be serial killers that they might meet a fate such as Bundy's. Rather, the journalists who compared this celebration to a typical college football tailgate more accurately captured the function of the festival that marked Bundy's death. Timothy R. Steffensmeier characterizes tailgates as rituals that "take on sacred status, in that the rhetoric of college football spills into everyday interactions and popular culture."[84] Whereas the tailgates to which many Floridians were accustomed derive meaning from the football stadium and project it onto the bodies and spaces of fans, the carnival on January 24, 1989 outside Florida State Prison figured the execution as the game. That ritual functioned to claim Bundy's death for the masses and distinguish his crimes not only from his own execution, but from the quotidian forms of gendered violence that permeated the site of the university, in whose name so many attendees claimed the serial killer's demise. Describing the festive scene and its cultural legacy, Schmid writes, "Bundy is the contemporary equivalent of Frankenstein's monster: something we have made that has to be destroyed to protect ourselves from the knowledge of our own involvement in the creation of monsters."[85] Killing Bundy was the antidote to the anxiety he inspired.

Susan Sontag wrote, "No 'we' should be taken for granted when viewing representations of other people's pain."[86] For her purposes, Sontag described the suffering of far-off victims of war or otherwise marginalized communities whose violent deaths might not warrant grief from Western audiences.[87] The "we" Schmid presumes is not confronting such pain. It is, in one sense, taking stock in Bundy's convulsing body strapped to a large wooden chair while an electric charge shuts down his organs. But that "we" also recalls the pain Bundy caused and, for Schmid, that "we" is complicit. But the "we" outside Florida State Prison during the early morning of January 24, 1989, to the extent that it is a universal subject, is a function of the exclusions that characterize any deployment of the royal *we*. The crowd that celebrated Bundy's end, just as the lawyers who prosecuted him, the authors who write about him, and the women and girls he murdered, was, it seems, almost fully white in its composition. Of course, one cannot say for sure that there were no people of color among the 300 individuals who swung crude effigies from nooses outside the prison, but the visual archive of that morning reveals none. Those who most eagerly cheered Bundy on his walk from his prison cell to the electric chair were decidedly white. And given that the ritual outside the prison was formally homologous to a lynch mob, it prefigures its own whiteness.[88] This royal *we*, like so many others, functions to universalize the white subject.

What, then, did the crowd outside Florida State Prison seek to destroy that it could not bear to face in itself? What inspired their anxiety? During the final episode of Berlinger's *Conversations with a Killer*, Aynesworth comments, "I was interested that there were a lot of drunken college kids there. Uh, young men who were age ten or so when Ted had killed the girls at Chi Omega." He characterized their celebration as an "excuse to get drunk and hoop it up." But Conquergood and others would challenge the notion that the crowd's Bacchanalian excess was so vacuous. While the massacre Bundy unleashed at the Chi Omega house in 1978 figured legally and culturally as a crime warranting death, the opportunistic acts of sexual predation in which many of the men screaming "Burn Bundy, burn" undoubtedly engaged at various parties and other collegiate social settings did not register at all. One of Bundy's greatest sins was disrupting the gendered norms of the university and of Western modernity in general. Describing the campus climate when Bundy kidnapped and murdered George Anne Hawkins in 1974, Rule wrote, "There are always high jinks during finals week, anything to break the tension, and strong young men frequently pick up giggling, squealing girls, playing 'cave man.'"[89] For this true crime author, whose narrative of her friendship with Bundy launched her lucrative career, such performances of masculinity and femininity in dormitories, apartments, and bars near so many college campuses across the United States were perfectly normal sources of nostalgia. Bundy was a monster who knocked women unconscious, brought them to isolated wooded areas, raped and strangled them, and often returned to defile their corpses. Such monstrosity, in Rule's telling, disrupted traditions that included young men mimicking club-wielding cavemen who slung docile women over their shoulders and brought them to a dark cave for their onanistic sexual exploits. The Otters of the world had long been stalking US campuses before Bundy's arrival, but the fates of so many Clorettes did not register as salient when juxtaposed with Bundy's monstrosity.

Conclusion

As the hearse containing Bundy's corpse drove from the prison grounds, the crowd cheered loudly. Some even briefly gave chase. The camera crews packed up and, as is the case with all tailgates, the revelers gradually made their ways home. Some returned to nearby Gainesville, where many of them attended the University of Florida. Others drove the 150 miles to Tallahassee. I picture some of the young men in attendance returning to their campuses that Tuesday, going about their weeks satisfied that they had honored the memories of so many slain coeds, and then attending parties where they drank and cheered each other on as they sought young women growing more docile with each drink.

National Lampoon's Animal House ended 1978 as the year's third highest-grossing film, just behind Grease and Superman. Curiously, all three films traded in nostalgia. Superman invited its audience to find solace in the promise of normative white masculine heroism. The musical Grease offered an exuberant performance of whiteness portrayed as 1950s charm, and itself performed humorous abandon regarding consent and sexual violence.[90] Both exalted a mythic bygone era in the context of a US-based white civil society languishing from its many failures. The aftermaths of Vietnam, Watergate, and an increasingly militant antiracist movement coalesced with recession to produce a national narrative of malaise into which Ronald Wilson Reagan would offer himself as the paternal hero.[91] While it is highly unlikely that the reveler wearing the Reagan mask outside Bundy's execution gave his decision quite so much thought, his invocation of a self-fashioned national savior whose regimes of austerity, deregulation, and mass incarceration devasted poor and working-class Black and other communities of color while successfully selling a narrative of national uplift to a white voting public was apropos (figure 19).[92] If Reagan gave white US Americans cause to embrace and proclaim patriotism, then vanquishing Ted Bundy as the Gipper's second term ended slayed a sacrificial monster who risked disclosing the monstrosity of the modernist project Reagan helped refine through neoliberal logics. That Bundy himself was once a politically active Republican in the mold of the so-called Reagan Revolution was a potentially delicious irony few chose to address.

But Animal House mocked nostalgia by refusing the mythos of a US collegiate tradition whose normative gendered structures never wavered. As Ted Bundy sat in jail awaiting trial for murdering two college students, severely injuring three others, and kidnapping, raping, and murdering a girl one year younger than Clorette, audiences laughed aloud as Pinto contemplated a variation on Bundy's modus operandi and the camera's gaze enabled others to indulge from a distance. I am not suggesting a cosmic connection between Bundy's rampage at the Chi Omega house, his 1989 execution, National Lampoon's Animal House, the rise of Reaganism, and the gendered

Figure 19. Celebrant outside Bundy's execution channeling Ronald Reagan. Fox 13 Tampa Bay, 1989.

and racial politics of the US university. Nor am I positing a crude ethical homology. Still, I imagine Pinto is purer than many who gazed at Clorette, or those who accepted Reagan's inducement to mock Black women as "welfare queens" and parasites to civil society, or those of us who labor in the academy and enforce the docility of Black women and other feminine bodies of color.[93] Yes, Pinto eventually slept with "jailbait" and is therefore a rapist, but he resisted the temptation to consume her fully prone body. Bundy, on the other hand, was obsessed with the prone feminine body. And those who watched *Animal House* and did so repeatedly if they purchased it as a VHS, DVD, or, more recently, viewed it via streaming services, could return to Clorette's prone and naked body again and again.

And this fictional, sexualized child also coalesced with *Animal House*'s myriad other gags about white masculine collegiate hijinks to constitute a hugely successful film that helped propel the acting careers of young men such as Kevin Bacon, Belushi, Stephen Furst, Tom Hulce, Tim Matheson, Bruce McGill, and Peter Riegert. Karen Allen also proceeded to be a conspicuous talent in popular 1980s cinema. But Sarah Holcomb, who portrayed Clorette, found a less lucrative career following *Animal House*. After the film's 1978 release, Holcomb appeared in three movies. Only *Caddyshack*, released in 1980, was significantly successful. Afterward, she vanished from public life. In her wake were rumors about drug addiction, mental illness, and institutionalization.[94] A brief 2006 article in *The New York Post* explained that she "tragically fell off the map."[95] The author cites an interview with one of *Animal House*'s screenwriters, Chris Miller. Speaking with Mr. Skin, a website specializing in nude images of celebrities, Miller explains, "She was young, younger than the rest of us. We were a fast crowd. Drugs were everywhere. She fell into what, for lack of a better term, you would have to call bad company. And got [bleeped] up on drugs. Coke, primarily, if memory serves."[96] Notably, Miller's early use of the first-person plural ("We were a fast crowd") pivots into a passive third person that names Holcomb's falling in with the very "bad company" of which Miller and others were part, as decisive in her disintegration. He also shares that Holcomb "wound up in some home for [bleeped]-up young girls."[97] The screenwriter adds, "I don't know what became of her. Sad story." In popular renderings, men such as Bundy manufacture tragedies—nearly unspeakable perversions of a normative gendered order that require swift and decisive state and communal action.[98] But to the extent that conquests by men such as Otter and Pinto, the young men gleefully shepherding Bundy to the electric chair, other young men "playing cave man" during finals week, or those who frequently, albeit to different degrees, acquiesce to the professoriate's pornographic form result in collateral damage, it is sad. As Mack and I argue in our work on affective divestment, publics can acknowledge violence against Others as sad, even tragic, without experiencing the affective pull of accountability.[99] Whatever clarity or compassion Miller's hindsight may afford him (that is, "if memory serves") from the standpoint of a lucrative writing career since 1978, his presence as a nineteen-year-old actress indulged in the excesses of "bad company" register simply as unfortunate stumbles by a "[bleeped]-up" young girl.

And while I doubt anywhere near a significant number of US fraternity members or other college-aged men truly fantasize about necrophilia, their invocation of such excesses as a means of marking their carnal territory early in the semester, as well as the *modus operandi* of so many campus rapists, discloses a common investment in sexually possessing the docile feminine.[100] Most white college and university faculty surely express disgust that their students traffic in such overt rituals of gendered violence. Professors, administrators, and others who participate in academic governance prefer more ephemeral and subtle forms of such violence. While one surely should never sing of necrophilia, using performance reviews, promotion and tenure processes, search committees, and other bureaucratic norms to discipline and expunge racialized feminine bodies that are anything besides docile often figures as legitimate.[101] Indeed, the university should be grateful for monsters such as Ted Bundy and frat boy rapists, for they perform monstrosity so overtly that the academy, the state, and other sites of sadistic gendered violence can operate with impunity and name it tradition and rigor.

Chapter 5

MY ART SHALL BE MY REVENGE

For six years, I lived, worked, and learned in central Illinois. I earned a bachelor's and master's degree, won many trophies by way of the speech team, and began drinking in ways that would lead me to a twelve-step program in my late thirties. And I finally got laid. I arrived in central Illinois an awkward kid and would continue to oscillate inside and outside of closets regarding much more than my sexuality. My first sexual experiences involved excessive amounts of booze and an exuberant feeling that I had finally arrived at a libertine place I fetishized for so long in middle and high school. But what became a badge of honor began as confusion and acquiescence to a blur that seemed to promise deliverance from shame.

Sex in central Illinois was often invigorating. It could also be devastating. During an evening in the summer of 2003, I sped through the rural roads just outside of town. The only source of light was my headlights, and, besides the engine of my modest white Ford Escort, the only sounds were the songs I used to perform confusion and pain that summer. For a significant portion of the months between the spring and fall semesters, I was sleeping with a woman with whom I believed had no business sleeping. She was gorgeous. I did not know a single man attracted to women who did not lust after her. She had the face and body of a model, drank hard, chain smoked, and spoke with a raspy Kathleen Turner–like voice. When she and I first locked lips, I could not believe it was happening. Later, when we first had intercourse, I felt as if I had crossed a threshold. A woman like this desired me.

I spent that summer attached to her and the fantasy of a life together. We spoke or saw each other virtually every day. We did not have sex all or even most of those days. We often kissed. I awkwardly expressed affection by touching the small of her back or holding her hand. Because I always doubted that she welcomed such gestures, I did so with a tightness between my throat and chest. I also knew, but did not care to admit to myself, that she was still sleeping with her ex. She was also very clearly still in love with a mutual friend she used to date. But there had to be a chance for us, and I was intent on pursuing that chance. And in a pattern that predominated most of my romantic and sexual attachments, I was willing to become whoever I concluded I needed to be to realize that chance.

That night I sped through the rural roads of central Illinois was the evening she told me at a party that we had to stop sleeping together. I halfheartedly asked her why she was giving up on the possibility of something between us, but I immediately recognized the inevitability of this end. I promptly left and sought ways to perform my grief in a dignified way. I was uninterested in where I was going. I was speeding down this road for effect, even if I was my only audience. I performed my grief in such a way that it would feel worthy. It was a way to persuade myself that I was feeling a kind of pain that was only possible if I had triumphed over the pathetic teenage version of myself who wandered confused through the Chicago suburbs located about two hours north of where I now sped through cornfields blasting music loudly on my car stereo. Anything that has a soundtrack has dignity, right?

Rural roads, pristine nature, and other isolated places outside the cacophony of cities and suburbs often function as enclaves for performing and fleetingly exorcising white masculine shame. It is where the humiliated can assert sovereignty. Prior to his execution, Bundy asked that his survivors scatter his cremated remains in the picturesque Cascade Mountains—a mountain range in the northwest United States where Bundy abandoned many of his victims' corpses.[1] Heavily wooded areas, snowy mountain ranges, and at times, his apartment or hotel rooms served as sites for sadistic expressions of sovereignty.[2] They were his Terrible Place.[3] Most versions of the Bundy saga characterize his pursuit of dominion as a response to deep insecurities and crushing humiliations, especially regarding his relationships with women. Previously, I explained how his vexed relationship with his genealogy figures prominently as a source of shame in the Bundy archive. Equally important are his shortcomings as a heterosexual man. Texts that underscore this dimension of Bundy's biography characterize his crimes as part of a melancholic shame-vengeance cycle enacted upon young women's and girls' bodies.[4]

In his work on the cultural politics of shame, Donovan O. Schaefer explains, "Shame is best understood as a hyperdense distillation of disappointment that has been injected into a particular object in mind."[5] In Sara Ahmed's characterization of shame, it is a function of failure in relation to a normative ideal—an affective response to anxiety. Myriad versions of the Bundy saga position the serial killer's shame at the many points where he fell short of a normative white masculine ideal. While implicit in shame is a critique of the very forces that induce it, many of its expressions manifest as vengeful sadism.[6] At its worst, shame functions as a melancholic feedback loop wherein the cycle repeats indefinitely. In most tellings of the saga, a potentially infinite array of young white women and girls bore the consequences of Bundy's shame. In the Burkean lexicon, they were scapegoats.[7] Schaefer continues, "It resurfaces when we re-encounter that object, extinguishing the joy that once attached to it and leaving a radioactive residue behind."[8] Shame, therefore, is capable of adhering to an array of fungible bodies that must bear its violent consequences.

In this way, Bundy and other white masculine subjects stage shame through various rhetorical modes. These include sadistic rituals, resentful manifestos, private musings, teenage poetry, and popular performances. In so doing, shame functions rhetorically to, if only briefly, extract satisfaction from fungible feminine bodies. Shame's expressions are serial. And they are often monstrous. Texts that presume to recall the Bundy saga and other expressions of white masculine shame likewise render feminine bodies interchangeable and therefore anonymous.[9] They do not register as salient outside the angry expressions of shame in which they are merely supporting characters. All such fragments of the Bundy archive subordinate the feminine so that the white masculine might, if only fleetingly, secure satisfaction in the face of shame.[10] Bundy never penned a misogynistic diatribe to accompany his murders. Whereas many other resentful men painstakingly frame their crimes as part of a broader project of vengeance against a despised, humiliating feminine, Bundy must rely on filmmakers, authors, podcasters, scholars, and other third parties for explanatory coherence. Such texts coalesce within the archive to express misogynistic rage.

She Makes Sure You Saw Her

Twenty-two-year-old Elliot Rodger massacred six people and injured fourteen in Isla Vista, California, on May 23, 2014. Like Bundy often did, Rodger targeted a campus, the University of California, Santa Barbara, to take his revenge against all those who humiliated him—especially women.[11] In the aftermath of Rodger's attack and suicide was an archive of misogynistic discourse expressing contempt for attractive women, and the men with whom they consented to sex.[12] Absent the benefit of hindsight, Rodger's rhetoric seems hyperbolic and almost comical. It reads as parody. But while his words indeed amplify the lexicon of white masculine resentment, therefore "exceeding tacit limits on expression," they ultimately express a macabre sincerity.[13]

According to Rodger, despite his efforts at being "the supreme gentleman," the women to whom he believed he was carnally entitled for adhering to the normative masculine ideal rejected him.[14] In his lengthy manifesto explaining his rationale for the attack, Rodger recalled a time when, at age sixteen, he watched a twelve-year old boy making out with an older girl. He writes, "They made out for a long time, and I could see them tongue kiss. They knew I was watching with envy, and they still did it. I bet that lucky bastard took great satisfaction from my envy."[15] Rodger cannot imagine any pleasure the "lucky bastard" might experience while locking lips with an older girl that exceeded the joys of humiliating him.

Mulvey describes the cinematic diegesis as "a hermetically sealed world which unwinds magically, indifferent to the presence of the audience, producing for them a sense of separation and playing on their voyeuristic phantasy."[16] She adds, "Among other things, the position of the spectators in the cinema is blatantly one of repression of their exhibitionism and projection of the repressed desire on the performer."[17] Rodger's twisted world was not a Hollywood film, but he readily projected his shame onto others.[18] His narrativization of his gendered becoming is aesthetically cinematic and laden with melodrama. Throughout, he posits stark antagonisms between himself and women, as well as the more attractive and confident men with whom they slept. In the vernacular of the involuntary celibate, or incel, movement that often claims Rodger, as well as Bundy, among its patron saints, such men are Chads.[19] The movement characterizes women and the attractive men they date as embodied mockeries warranting contempt, sexual violence, and, quite often, extermination.[20]

Much like the women in Rodger's morbid tale, Chads lack agency outside the incel's shame. They exist solely to conspire with women to humiliate men like Rodger. His voyeuristic fantasy is one in which the rest of the world seeks to heighten his shame's intensity. Their every act taunts him, as he must watch them enjoy puberty's social and carnal trappings. Similarly, in the 2008 song "Sometime Around Midnight," the Airborne Toxic Event's front man Mikel Jollet describes an evening at a bar where he encounters his ex-girlfriend. The song begins with a melancholic, minute-long orchestral string arrangement that imbues what might seem an otherwise benign night at the club with the grandiosity Jollet believes it warrants. The track then settles into a high-pitched, moody guitar melody that carries the rest of the song. Near the song's conclusion, when his nameless ex appears to leave the bar with another man, Jollet, whose voice has escalated in volume and frequently breaks as if screaming, sings, "Then she leaves with someone you don't know, but she makes sure you saw her. She looks right at you and bolts as she walks out the door."[21] On the lyrics website Genius, a commenter offers one interpretation of this passage. Smileforthem22 writes, "Another classic girl move. You want your ex to know you've moved on, whether you have or not. You want him to see you leaving with another man."[22] Whereas one reply to the post states, "The 'classic girl move' bit is pretty sexist," another posits, "His ex wants him to feel pain."[23] Two thirds of the contributors to this thread take Jollet's words as a given. That is, they believe his claim that his ex-girlfriend, whose voice is entirely absent from the song, seeks to humiliate him with a sustained gaze and sadistic desire to make sure he sees her.

Popular music written by men to lament rejection by women is a theme stretching back to Mississippi Delta blues and other foundational genres for contemporary Western music.[24] Chief among such art during the late twentieth and early twenty-first centuries has been emo, or emotional hardcore. Originating in Washington, DC, with groups such as Rites of Spring and Fugazi, emo is a contested term that many of its associated acts forcefully disavow—after all, isn't all music emotional? Early emo typically employed harsh hardcore or post-hardcore instrumentals with confessional lyrics. Later iterations, such as the bands Dashboard Confessional, Jimmy Eat World, and My Chemical Romance, adopted a more melodic and, at times, operatic approach.[25] Emily Ryalls writes, "A common theme in emo music is the girl who treats a boy badly, emasculating him along the way, only to be rewarded by a pathological commitment from the boy."[26] In other words, emo functions as a musical cry from a masculine wound that quixotically seeks to resolve shame through women's bodies. Archiving these fruitless quests are analog and digital musical media, live performances, celebrity culture, and other popular modalities. Regarding the role of women in emo, music critic Jessica Hopper laments, "Our existences, our actions are portrayed SOLELY through the detailing of neurotic self-entanglements of the boy singer—our region of personal power, simply, is our breadth of impact on his romantic life."[27] Young girls make out with younger boys only to mock other boys. A woman who has committed the unpardonable sin of moving on after a breakup conspicuously laughs, smiles, and "leaves with someone you don't know" during a night out. The love object's every gesture functions to torture the masculine narrator.

For my purposes, I want to stretch emo's definitional boundaries to accommodate any music that lyrically and aesthetically expresses white masculine shame as a vengeful lament. For example, the Airborne Toxic Event is not strictly an emo group. Nor are many of the ones I describe below. But Hopper's and Ryalls's above descriptions of music called emo cohere with other sonic arrangements. I want to bend the term to my will so that it might support a larger point about the cultural politics of white masculine shame. After all, artists such as the Airborne Toxic Event, Afghan Whigs, Nine Inch Nails, and Panic! At the Disco perform work that is no less obsessive in its melancholy yearnings than traditional emo bands such as My Chemical Romance and Weezer.[28] Emo logic also propels the narratives of cinematic texts such as *High Fidelity*, *500 Days of Summer*, and *Love, Actually*.[29] In other words, I want to suggest that emo is a rhetorical genre whose patterned elements most conspicuously originate in a key instantiation of punk, but traverse distinct categories of public address to disclose a mode of white masculine lament characterized by voyeuristic shame and sadistic vengeance.[30]

More Woman Than He Could Handle

While long brown hair parted down the middle was hardly a unique hairstyle among white US women in the late 1960s and early 1970s, writers such as Rule characterize the look as a crucial part of Bundy's modus operandi.[31] They claim it was central to the sadistic form that framed his cycle of revenge—his emo drama, if you will. During 1967, Bundy attended the University of Washington. There he met Diane Edwards. Fragments of the Bundy archive that address

Edwards's role in the serial killer's life describe her as a beautiful and promising young woman from an affluent family. Using a pseudonym in place of her real name, Michaud and Aynesworth write, "Marjorie was from a class into which Ted previously had enjoyed only upward glimpses."[32] Describing her as "the coed of his dreams," Sullivan writes of Edwards, who he names Carla Browning, "She was, perhaps, everything he ever wanted, or thought he wanted out of life."[33] For these writers, Edwards's place in the Bundy saga was to personify the serial killer's aspirations, as well as his shortcomings.

Central to Bundy's infatuation with Edwards, at least the version found in most texts about him, was deep insecurity regarding his economic and social standing. He was thrilled that Edwards evidentially returned his affections, but he was equally overwhelmed by a suspicion that he had no business dating this embodied fantasy.[34] For Bundy, his upbringing in a working-class household was a frequent source of shame. Furthermore, his discovery of his fraught genealogy left him devastated and resentful toward his mother.[35] By most accounts, his educational, professional, and romantic ambitions expressed his desire to transcend his humble origins. By his calculations, winning Edwards's love would deliver him from the shameful Cowell and Bundy legacies.

Women therefore functioned as media for Bundy's idealized and elusive sense of self. Sandi Holt, one of Bundy's childhood playmates, recalls in *Conversations*, "In high school, he wanted to be something he wasn't."[36] She continues, "He was going to show the world that Ted was the one to be dealt with."[37] But Holt, like others in his orbit early in life, rarely took his espoused ambitions seriously. She explains, "He wanted to be the number one in class, but he wasn't."[38] Whereas many mainstream mediated texts about the killer characterize him as a cunning criminal, others narrativize Bundy's desperation to thrive in a world where he was agonizingly average. In an article for *Rolling Stone*, journalist Tara Telfer writes, "He was a nose-picker, a law school dropout, and a necrophiliac who mispronounced words."[39] Far more frequent in the Bundy archive is the story of a man clever enough to feign charisma and intellect to conceal the pathetic monster therein. MacPherson claims, "Bundy was merely smart, not brilliant."[40] Someone would have to pay for the resulting shame.

Michael Feifer's film *Bundy: A Legacy of Evil* chronicles Bundy's experiences with Edwards more than any other cinematic text in the archive.[41] It is, in my view, among the worst of the Bundy movies. A reviewer on the horror entertainment news site Dread Central (I searched in vain for a mainstream source that deigned to review the direct-to-video film) captures *Bundy*'s essence better than I can. They write, "This film plays like a series of mostly mundane vignettes and musical montages that randomly drift from place-to-place and year-to-year throughout Bundy's serial killing career, never staying focused on any particular segment long enough for it to develop any true significance."[42] *Bundy* is a mess.

Early in the film, Corin Nemec's Bundy awkwardly flirts with Edwards, or "Stephanie," inside a building at the University of Washington. Dressed in pressed khakis and a collared shirt underneath a sweater, he clumsily recites Shakespeare, depreciates himself, and struggles to sit still or make consistent eye contact before this gorgeous woman. He seeks to look and sound the part of a sophisticated student worthy of this young woman's love. His is a romantic performance approximating that of a middle school boy asking his crush to dance. But actress Jen Nikolaisen's Stephanie, who, despite her basis on an affluent, ambitious, and educated young woman, seems every bit as giggly and easily charmed as the average cinematic coed—or most of Bundy's victims as most filmmakers portray them.[43] Regarding her suitor's Shakespearian courting, Stephanie responds, "That may be the sweetest thing anyone has ever said to me." This sequence, while horribly acted and written, establishes, as do other Bundy texts, the killer's infatuation with Edwards as a foundational moment in the broader saga.[44]

During *Conversations*' first episode, Michaud describes the conditions that led to Edwards's decision to abandon her brief romance with Bundy. The journalist explains, "She was frankly more woman than he could handle. He didn't have any money, and that kind of opened up a lot of the old self-doubt." Crucially, Michaud genders Bundy's failings vis-à-vis Edwards's stature. She was not merely someone of greater social standing than Bundy, but her very womanhood exceeded Bundy's limited capacity for courtship and, therefore, concretized his shame. Decades later, Elliot Rodger similarly rendered his romantic and other personal failings to women.[45] In an article for the online feminist periodical *Pulp Magazine*, Jessica Wildfire describes Bundy as "the first incel."[46] And for incels, shame flows as vitriol through women's bodies. They are the problem.

During the portion of Feifer's film that focuses on the downturn in Bundy and Edwards's romance, the couple begins kissing while sitting on a bed. They then lie down, falling out of scene. Feifer briefly cuts to black and returns to the scene only for Bundy to promptly sit up and begin berating himself for prematurely ejaculating. Edwards's capacity for normative white womanhood was such that Bundy could not contain his own pleasure, while failing to provide any for her. In so doing, he failed at normative white manhood.[47] Edwards was more woman than Bundy could handle. She later tells him, "I need a man in my life. You're a boy!" Rule frames the romance in similar ways, writing, "Stephanie was like no girl he had seen before, and he considered her the most sophisticated, the most beautiful creature possible."[48]

Over the course of his first and only year dating Edwards, Bundy struggled academically and professionally. Interpreting this as a lack of ambition and maturity, Edwards broke up with him shortly after he followed her to San Francisco. The breakup crushed Bundy, seeming to confirm every fear of inadequacy he harbored about himself.[49] Michaud and Aynesworth summarize his state of mind at the time, explaining, "This first tentative foray into the sophisticated world had ended in disaster."[50] During an interview with a psychologist in the 2000 televised adaptation of *The Stranger Beside Me*, Billy Campbell's Bundy claims that humiliation caused him the most hurt. When the therapist asks who humiliates him, Bundy briefly loses composure, pursing his lips and looking to the side. He says, "It doesn't matter." By the film's conclusion, just as in Rule's book, Bundy's brief romance with Edwards figures as a foundational shame. During recorded footage from *Conversations*, Bundy told Michaud and Aynesworth, "I had this overwhelming feeling of rejection that stemmed not just from her, but everything." Emerging from these narratives of the Bundy saga is a scorned man quickly concluding that the world stood against him. He began to emotionally unravel. And therein lay the origins of his monstrosity.[51]

Edwards was, by archival consensus, out of Bundy's league. But in so being, she was also something less than human. She was a "creature"—a fleshy metonym of Bundy's many failings.[52] Her successes functioned to confirm Bundy's failures. They have no apparent value on their own. Edwards was what Bundy saw when he gazed upward, voyeuristically yearning for a life that could never be his. In this telling of the Bundy saga, his pornographic gaze is a function of deep insecurity. He gazed at Edwards as he would pornographic magazines, young women disrobing through their bedroom windows, prospective victims walking confidently through college campuses, or their lifeless bodies posed as if on the cover of a detective magazine in an isolated wooded area. In efforts to protect her identity, many Bundy rhetors vanquished it by assigning seemingly interchangeable pseudonyms. Apropos of Bundy's modus operandi, many contributors to the Bundy archive reified it by rendering Edwards and the scores of women and girls Bundy murdered as fungible bodies slightly altered to bear the burden of one man's shame and the story thereof.

The Anger's Better Than the Kiss

I cycled through many angry songs about heartbreak during my nighttime drive in rural central Illinois. Some expressed sadness, others self-loathing, and still others unmitigated rage toward an elusive love object.[53] But the track I played the loudest and repeated most often that night was one I think I was waiting to use for a moment such as this. Appearing on the band's 1993 album *Gentlemen*, Afghan Whigs' "Debonair" is the record's fourth track. It pulsates with a kind of righteous indignation underwritten with self-loathing toward which I found myself aspiring. Romantic and carnal pain are aesthetic sacraments for so many of us. Describing what she calls reflexive sadomasochism, Ryalls explains that genres such as emo seek to turn humiliation into pleasure by reconfiguring shame into vengeance. She explains, "The process of reflexive sadomasochism allows emos to make themselves victims and then to re-assert masculine dominance."[54] I was disappointed that I had not yet experienced the kind of heartbreak that could make a line such as "Feel it now and don't resist / This time the anger's better than the kiss" possible. But now it was time to perform a victimhood that preceded vengeance.[55]

"Debonair's" opening guitar riff, based on the chord progression of the theme song from David Lynch's *Twin Peaks*—itself a surreal narrative about frustrated attempts to possess the feminine—pierced my sadness and shame and nurtured them into a dignified rage.[56] Surrendering to the song's sonorous envelope gave form to my humiliation.[57] Indeed, the anger was better than the kiss. "Debonair" performs white masculine reckoning with heartache in ways attuned to the intensities of aggrieved entitlement. Music journalist Bob Gendron writes of "Debonair," "He's out for blood, bent on revenge, resolved to humiliate, eager to abuse."[58] Songwriter and lead singer Greg Dulli tauntingly sings, "This time I won't repent / Somebody's going down." "Debonair" functioned for me aesthetically as what Rodger called a Day of Retribution.[59]

I was a nice guy—what Rodger called a supreme gentleman who adhered dutifully to white masculinity's normative ideals. In this moment, it seemed that decency and sensitivity had provided me with precisely shit. This woman was my Diane Edwards—a carnal and romantic sun to my bumbling Icarus. Such is a revelation that generations of sensitive white men experience at such moments and express through myriad rhetorical modes. Some of us drive through cornfields blasting angry music. A sufficiently motivated few join rock bands and write songs of sadness and rage.[60] Others kidnap, rape, and murder young women and girls. And young men such as Rodger attempt to deliver on the promise, "I'll take great pleasure in slaughtering all of you." Still others find meaning in the misogynistic musings of men such as Nick Fuentes, Jordan Peterson, and Andrew Tate.[61] I too wanted revenge, even if not in an explicitly violent or even public way. I desired satisfaction. Dulli sings of a monster awoken by the pain of abandonment: "And once again the monster speaks / Reveals its face and searches for release." Even if this evening's drive through the rural roads of central Illinois would be the only release this monster would find, I was happy to provide it and grateful for Dulli's help.

And such help was something I had sought many times before. Popular music, poetry, and other cultural artifacts had long helped me mold my suffering as emo. On New Year's Eve, 1995, I attended my first house party with peers to mark the new year. By the standards of the parties I attended in college and afterward, this was quite tame. The host did not serve booze and, to my knowledge, there were no drugs on the premises. Several of my friends, or those I aspired to call friends, were at the party with dates or romantic prospects. Even before midnight, several of them awkwardly and conspicuously locked lips while 1990s R&B played on a nearby stereo.

I had my eyes on one person. She was my crush at the time and the first I had conjured the will to ask on a date. Several days before the party, some mutual friends played interference and urged me not to ask her out when they learned that she was firmly uninterested in anything other than friendship with me. So, I attended that New Year's Eve party, heavy with others' expectations of midnight kisses, with every reason to expect I would not be making out with the object of my desire or anyone else.

The disappointments of that evening and so many others that would populate my high school social calendar coalesced and calcified as shame. As crowded as my friends' house was as 1995 ended, my shame built a boundary between myself and the affects that circulated through the party—affects whose expressions were joy, pleasure, and, albeit in distinctly immature form, love. My body experienced this full house as solitude. To my understanding, whatever joy occurred that night merely conspired to heighten my misery.

Silvan Tomkins writes, "In contrast to all other affects, shame is an experience of the self by the self."[62] Indeed, to observe a world where others seemingly mock you by proceeding through their days effortlessly is to encounter infinite reminders of one's inadequacy. Of course, as Rodger explains in his manifesto, two peers making out or holding hands registers as mockery. Any reciprocal erotics my peers performed together were secondary to the humiliation with which they bombarded me.

But solitude need not negate expression. Kelly explains, "Despite at times being private and ineffable, pain is an intersubjective experience."[63] Its legibility to others requires the work of translation, whatever form it may take.[64] Shortly following my father's death, I discovered my own archive of shame and other anxious affects in the form of dusty notebooks in what had been my childhood bedroom. On the cover of one, a Mead Composition notebook, my younger self wrote, "Notes from Hell" and "for my eyes only" (figure 20). The journal is quite explicitly for an audience of one. But in each entry's original orbit were various personae that I addressed with longing, envy, intense insecurity, and sometimes rage.[65] The notebook amounted to an anthropologist's journal he kept while observing an unfamiliar culture.[66] It also operated in a discursive environment of popular cultural artifacts whose renderings of white masculine pain provided the generic grounds from which I wrote. Those grounds found expression as sadistic form. As such, these artifacts from my archive are also part of the Bundy archive.

On January 30, 1996, I wrote, "I slipped on an ice patch on the way back from PE today. For some reason, it was more embarrassing than it usually would be. It was degrading to hear this jock say, 'Hey, buddy, you've got to watch out, it's slippery there.' 'Buddy.' Every time someone calls me that, I want to hurt them, even kill them. Also, [Rachel] was there. I was embarrassed by the fact that she saw me in that situation. I care about her, I just don't know how much."

My current memories of Rachel are hazy. She was a girl and we hung out with the same people. Some entries in the journal report that I had a crush on her. Her name was not Rachel, nor are the names I list below real. Just as decades of authors and filmmakers have christened Diane Edwards with pseudonyms, I am taking measures to protect the innocent. But in so doing, I am also rendering them fungible. They function as now-anonymous signifiers of shame. Their purpose is to propel my narrative, just as Edwards is an essential character in a story whose apotheosis is the kidnapping, raping,

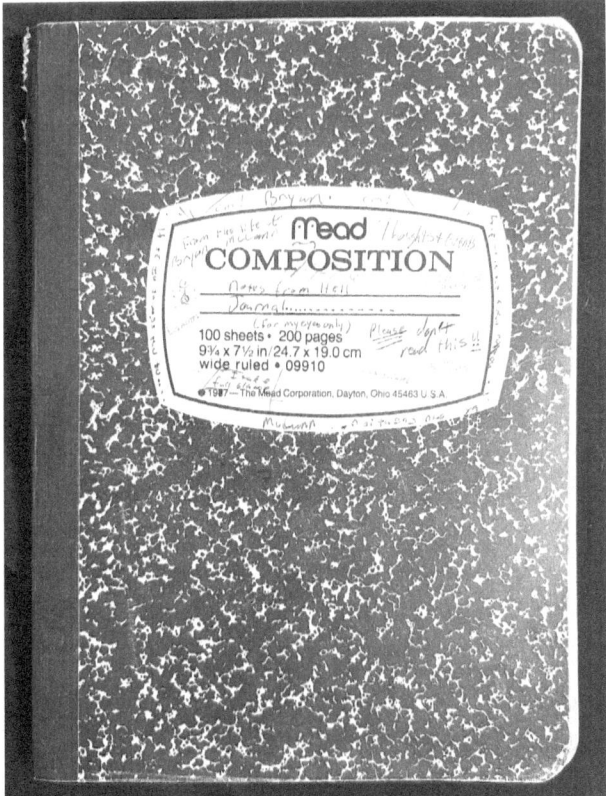

Figure 20. Cover of the author's teenage journal. Author, 2023.

and murdering of at least thirty white women and girls whose function was to atone for her original sin. Rachel and her peers similarly functioned as avatars from which I sought a measure of attention and justice.

But whereas this memory of unrequited love no longer resonates, the humiliation of "this jock" calling me "buddy" still stings. I can appreciate the way it felt like condescension from somebody on a higher social plane than me. He probably had a girlfriend. His parents probably made more money than mine. And the house they shared was likely nicer than my family home. His brief address, delivered toward my clumsy body, activated myriad anxieties that took shape as shame. In hindsight, slipping on the Midwest ice as a teenager recalls my father's own embarrassments. He was prone to snapping when other men offered him assistance in good faith. He would show them he required no help! As an adult, I have often responded to others' kindness in such a way. At the time I slipped on the patch of ice, I lacked the capacity to confront this young man, whose ability to further embarrass and perhaps even physically hurt me inspired caution. But the prospect that this "jock," or Chad, sought sincerely to offer aid as I navigated an icy Chicagoland winter day was unimaginable. In my emo telling of this experience, his sole purpose was to humiliate me.

After Rachel, I developed a crush on Tina. Later, my journal chronicles feelings for Natalie, Claire, Justin, and Tyler. Regarding Claire, I wrote on April 20, "I was surprised to learn that she was a poet, something I didn't expect from her. I suddenly feel attracted to her now, not that anything could happen. She seems out of my league." This too was a time when I devoured books by the often-misogynistic likes of Jack Kerouac, Ginsberg, and David Foster Wallace largely in the service of cultivating a white masculine bohemian ethos that I still chase through the professional circuitries of academia.[67] Such men provided written and embodied instructions in sophisticated, if often tortured, white masculinity. In one string of sentences, I both affirmed that, because she wrote teenage poetry, Claire warranted my attention while also speculating that she was "out of my league." And so, it often went, a cycle of demanding expectations and pessimistic self-loathing that structured my affective linkages with various objects of my desire.[68]

But even as 1996 was evidently a year of many romantic investments, Tina was the one who featured most prominently. She was the one I wished to kiss that New Year's Eve and the one about whom I wrote on April 1, "Why can't I have her!!!!" On March 20, I disclosed, "Every time I see [Tina], I want to take her by the hand and kiss her. Of course, I dare not do that. It's been five months since I first fell head over heels for her. The only person I've yet to truly fall in love with is someone that I cannot have." These entries read as cliché. They are comically melodramatic in ways that teenagers are distinctly capable of achieving without a hint of irony. Unrequited love is obviously a familiar trope in Western narrative traditions. But equally persistent in my reflections on my longings for Tina is a logic of possession. A reader of my journal would learn very little about Tina or why I desired her so much. They would only know that I wanted her. My teenage words' resonance with Rodger's manifesto or Bundy's brutality against so many replicas of a founding heartbreak is chilling. Why can't we have them?

The final clause of my March 20 entry recalls one of my favorite songs at the time (and still). Appearing on their debut album, *Pretty Hate Machine*,

Nine Inch Nails' "Something I Can Never Have" is itself a lament about yearning for that which the white masculine subject cannot possess. Critic Tom Breihan describes the song's haunted sonic aesthetic, writing, "Starting with nothing but a haunted, minimal piano figure and a few hushed synth tones, the track slowly lets in sputtering static, faraway door-slam drums, and quiet little counter-melodies."[69] He also notes that, unlike so much of Nine Inch Nails' catalogue at the time and since, the song incorporates no electric guitar. It begins quietly and builds to a crescendo punctuated by intensifying drums and front man Trent Reznor's voice. By the final chorus, he is practically screaming. His already nasally voice cracks as he sings, "You make this all go away. I'm down to just one thing and I'm starting to scare myself." While more amorous in its pretenses since Reznor claims the love object makes that which is dark and painful "go away," he, like Afghan Whigs singer Dulli, ultimately discloses his awareness of his capacity and barely latent desire to do harm.

Searching for Release

When privileged bodies experience pain, the resulting discourse often mitigates Others' suffering even as it names them complicit in the pain in question.[70] Therein lies the compulsion for vengeance. If shame is a function of anxiety born of frustrated desires, vengeance is chief among its public expressions. Emily L. King explains that vengeance offers fleeting moments of satisfaction that, like any other addiction, requires another hit once the buzz inevitably wears off.[71] Bundy, Rodger, and other vengeful subjects seek to punish their enemy, but also wish to prolong the pleasure of doing so. The work of revenge therefore is never complete. It is, by definition, serial.[72] The bodies that bear the burdens of white masculine shame are therefore fungible. If one victim is insufficient to satiate monstrous urges born of shame, others must materialize. What proceeds is an industrial, fascistic logic—a mass (re)production of fungible bodies marked for annihilation.[73] Because one target is never enough, more and more people begin looking like targets. For this reason, the vengeful emo subject requires more victims for his songs, poems, and murders.

In 1973, one year before Bundy's first confirmed attacks and murders, he and Edwards began dating again. During their four years apart, Bundy reentered school, became involved in Washington State Republican politics, and secured admission to law school. He had gotten his act together. Regarding their rekindled romance, Rule speculates about Edwards's impression of the new and improved Bundy. She writes, "Where he had been a boy, uncertain and wavering, with no foreseeable prospects, he was now urbane, smooth, and confident."[74] They promptly began talking of marriage. Following a scene portraying Bundy's ascendance in Washington GOP politics, Feifer films a lengthy montage of Bundy and Edwards walking the streets of San Francisco together. The scene is idyllic, punctuated by a brief exchange in which Edwards praises Bundy for his newfound maturity. She stares at him longingly as she speaks. The sequence culminates at a high-end restaurant. During the meal, Bundy proposes to Edwards. Much to the other guests' pleasure, she says "Yes." Immediately after Edwards accepts the proposal, Bundy excuses himself to use the restroom. He promises his new fiancé, "When I get back, I have an even bigger surprise for you." He then leaves the restaurant, forcing Elizabeth to wait alone, humiliated, as other guests leave. It becomes clear to her that Bundy will not return. Her mediated solitude projects a shame that is itself a function of Bundy's shame.

While Feifer takes great narrative liberties in telling this story, he captures the essence of the relationship's second chapter. In a version that corresponds with most others in the Bundy archive, Rule explains that, following their reconciliation, Bundy quickly grew cold toward Edwards. Describing the final weeks of the relationship, Rule writes, "He had chased after her for six years. Now, he seemed uninterested, almost hostile. She had thought they were engaged, yet he had acted as if he could hardly wait to be rid of her."[75] When Edwards confronted Bundy over the phone regarding his behavior, Rule reports that he coldly said, "Stephanie, I have no idea what you mean."[76] He then hung up the receiver.

More important than the specifics of Bundy's vengeful bait and switch with a woman who he first adored and then resented is how the narrative functions within the broader archive. Immediately after the proposal in Feifer's film, Bundy declares, "You don't know what you've done for me, Stephanie!" In a run-of-the mill romantic comedy or sentimental drama, such a statement would indicate that the woman he courted made him a better man or taught him how to love again. But the film's diegesis and other versions of the Edwards saga in the Bundy archive imbue such language with irony. What she evidently did for him was transform him into a serial killer, or his true self.

In a recorded interview segment during *Conversations*' first episode, Bundy describes his feelings regarding Edwards to Michaud and Aynesworth.

He shares, "In there somewhere was a desire to have some sort of revenge on Diane." Referring to an earlier attempt by Bundy to win Edwards back, Rule writes, "Had she accepted him back at that point, some of his humiliation might have been tempered. But she couldn't."[77] In a scene from the televised adaptation of Rule's book, Rule meets Edwards (named Victoria in the film) at night in a nondescript city locale. Edwards tells Rule about Bundy's cruel act of revenge. Rule then asks when the events transpired. After Edwards shares the exact date, Rule pauses, then says, "The first girl was attacked three days later." Though narratively contrived, this sequence reifies the other versions of the Edwards story. In such accounts, Edwards could have spared scores of women her just punishment had she taken Bundy back.

This is not to suggest that Rule or any other rhetor in the Bundy archive believe Edwards's choices were unreasonable. To the contrary, they universally affirm that Bundy was beneath a woman of her stature. But equally prominent in the Bundy archive is the claim that the Edwards saga, coupled with his concurrent discoveries regarding his genealogy, were primal scenes for Bundy's subsequent series of murders. While some individuals with proximity to the case suspect Bundy began murdering women and girls earlier in life, his first confirmed killings undoubtedly began in the immediate aftermath of his revenge against Edwards. And for Rule, whose true crime memoir about the Bundy case remains the most prominent, his desire for vengeance never ceased. Regarding the women and girls Bundy killed, Rule writes, "The victims are all prototypes of Stephanie. The same long hair, parted in the middle, the same perfectly even features."[78] In other words, each murder functioned as an expression of Bundy's contempt for a singular woman who humiliated him. In her *Vanity Fair* piece about Bundy, MacPherson repeatedly refers to his murders as "symbolic" repetitions of his rage against Edwards.[79] Writes Rule, "None of the crimes filled the emptiness. He had to keep killing Stephanie over and over again, hoping that each time would be the time that would bring surcease."[80] As surely as William E. Connolly argues that the drive for revenge quickly becomes generic, Bundy, at least in Rule's telling, never sutured the shameful wound for which he blamed Edwards. Similarly, MacPherson writes, "His great romance, and one that some speculate may have triggered his symbolic killings, was with a beautiful coed who jilted Bundy when he was a junior in college."[81] Such a characterization of Bundy's motives itself anonymizes the at least thirty young women and girls he murdered. Rather than individuals with rich histories and ambitions, they most often function in the archive as scapegoats for this foundational heartbreak. Their murders are "symbolic" acts of revenge against Edwards, not calculated corporeal acts of cruelty against women and girls with histories and agency.

To Dream of Malicious Consequences

For the emo subject, love objects cause pain. Cultural critic Hanif Abdurraqib explains, "It's in the spirit of male loneliness to imagine that someone has to suffer for it."[82] Vengeance is a kind of inevitability in the stories the men of this chapter tell. The monster inside Dulli, Reznor's espoused helpless fear of the horrible things he might do, Jollett's paranoid surveillance of his ex-girlfriend at a bar, Rodger's escalating rage that eventually arrived at his poisonous words' limits, or the mythos of Bundy murdering Diane Edwards *ad infinitum* all gesture toward diminished culpability for the white masculine subject who avenges his many humiliations.[83] There is always some body to blame. Describing this dynamic in popular music, Eli Davies writes, "The whole thing is a deep, thick pool of jealousy and pain; desire is transformed into something sinister and violent, a woman is sneered at, dismissed, her body instrumentalised, but none of this is hidden; it's all on plain, ugly show."[84]

In his manifesto, Rodger imagined what this show might entail. He writes, "The first strike against women will be to quarantine all of them in concentration camps. At these camps, the vast majority of the female population will be deliberately starved to death." He adds, "I would have an enormous tower built just for myself, where I can oversee the entire concentration camp and gleefully watch them all die."[85] Justice, for Rodger, was humiliating those who humiliated him. He concludes his fantasy with as lucid an articulation of his misogynistic worldview as one can expect to find in his archive. Writes Rodger, "*If I can't have them, no one will*, I'd imagine thinking to myself as I oversee this. Women represent everything that is unfair with this world, and in order to make the world a fair place, they must all be eradicated."[86] Rodger engages in a worldmaking endeavor wherein utopia arises from the corpses of those who have humiliated him. It is, as Kelly illustrates, "a large-scale industrial project of sexual repression, and ultimately, feminicide."[87] It is a fascist enterprise that seeks to recuperate the anxious white masculine subject's rightful sovereignty.[88]

For my part, I was no more capable of harming my love objects as a teenager in the Chicago suburbs than as a graduate student in central Illinois. I used poetry instead. In fact, my first publication chronicled my shame on New Year's Eve, 1995. Appearing in my high school's student-run literary magazine, the poem reads in part,

> You have me contained in that distant
>   corner's perpetual embrace
>   staring at you with magnetized vision
>   through a transparent tear.[89]

Ginsberg it is not, but it was my clumsy attempt to crystallize experiencing myself as hopeless and helpless as I watched Tina enjoy an evening without any midnight kisses and my peers secure theirs with seemingly no effort. All of it conspired to mock me. The poem concludes,

> I want to hurt you,
> to scar you
> and bruise you,
> I want to cement you in my filth,
> my longing
> and my contempt.[90]

Fortunately, I added,

> But to look into your eyes and dream of malicious
> consequences is one of those hopeless impossibilities.[91]

I do not recall what I thought "malicious consequences" meant at the time. So much of this work was derivative of my literary and musical idols—most of them white men. Indeed, what I performed in this poem was an iteration of a broader white masculine performativity that tethered creativity to pain.[92]

And for me, my poem was my revenge against a world full of love objects who would not return desire in kind. I do not believe it was ever in my capacity to inflict violent retribution on a world that denied me. That said, I am likely fortunate to have graduated high school in spring 1998, several months before the mass shooting at Columbine High School in Littleton, Colorado, transformed the disciplinary apparatuses of so many US high schools.[93] White teenage boys who dressed in black, wrote poetry, and listened to Nine Inch Nails became, however fleetingly, objects of moral panic.[94] And while an angry teenage poem is not an assault rifle, it is a weapon. It crystallizes white masculine shame and demands that others experience it.

The Truth Is Terrible

Teenage poetry expresses shame. It is also a source of shame. As I have read through my old journals and poetry, I often cringe. Whatever embarrassment I lacked at the time for my bohemian aspirations and morbid meditations on loneliness, I make up for it in the present. That is, my response to shame is itself a source of shame. I am ashamed of my younger self, as well as the adult he became. It is cyclical.

Bundy kidnapped, raped, and murdered scores of young white women and girls. He also had sex with their corpses. Most renderings of the Bundy saga characterize this latter excess as the most disturbing among the serial killer's cruelties.[95] If Bundy were a garden variety rapist and murderer, he might not have caused as much disgust or even attracted so much notoriety in mainstream public culture.[96] Sexual violence against feminine bodies is, after all, quite normative in the context of white Western modernity. It is practically a redundancy.[97] Sarah Marshall writes regarding sexual violence against women, "Once you were dead, you could be loved forever. Once you were dead, no one asked if you had fought back hard enough, if you hadn't really wanted it after all."[98] But necrophilia is a step too far. Even as sexually defiling corpses violently asserts sovereignty, it also registers in public discourse as a symptom of extreme depravity.[99] It is what separates men such as Bundy from college-aged men with no regard for consent, architects of imperial projects, or even lonely young men whose shame manifests as mass violence or vengeful artistry. Amplifying the depths of Bundy's depravities helps alleviate what anxiety might emerge from his resonances with normative white masculinity.

The true crime writers who chronicled Bundy's death row confessions in detail agree that he was especially evasive regarding necrophilia. During his original conversations with Michaud and Aynesworth, Bundy presented himself as an expert on serial killers, speaking only in the third person when describing what all three men knew were his crimes.[100] Later, during his meetings with Hagmaier, Keppel, and other constabulary visitors eager to close many cold murder cases before the execution, Bundy only reluctantly disclosed his onanistic rituals with dead women and girls.[101] Regarding these disclosures, Hagmaier explained during *Conversations*' final episode, "That was something he never talked about even in the third person." The FBI profiler added, "You know, the truth is—is terrible." Bundy's monstrous truths are of course terrible, as are the scores of other manifestations of sadistic form that constitute white Western modernity. But whether it be from Hagmaier's mouth, Berlinger's editing, or both, this sequence within the documentary series' last fifteen minutes saves the worst for last. The cruelties Bundy inflicted on young white women and girls after their death figure as far more upsetting than the torture he inflicted on them when they were alive and conscious of what was happening to them.

Bundy's necrophilia also positions him as a freak warranting mockery. In his recollection of death row meetings with Bundy, Keppel writes of the serial killer who murdered scores of women in his jurisdiction, "Not only was he a chickenshit who coldcocked his victims before he carted them away and strangled them, he was a necrophile who sexually aroused himself with their remains as he spent time with them at their resting places, even as they were decomposing into skeletal shadows of what they once were."[102]

This sentence's structure is illustrative. Not only was he a "chickenshit" who raped and murdered young women and girls; that would be bad enough. But he also had sex with their rotting corpses. Similarly, after cataloging several of the cruelties Bundy inflicted on his victims while they were alive, Rubin writes in her memoir, "Even once the women were dead, he couldn't stop himself from wanting to rape their cold corpses."[103] Such is the mark of a true monster, if also a coward whose pathetic pursuits of normative white masculinity ultimately excluded him from its idealized domains.

In the film adaptation of Keppel's book, the detective, portrayed by actor Bruce Greenwood, presses Cary Elwes's Bundy regarding Hawkins's murder as the men sit inside a prison interrogation room. The condemned killer evades Keppel's inquiries regarding his time with Hawkins and her corpse, squirming, chain-smoking, and changing the subject. As Keppel presses Bundy about the fates of the many women's heads he decapitated, Bundy eventually relents and explains that he used the heads to remind himself of his power over his victims. He did so by "beating off to their skulls." As he utters the words, the soundtrack's muted, moody soundtrack briefly escalates to a few distant drumbeats. Director Bill Eagles wants viewers to appreciate this scene's salience. The entire film, which chronicles Keppel's hunt for Gary Ridgway and his attempts to extract confessions from Bundy, was building toward this moment when the extent of Bundy's depravities became clear.[104]

And here I am, saving the worst for last. At the conclusion of a chapter that dwells in rape and murder, and misogynistic shame, which is itself near the end of a book that navigates myriad disturbing domains, I position Bundy's necrophilia as a culmination. This is apparently where the road through the Bundy archive leads—sex with corpses. And as with other chronicles of shame that populate the Bundy archive, the fungible feminine bodies that endure white masculine shame's violent expressions remain mostly silent. For by the time Bundy's vengeance against the women who humiliate him reaches its depraved culmination, they are long gone. And dead feminine flesh is quintessentially fungible. They can, as Bundy told Hagmaier, "be anything you want them to be."[105] This ubiquitous serial killer's ritualized uses of dead feminine flesh function in the archive not as claims made to the women and girls he murdered. They are media incidental to the ritualized expression of white masculine dominion.[106] Bundy's necrophilia instead addresses the publics that consume his saga while enacting homologous cruelties. And this shameful excess often assures publics whose revenge flows from pens, musical instruments, and assault rifles that their own monstrosity has its limits. But formally, the necrophile, the teenage poet, the emo musician, and the mass shooter occupy a common plane wherein objects of desire, despite their intoxicating allure, hover in a state of mute malleability so that our shame may have its say.

CONCLUSION

In the final episode of *Conversations*, Aynesworth recalls feeling relief at the prospect of Bundy's execution when he arrived at Florida State Prison on January 24, 1989. This was not a man foaming at the mouth such as those reveling outside the prison, nor does he appear particularly invested in retribution for Bundy's many victims. After interviewing Bundy and collaborating with Michaud on two books about the serial killer, Aynesworth simply sounded exhausted. He explained, "I was just happy to see him go."

I do not support the death penalty, nor have I ever in my adult life. At times, I have been deeply involved in efforts to end state killing. But Aynesworth's relief at Bundy's electrocution resonates, especially as this project draws to a close. I also empathize with Liz Kendall who, at the close of *Ted Bundy: Falling for a Killer*, says, "I'm hoping that this is the end of my participation in anything related to Ted." The character Pamela in Jessica Knoll's Bundy themed novel *Bright Young Women* is on to something when she compares experiencing the Bundy archive to life during the COVID-19 lockdown. Writes Knoll, "I was held captive by a virus that had been around a long time, that had finally mutated to infect me. Him."[1] In the final pages of her memoir, Rubin writes, "Bundy does not deserve to live on in the collective memory as a charming and brilliant man when he was neither."[2] Ted Bundy is a creep. His ubiquity is, by so many measures, nauseating and exhausting.[3]

Since committing to this project in 2019, I have thought about Bundy every day without exception. To flip through the pages of my various notebooks during this time is to see ubiquitous, often daily, references to him.

As I note in earlier pages, I often walk across campus, as well as other public spaces, and briefly register young women who fit Bundy's victim profile. At times, I grow self-conscious in crowded coffeeshops or aboard airplanes as I type entire paragraphs about disturbing misogynistic cruelties. And, of course, writing about Bundy has also entailed recounting difficult memories and uncomfortable self-appraisals. While completing manuscript revisions, I experienced a mental health crisis that resulted in a brief hospitalization and a period of medical leave from work. While the origins of such troubles are varied, my spouse makes a reasonable point when they have suggested that perhaps there are psychological perils to, in their words, filling my head with Ted Bundy. This man is exhausting, as is his archive. I am ready to see Ted Bundy go.

But I am not counting on his disappearance from US public culture soon, nor fanfare about serial murder in general.[4] The nine feature or television films, numerous documentaries or episodes of true crime series, podcasts, books, social media fandom, and myriad other texts that circulate the Bundy saga form part of the broader rhetorical ecology that is the Bundy archive.[5] They attest to this saga's staying power. Suffice it to say, Bundy is unlikely to lose his place atop the serial killer pantheon.[6] The objective for critics and rhetors interested in disclosing the sadism and depravity that characterizes Western modernity is to hasten the rupturing of the rhetorical alibis that frame the cruelties that Bundy, the state, and other purveyors of gendered modernist violence enact. This does not mean turning away from the Bundy archive so that others can extract pleasure and rhetorical cover from it. As King explains, celebrity culture is a potentially fecund site for critical practice because celebrities themselves are metonyms for myriad social investments. Because, as Schmid reminds us, serial killers such as Bundy are indeed celebrities, we ought not relegate such archives to the modernist logics whose investments in white masculinity's violent dominion marginalize potentially transgressive readings thereof. Rather, our readings of Bundy should amplify the anxieties his ubiquity betrays in the service of critique.

It is not particularly useful to produce a hierarchy of popular texts trading in the Bundy saga to distinguish the most problematic portrayals from more promising ones. After all, I opened this book with reference to a Bundy film that fails at virtually all normative criteria regarding quality cinema. And yet, its many failings render it a more valuable Bundy text than many others from more talented and better-resourced artists. This book's core arguments rest on the premise that even the most problematic texts function heuristically to disclose the cruelties that find expression through modernist white masculinity. There is no burning Bundy bush that can clean up the mess of which he is but one expression. But in closing, I advance trajectories of thought and practice, which several key Bundy texts concretize, that might help us do Bundy differently.

Identification's Aporia

I have only dreamed of Bundy once that I can remember. I am grateful that at least my dreaming mind perhaps enjoyed a degree of independence from this volume's primary focus. The dream placed me in Florida during what had to be the early morning hours of January 24, 1989. I stood against a wall inside Bundy's death row cell. If anyone else there, least of all Bundy, knew I was present, they did not indicate as much. It was time for Bundy to walk from his cell into the room where prison staff would strap him to the electric chair and murder him. Every account I have read about Bundy's execution suggests that the man who murdered several dozen white women and girls did not resist his final walk. Although many witnesses reported that he appeared petrified by what was to come, he acquiesced to the state's macabre ritual just as he forced so many young women and girls to perform their role in the rituals he enacted in various parking lots, alleys, wooded areas, sorority houses, and hog pens.[7]

Inside the cell, Bundy sat on the cell bed with his back against the wall. His shoulders slumped and his head hung as he sobbed and shook his head. He spat out things such as, "This is bullshit!" while prison staff surrounded him and made clear that his walk to Old Sparky was not optional. A man who crushed two sorority sisters' skulls and severely injured two other Chi Omega residents in the span of fifteen minutes was now reduced to a scared, crying man. This characterization of a cowering condemned killer appears in several versions of the Bundy saga. In the televised adaptation of *The Stranger Beside Me*, Billy Campbell's Bundy wiggles and pleads as the prison staff leads him on his final walk toward the death chamber. In Bright's *Ted Bundy*, Burke portrays the titular character during his final hours as prone to sobbing, but mostly in a state of barely coherent shock. Bright also subjects him to humiliation from prison staff, including a scene wherein guards shove cotton up his anus to minimize the effects of electrocution-induced defecation. The director treats a man who raped scores of women and girls in kind, reifying the very logics of vengeance and gendered degradation Bundy himself performed. Describing such protocols in her memoir, Rubin writes, "Bundy was pushed into a position of shame."[8] During the execution scene itself, Burke's Bundy is pale with fear and seems barely aware of what is happening. If the legal threshold for a humane execution is the condemned's capacity to understand what is happening to him and why, this Bundy may have had grounds for another appeal.[9] The Bundy that resonates most with the broken man in my dream is Luke Kirby's portrayal of the killer in Sealey's *No Man of God*. During the film's final minutes, Hagmaier, portrayed by actor Elijah Wood, looks through a prison door window, watching Bundy and several supporters holding hands and praying in anticipation of his execution. Bundy cannot sit still, eventually breaking down and screaming expletives. Throughout the movie's final moments, Bundy anxiously rubs his newly shaved (and therefore electrocution-ready) head, is quick to anger, appears exhausted, and is, above all, palpably desperate. He is pathetic.

The Bundy I watched process his imminent death recalled a child in an unpleasant situation who simply wanted out. The child lacks the faculties to reckon with certain kinds of fear, anger, or other unpleasant emotions. As an alternative, they deteriorate to an infantile condition in which they utter some variation on "It's not fair!" Perhaps it was my identification with a masculine body ill-equipped to handle overwhelming emotion that caused me to feel mostly fear as I watched Bundy disintegrate inside his cell. In the weeks preceding my decision to enter an intensive outpatient psychiatric program and abstain from alcohol, I rebuked my spouse's reasonable exhaustion at my behavior by screaming, "I have a chronic condition!" During a car ride home, during which my mood spiraled from the indignity of not having enough funds in our checking account to pay for a fast-food dinner, I threatened to jump out of the moving car as if physically fleeing emotional discomfort. In his novel *Infinite Jest*, David Foster Wallace compares self-harm and suicide to jumping out of a burning building. It is not about hurting oneself, but about mitigating pain by ending it—or, as the late rock musician David Berman suggests, passing the pain to those left behind.[10] It is a means of escape that appears perfectly logical in the moment given the overpowering affects coursing through one's body.[11] Such is the motivation behind my own suicidal ideations and other kinds of acting out. I want to escape the flesh trapping me inside the body that languishes in a brutal cross-section of myriad anxieties. And I suspect the Bundy of whom I dreamed not only desired to flee his imminent death but grew infantile to avoid the anxiety of reckoning with the fact thereof. Broken men yearn for escape.[12]

The week my father died was humiliating for both of us. When he fell head-first and ass-up into the bathtub while taking one of many daily, slow, and likely painful shits, he was too weak to call for help. Thankfully his emaciated body was still capable of making a loud noise. I rushed in, picked him up, and helped reposition him on the toilet, smelled his feces, and saw his shriveled penis. Because minds go to strange places in the face of corporeal death, I reflected for a moment on how my father would never again experience or give sexual pleasure. I recalled my own capabilities while watching his porn tapes, which also instilled in me myriad unrealistic standards about size, endurance, and other signifiers of adequate virility, and therefore masculinity.[13] And those videos were a secret we shared even as we kept it from each other.

During one of my adult visits home before he got sick, I borrowed my father's hoodie to walk the family dog around the block. I often enjoyed this chore because it allowed me a brief respite from the tensions that still characterized so many of my familial dynamics. And at times when I was off the wagon with regard to smoking or vaping, I could indulge my habit without scrutiny. Home and secrecy remained tethered well into adulthood. During this walk, I stuck my hand in one of the pockets and immediately recognized what I touched as an unopened condom wrapper. Finding hidden beer or porno around the house was old hat, but this was new. It had been decades since monogamous sex between my father and mother would require a prophylactic. And while my dad was a bit of an oddball collector who picked things up from off the street (and stole things from his mail route), that explanation did not strike me as credible. So, I wondered about his plans for this condom. Because my father had long since given up on attractiveness and self-care, I doubted that this was for a lover. Far more likely, in my estimation, was transactional sex. What kind of john was my father? Was he simply businesslike? Did he and the sex worker meet at some cheap hotel, go about their business, and part ways? Was he a sweetheart who performed tenderness in ways he struggled to around his family? Maybe he was a weirdo who enacted various fetishes he never dared explore with my mom. Or maybe he was cruel. Surely it was conceivable, even likely, that the man whose capacity for physical violence kept me in a state of suspended fear for much of my childhood and adulthood also expressed his capacity for rage through sex. Did he call the sex worker a slut or a whore? Was she a Black or non-Black woman of color and, if so, did he pay enough for her to endure the various racial epithets he had used so often over the course of his life? And how did my father, the cheapest man I have ever known, come to willingly spend money on sex? And how did he conceal doing so from the rest of us? Then again, secrecy was a skill on which he relied so heavily and developed over a lifetime. If Bundy could convince an otherwise intelligent young white woman to help him carry his books to his car, then my father could likely hide his own proclivities amid the chaos and distraction of my family unit.

"Father and son bonding," he mumbled as it became apparent to both of us the profound reversal of roles taking place upon the toilet on which I would sometimes discretely masturbate as a teenager. I chuckled politely. He was right in ways that exceeded the morbid humor of the moment—a moment I wanted desperately to escape. My encounters with my dying father as bare life brought me closer to him than I had ever been.[14] This closeness was unfamiliar, as was the proximity to imminent death. It was a moment of vulnerability that, as bell hooks writes, hegemonic modes of masculinity conspire to violently suppress.[15] Whereas my father had disappeared into the abyss of his failing body, I had no such luxury. And newly sober, the drinking that temporarily eased the tension of visits home was no longer an option. Of course, he and I were always close in that we performed strikingly homologous alcoholic repertoires even if at different junctures in our lives. And that knowledge is what fucked with me so profoundly as he slouched toward the end.

The day he died, I injected a dose of morphine into his nearly toothless mouth as it hung ever-so-open. I envied him not because I had an affinity for opiates, but because I would have welcomed anything to numb me at this time. After dispensing the morphine and leaving him with some canned pears I knew he would not eat following months of chemotherapy and radiation, I left for an hour to run errands with my mother. I had traveled to Chicagoland for several days to lend support and ease some of the care burdens my sister and mother disproportionately carried. My mother and I returned home to his vacant eyes and desperate breaths punctuated by ever-longer silences.

Describing Bundy's electrocution in the final episode of *Conversations*, Deckle recalls seeing Bundy's fist clench tightly as electricity coursed through his body. He explains that, at the time, he wondered how many throats that fist had clenched to the point of death. In my dream, the Bundy I witnessed before the prosecutor and other witnesses watched him die was somehow, if even briefly, apart from his most heinous acts. The prospect of death had so reduced him that he now seemed to embody a Levinasian Other for whom I had ultimate responsibility.[16] Similarly, despite his many cruelties over the course of my life, my father's reduced state also inspired pity and a sense of responsibility. It recalled his kinder capacities. Perhaps it made the stark duplicities of the familial grieving process easier to bear.

Intellectually, I take issue with experiencing felt responsibility for the man whose alcoholism caused me so much pain. The man who kept an unopened condom in his pocket, stolen pornos in the garage, and a beer cooler in the backseat of the car with which he drove me to and from various childhood destinations was not trustworthy or necessarily grieveable. Viewed through the lens of those behaviors, he deserved the humiliation he experienced at the end. Such is the logic that assembled so many exuberant bodies outside Bundy's 1989 execution. But I also know that my father's painful death from cancer was merely a final humiliation during a lifetime of humiliations born in part of authentic affinity and felt responsibility for family. And I wonder if whatever he did with that condom in his hoodie made him feel, if only briefly, like the man modernity promised him he could be. By most accounts, Bundy enjoyed sovereignty when he kidnapped, raped, murdered, and desecrated the corpses of young women and girls. And the very character of sovereignty is one of violent yearnings for fungible feminine flesh—bodies, that in their submission, assure the sovereign of his dignity. To spy in the confident sovereign a fundamental brokenness discloses the ultimately untenable character of white masculinity for the vast majority of bodies that mediate it.[17]

Having and Wanting

In her meditation on Bundy's mental health and the question of evil, Marshall characterizes him as a confused and broken soul. Based on several interviews with lawyers and mental health professionals who worked with Bundy in the years preceding his execution, she found stories not of the psychopathic narcissist so prominent in US popular culture, but of a bipolar man with little control over his impulses. She writes, "We can say that Ted Bundy was a psychopath, but we can also attribute his behaviors to the mental illness his lawyers observed in him, and doing so reveals a very different picture from the one we know."[18] Describing that picture, she continues, "It shows us a man who appears to have been unable to control his actions or make the decisions that would have saved his life, who put on shows of competence and superiority because he needed to force the world to see a version of himself that he was no longer sure existed."[19]

More than most artifacts in the Bundy archive, this description of Bundy resonates with my experiences as a white masculine subject. Throughout this volume, I have described my experiences with addiction and mental illness during my academic career.[20] Whatever internal rot I aimed to silence with booze and self-harm, my concurrent professional trajectory did not visibly suffer. I worked desperately to project competence, even excellence. For I was sure the talented thinker and writer I portrayed to the world would evaporate if I allowed myself a moment's respite from my careful curatorial work. The broken man who drank himself into oblivion most nights, often thought of suicide, engaged in self-harm, and came dreadfully close to destroying his marriage needed to remain hidden.

My father shifted violently from enacting the role of a dedicated working-class father to a bitter man who no longer cared to nurture such facades. I have compassion for my father and, even if in fleeting moments, for myself. But Bundy seems a step too far. To call for compassion toward the man who kidnapped, raped, and murdered over two dozen young women and girls is to imply that those so often crushed by modernity's violent gendered heel should also do so. Whatever metaphysical value compassion and forgiveness may hold for a shared future, such is not my demand to make. And most chronicles of the Bundy saga argue forcefully against compassion. In their books, Michaud and Aynesworth frequently comment on Bundy's cockiness and audacity during their interviews.[21] Keppel diminished Bundy's masculinity and raged against his depravities in *The Riverman*.[22] Despite her pretense of friendship with Bundy, Rule ultimately characterizes him as irredeemably monstrous. For example, she played a prominent role in circulating the claim that, as a teenager, Bundy murdered his eight-year-old neighbor Ann Marie Burr.[23] And Liz Kendall concluded that the man she once thought she would marry was ultimately reducible to his worst actions.[24]

But there is another narrative of Bundy—one that disrupts the coherence of an archive that employs his unmitigated evil to rationalize other kinds of white masculine violence. During the final act of the 2020 Max documentary *Crazy, Not Insane*, Dorothy Otnow Lewis, a psychiatrist who worked closely with Bundy during his death row appeals, recalls that the condemned killer admitted to a childhood sexual encounter with his sister.[25] Coupled with abuse from his grandfather, his confusing genealogy, and insecurity regarding his family's economic status, Lewis's discovery reveals considerable childhood trauma. Moreover, the psychiatrist's broader program of research, and the topic of the Max documentary, finds that childhood trauma affects brain development in ways that reduce impulse control and other executive functions. If we accept Lewis's conclusions, Bundy's capacity to refrain from enacting his fantasies was minimal—virtually nonexistent.

Nelson, who enlisted Lewis's help in hopes of stopping her client's execution, also characterizes the Bundy case as a tragedy for all participants rather than a Manichean conflict between a violent, brilliant misogynist and his feminine prey. For her, executing a man whose mental illness caused him to sabotage his own defense during two capital murder trials was a constitutional nonstarter. This manifestation of Bundy, an impulsive man who tried in vain to cultivate a version of himself capable of responding to the demands of the moment, appears elsewhere in the Bundy archive. In a widely circulated television interview during his murder trial in Colorado, Bundy's eyes often shift between the camera and the interviewer, as if he is a child seeking the approval of both.[26] In his infamous final interview with Dobson, Bundy begins with a nuanced description of pornography's role in his cruelties, but, by the end, as if to please Dobson, has fully adopted the culture warrior's belief in a stark causal relationship between such material and his murders. And during the first sequence of the movie that opens this book, Bright's *Ted Bundy*, the director displays a series of childhood and teenage photographs of the man who he would spend the rest of the film portraying performing ghastly violent acts. Burke's first scene as Bundy shows him awkwardly rehearsing normalcy, such as introducing himself, in front of a mirror. Such an inaugural characterization of the film's titular character implies that all involved in the Bundy saga are victims of the cruel forces that mobilized his crimes. Similarly, Feifer's film uses flashbacks to establish Bundy's traumatic childhood and later underscores the heartbreak of discovering he was an "illegitimate" child. At several points in *The Deliberate Stranger* and *Extremely Wicked*, Harmon and Efron's Bundys abruptly and briefly shift from the assured charming man they impersonate to a confused and sometimes fearful man who fundamentally misunderstands the world around him. And although they err on the side of monstrosity, Kendall and Rule nonetheless characterize Bundy as inherently pathetic, if also evil.

As she concludes her article about the question of evil and the nature of psychopathy in the Bundy saga, Marshall imagines herself as a potential Bundy victim. She writes, "*Listen*, I said, when I imagined him driving me up the mountain some dark night, a narrow logging road, the way long, the radio gone to static. *Listen*, I'd say. *Just tell me what you need from me. Why is my body the one you have to tear apart? What do you think you'll find?*"[27] If Marshall's Bundy is not, contrary to most popular portrayals, a psychopath incapable of genuine human feelings, then, she concludes, he is someone with whom she could reason and maybe even reach. He is someone who others, had they tried, could have reached. She could convince him that he has a choice. He does not *have* to kill her. For this journalist, Bundy's depravities are the result of his virtually nonexistent impulse control. Were it not for childhood trauma, the unpredictable destinies of neurology, or the inadequacies of mental healthcare, dozens of young white women and girls, and one Theodore Robert Bundy, might still be among us.

On the evening my father provided my sister and I alcohol, only to grow enraged at our subsequent behavior, he chased us to the car as we left my aunt's condominium. He had already physically punished us in her presence. Now, under the cover of his own domain, free of surveillance and judgment, he could presumably enact greater cruelties on his young children. After we buckled ourselves into the back seat of the family Buick Regal, he punched both of us repeatedly in the face. We both sobbed. Then he, likely drunk himself, started the car and proceeded to drive. I looked forward and frequently saw his bloodshot eyes glance at us via the rearview mirror. His visceral anger nearly made him unrecognizable. As surely as Molly Kendall observed the man she regarded as a father figure enter a trancelike state when she discovered him naked, my father, whose violence I already knew at this young age, was evidently in an altered state.[28] Perhaps I could have reasoned with him. I might have asked him what he needed from me. Or, what he needed from a world in which he labored in vain to arrive at a place of contentment. And I still want to know what he believed beating his children would provide him.

For my part, when I explode with my own gendered rage, I am looking for a scapegoat. With the cruel world itself out of reach, I choose others in my orbit, especially my spouse, to hear my bitter complaints. But throughout the process of writing this book, my spouse has urged me against writing myself as a monster. And I know my father too well to posit him as one. I recall learning about film and music from him, therefore acquiring curiosities that were a precondition for this book. And he loved my sister-in-law's intellectually disabled son, eagerly spending time with him whenever the two families came together. I sit here wondering what kind of grandfather he may have been to my adopted children. He would have been a good one, I think. And I recall overhearing him say to my spouse, less than a year before his death and mere months into my sobriety, "Thank you for taking care of my son." Especially difficult for me to grapple with is the recognition that the same felt obligations that motivated my father's shame and cruelty could also inspire kindness. A monster would be far easier to grieve.

My alcoholism helps me identify with my father. And, as I have repeated throughout this volume, my constitution as a white masculine subject helps me find resonance between Bundy's depravities and my own. Marshall makes the provocative argument that a kairotic interruption might have placed any of us on different courses. In Marshall's claim resides a theory of discourse positing the capacity of argument to interrupt compulsion. Seeing the world and its inhabitants differently, and to accept alternative means of reckoning with misery, helps white masculine subjects understand that we need not proceed sadistically through the world.

In *No Man of God*, director Sealey offers a different Bundy. Her film dramatizes the serial killer's many prison interviews with Hagmaier, especially in the days before his execution. Sealey never situates Bundy outside the prison. She portrays neither his murders nor his death. *No Man of God* also abandons longstanding tropes of Bundy being a charming, manipulative criminal genius. Instead, he appears as a broken, desperate narcissist in fear for his life. The film also crucially uses a variety of techniques to amplify the homologies between Bundy's sadism, Hagmaier's own fantasy life, and day-to-day enactments of misogyny that rarely register to many publics as such given their banality. At several times in the film, Sealey uses slow motion to accentuate Hagmaier's self-awareness regarding the ways he gazes at women's bodies as they walk down the street or through prison corridors. Near the end of the film, as Bundy viscerally describes a murder, Hagmaier jarringly alternates between horror at the killer's cruelties and identification with his investment in dominating fungible feminine flesh.

As their final conversation before the execution ends, Hagmaier begins leaving the interview room. Bundy calls out and asks him, "Did you get what you came here for? Do you know why I did it?" Bundy chroniclers such as Marshall and Nelson argue that this question haunted Bundy as much as anyone else.[29] The man they describe did not understand how he came to do the things he did and wished desperately to figure it out. During a sequence of *Falling for a Killer*, Bundy's younger brother Richard recalls a time when Ted abruptly sent him home early during a visit to Utah. Describing his brother's behavior as they awaited Richard's flight back to Washington, the younger Bundy shares, "I can see this look on his face, and he was horrified and disgusted about something." Struggling to maintain his composure during the interview, Richard continues, "I think he felt his urges coming on, knew he was about to murder somebody, and he had enough responsible attitude to get me out of the picture so I wouldn't be involved with it." Bundy's capacity to be a good big brother never waned, but his desire to kidnap, rape, and murder young women and girls was like any other addiction. Its dominion never ceased until it found satisfaction. Despite such powerful compulsions, the notorious killer had the clarity of mind to experience disgust at his own behavior.

But the Hagmaier of *No Man of God* does not indulge the compulsion narrative. Following Bundy's question, he looks at the condemned man, expressing with his face both disgust and sadness. "Because you wanted to," he says. Bundy inhales deeply at the unsatisfying answer. Sealey addresses what Marshall does not regarding Bundy's crimes. A failure to control actions presupposes a desire to commit them. Whatever interference Marshall imagines in the lives of Bundy or other sadistic men that might have avoided such disastrous outcomes are unnecessary absent desire. Sealey prepares her audience for Bundy's execution by offering only the insight that he wanted to kidnap, rape, and murder young women and girls. And he wanted to return to their corpses under the cover of night to continue dominating them. And within the Bundy archive, this blunt desire coexists with the serial killer's adoration of his little brother, the possibility that he truly loved Liz and Molly Kendall, his mental illness and childhood trauma, his potential remorse, and other variables that constitute a man and archive incapable of delivering a coherent composite of why men such as Bundy act as they do. In the end, the archive does not offer an essential Bundy, nor one that alleviates anxiety in audiences willing to occupy the complex expanse of the man and his monstrous legacies.

But what of the colonizer and other executors of white masculine dominion whose excesses liquidate entire peoples and ravage the planet? Frantz Fanon described whiteness as an absolute system that interpellates subjects racialized as white into whiteness itself, and therefore white supremacy.[30] Similarly, David Roediger documents how what W. E. B. Du Bois called the psychological wages of whiteness induce poor and working-class whites to invest in anti-Blackness and other regimes of domination even when it requires accepting an economic system that exploits their labor.[31] And James Baldwin frequently commented on the various neuroses that characterized whiteness in the United States.[32] The bodies that function as media for sadistic form do what they do because they want to. And their want is a function of white Western modernity's inducements. Such seemingly contradictory insights are coconstitutive. They are mutual preconditions for critiquing modernist white masculinity in ways that move ever so slowly toward its dismantling.

Sadism's Call

Bundy had a choice, as do we all. But sadism's suasive call often proves difficult to ignore.[33] In his 2014 one-man show, *The Ted Bundy Project*, performance artist Greg Wohead reckons with his own morbid curiosities regarding Bundy and other notorious sadists. In an informational packet for the show, Wohead writes, "*The Ted Bundy Project* is an exploration born of a curiosity about the nature of charm, the label of 'monster,' and the tension between attraction and repulsion."[34] Additionally, "Greg wants to ask what we are capable of imagining and doing, whether we are who we say we are and how much is too much."[35] Throughout the show, which runs just under one hour, Wohead wears a white polo shirt and tennis shorts, which is the outfit witnesses reported Bundy wore when he kidnapped Denise Naslund and Janice Ott at Lake Sammamish State Park in Issaquah.[36] The performer addresses his audience, who sit in a thrust configuration, with facts about Bundy, interpretations of his taped confessions, a Hall and Oates–accompanied reenactment of the first time Bundy and George Ann Hawkins made eye contact, and various uses of onstage props such as a pair of handcuffs, a pantyhose mask, a replica of the log Bundy used to attack five women in Tallahassee, a brown wig with long hair parted down the middle, and a projector.

In a favorable review of the performance, Lyn Gardner writes, "Of course this isn't really a show about Ted Bundy. It's a piece about our fascination with violence, murder and gore."[37] Indeed, Wohead's primary focus, besides coming to terms with his own morbid curiosities, is inviting his audience to confront theirs. A key thread during the show is Wohead's experiences with the viral video *1 Lunatic, 1 Ice Pick*. The controversial video shows Luka Magnotta murdering Jun Lin in Montreal, Canada.[38] Wohead never plays the grisly video, which portrays Magnotta stabbing Lin, who he had tied nude to a bed frame, to death, and then dismembering him and performing necrophilic acts. But the performer plays a reaction video of several teenage or college-aged men in a hotel room watching *1 Lunatic, 1 Ice Pick*. The young men behave as if they are cheering on a sports team, a fellow student pursuing a sexual conquest, or a state carceral apparatus executing a loathed serial killer. One man in the video repeatedly vomits in a trash can but continues lifting his eyes and frequently smiling as he continues watching and retching. While the reaction video plays, Wohead describes *1 Lunatic, 1 Ice Pick* in detail. He does not show his audience the murder, but he invites them to picture it as they watch several young men celebrate the very act he describes.

Later in the show, Wohead plays the first few seconds of the video but pauses it before the actual violence ensues. Because he pauses at a frame where no visible action is occurring besides Lin lying in bed under a duvet, it is unclear whether the audience is viewing a frozen frame or a sequence in the video just before Magnotta enters and tortures Lin to death. The camera operator filming the recording of the performance that Wohead shared with me pans to the audience, whose members appear pensive at the prospect of watching a murder unfold. One white man gently places his fingers against the middle of his eyes, as if to prepare to cover them. Others in the audience, including many white women, simply look on.

Wohead closes the show as he opened it, by playing a vinyl record of the Scottish band Middle of the Road's 1971 hit "Chirpy Chirpy Cheep Cheep" and dancing to it. The song itself is a mostly vacuous pop song about a baby bird calling out for its absentee parents. But its juxtaposition with Wohead dressed as Bundy and enthusiastically performing several popular dances from the 1950s and 1960s is unnerving. With his dancing, Wohead seems to say, I leave you to reckon with this aporia I have left on stage. The lights fade, with Wohead still dimly visible and dancing. The projection screen reads, "In case you want to Google it." The screen then transitions to the video's title, *1 Lunatic, 1 Icepick*. And the show ends.

The Ted Bundy Project confronts its audience with sadism's inducements.[39] The individuals who gather to watch Wohead perform social commentary, as well as young men in hotel rooms giddily watching a murder unfold, can choose whether they will answer the call. They can look away or gleefully gaze. They can vomit in trash cans. Or they can look and experience the ghastly recording as an artifact of a culture enamored with its own cruelties. Notably, Wohead is a US American performer based in the United Kingdom. His recorded performance, which I view from my home in the United States, occurred in Europe. Wohead therefore reminds us that the United States does not have a monopoly over the Bundy archive. The continent that men such as Ian Brady, Dennis Nilsen, Peter Sutcliffe, and Fred West surveyed for fungible bodies is also the grounds from which white Western masculinity and its broader modernist project spawned.[40] Thus, the macabre rituals of the Bundy archive ensnare audiences on both sides of the Atlantic. Members of any audience entrenched in modernity's cruel logics might return to their homes after Wohead's show and Google *1 Lunatic, 1 Icepick*.

Wohead leaves the publics he addresses with a choice between the curiosities that induce us to consume fragments from so many macabre archives and what he imagines to be the better angels of our nature. But to presume the presence of a better choice, at least a self-evidently better one, is to invest levels of confidence in a conspicuous good whose capacity to violently disappoint we should not underestimate. A fork in the road is often a point of divergence whose inevitable reunion awaits ahead. Anyone who left Wohead's performance that evening perhaps left with the impression that they had a relatively stark choice to make. They could follow their morbid tendencies and consume the Bundy archive, or they could live more thoughtfully and compassionately.

In *The Bundy Archive*, I have suggested public curiosities about Bundy are a function of a patterned logic of which Bundy the man is an expression. He is a name for a variation on a broader white masculine form. In such a rhetorical formation, divergences are often illusory. I write in the aftermath of the 2024 US presidential election, in which Donald J. Trump secured a second, nonconsecutive term in the White House. His Democratic opponent, Vice President Kamala Harris, a Black woman, selected Minnesota Governor Tim Walz as her running mate. Enthusiasts for Walz often characterized him as a refreshing alternative to Trump's toxic brand of white masculinity.[41] I confess that Walz's gentler disposition, his espoused feminism, and demonstrable support for queer and trans people in Minnesota were heartening amid the Republican carousel of sadistic form. But I also find deep resonance with Ruth Whippman's reservations about such characterizations. She writes, "Positive masculinity still draws on the old trappings and anxieties of traditional manliness, the same belief that there is such a thing as a 'real man' and the same fears of falling short."[42] In other words, just as in the duplicity narrative that frames so much Bundy discourse, even allegedly progressive expressions of masculinity risk trading in the same normative logics that name some masculine performances authentic in opposition to others. Furthermore, Walz represented an incumbent Democratic Party whose support of Israel's genocidal campaign against Palestinians in the Gaza Strip, as well as its broader colonial enterprise that finds expression through repeated euphemisms about its "right to defend itself," alienated many Arab, Muslim, and left-wing voters.[43] The men that numerous rhetors within the Bundy archive characterized as idealized expressions of white masculinity, especially those in law enforcement, were themselves complicit in quotidian regimes of gendered violence. Similarly, even the most sensitive expressions of manliness often occupy bodies whose entrenchment in state power and mainstream politics overdetermine their complicities in empire's gendered atrocities. The archive is a function of rhetorical invention, but it also ensnares the archivist and critic themselves. This is not to suggest that there is no way out. To suggest as much would be ahistorical, even as the preceding pages have argued that white masculinity's ideological scaffold is intricate, vast, and violent. Generations of Black and non-Black people of color, First Nations, women and femmes, queer and trans communities, and other publics reveal the presence of other archives that undermine the sadism whose logics so frequently masquerade behind the cover of normalcy.[44]

The Archive Looks Back

In fact, the very logics that structure sadism potentially enable its undoing. Matheson explains that empathy is inherent to sadistic fantasies. He writes, "The important dynamic in the affective ecology of sadism concealed from its subjects is not just the dependence on a victim, but the strong identification with them."[45] For sadistic form to function, the sadist must hold his victim close, but not too close. Sadism therefore functions as a delicate choreography wherein the sadist must be close enough to the victim to enjoy their suffering, but not so close that the fantasy begins to unravel and induce anxiety.[46] This is why prevailing renderings of the Bundy saga characterize the serial killer as duplicitous, especially depraved, or otherwise contrary to normative white masculinity. Such versions of Bundy enable the publics that consume him to enjoy violently possessing fungible feminine flesh without implicating the broader modernist enterprise that structures white masculine performativity. We can have our cake and eat it too.

But closeness to Bundy need not preclude alternative modes of empathy. Texts such as Sealey's feature film *No Man of God*, Wood's Amazon docuseries *Ted Bundy: Falling for a Killer*, Knoll's novel *Bright Young Women*, and Kendall and Rubin's memoirs are unique within the Bundy archive in that they invite their publics to confront the broader violent legacies to which Bundy gives expression through identification with victims and survivors. In addition to the scenes I describe above, which orient the viewer toward the homologies between Bundy's sadism and more quotidian enactments of white masculine violence, Sealey's film disrupts the masculine gaze by looking back. During the film's reenactment of Bundy's death row interview with Dobson, the director provides scant detail regarding the men's conversation. After panning across the prison visitation room where the interview occurs, the camera settles on a shot that frames Bundy and Dobson sitting on either side of a prison table. Between them and standing near one of the room's walls is a young white woman who appears to be in her early twenties. She has long blonde hair and wears a white baseball cap. She holds a clipboard and black leather padfolio tight against her chest. The camera slowly zooms toward the woman as the scene's ominous instrumental music increases in volume, eventually drowning out Bundy and Dobson's discourse about pornography. Her facial expression increasingly signals distress. Perhaps this young member of Dobson's film crew recognizes that she and women like her align with men such as Bundy's victim profiles, as well as the kinds of bodies Dobson and his brethren seek to subordinate in their culture war. Her eyes begin to well up with tears as she pivots her head from side to side, looking at Bundy and then Dobson as if to implicate both in the gendered violence that codifies her vulnerability. She then abruptly stares directly at the camera and therefore the viewer. In so doing, she implicates the film's audience as much as Bundy or Dobson. Forced to endure an opportunistic spectacle

Figure 21. Breaking the fourth wall in *No Man of God*. RLJE Films, 2021.

between two men invested in disciplining feminine flesh, this woman's quiet rage ultimately becomes this brief scene's centerpiece (figure 21).

Regarding the sequence, Sealey tells *Refinery 29*'s Ann Cohen, "What I was trying to represent with that woman is: What is it like to be a woman in a society, living in a world where we're obsessed with these guys?"[47] She adds, "I'm much more interested in her than I am in Bundy."[48] If feminine bodies are white masculinity's object, then Sealey's young woman exemplifies the object staring back. It implicates the viewer for whom so many artifacts in the Bundy archive, including mainstream films, direct-to-video exploitation flicks, classic cinematic portrayals of masculine collegiate hijinks, celebratory rallies outside executions, or so many young white men's pornographic fumblings provide opportunities to possess feminine flesh while disavowing the gratuity of Bundy himself. Instead, the young woman in this brief sequence stares at Bundy, Dobson, and the audience as if to map them onto a broad constellation of modernist gendered violence. What Sealey induces in this sequence is a proximity to Bundy that is too close for comfort. It invites, rather than alleviates, anxiety.[49]

Fundamental to the Bundy archive is mediating the affects that coalesce at the scene of the crime. Whereas rhetorics of victimhood risk trading in essentialisms that rationalize modes of carceral violence that are themselves concretizations of modernity's cruelties, texts such as Sealey's call on those who would consume Bundy to do so from alternative perspectives.[50] Similarly, in her novelization of the Bundy saga, Knoll writes from the imagined perspectives of two fictionalized versions of women involved with the case. One, Pamela, is chapter president of the Chi Omega sorority

Bundy attacked at Florida State University. The other, Ruth, is one of the two women Bundy kidnapped from Lake Sammamish State Park. Referring to Bundy only as "The Defendant" throughout *Bright Young Women*, Knoll, like Kendall, Rubin, and Wood, aspires to characterize the women Bundy murdered, injured, or otherwise traumatized as nuanced agents capable of powerful insights regarding one serial killer's homologies with a broader enterprise of masculine violence.[51] In the immediate aftermath of the Chi Omega attack, Pamela reflects, "There were men who cracked their knuckles while divulging to me what they would do to The Defendant if they got the chance, thinking this was somehow reassuring for me to hear. But all it did was make me realize that there wasn't so big a difference between the man who'd brutalized Denise and half the men I passed every day on the street."[52] Whereas Rule fashioned such "good ole boys" as Bundy's heroic antithesis, Knoll portrays such posturing as a tiresome expression of hypermasculine bluster.[53] Throughout the novel, Knoll's characters narrativize the ways the very misogyny that characterized Bundy's depravities also find expression in the day-to-day indignities of masculinist culture.

I have taken care in this volume to frequently identify Bundy's murder victims as young white women and girls. Whiteness, functioning as it does as white supremacy's invisible center, is strikingly inconspicuous despite its ubiquity in the Bundy archive.[54] While the normative category of "woman" looms large, the role of racialization in the Bundy saga does not. To be fair, during promotional interviews for *Extremely Wicked*, Berlinger and Efron claimed that the Bundy story is, in part, an object lesson in white privilege. According to Efron, "The fact is that the whole world, literally, all the media, everybody, was capable of believing that this guy was innocent. Talk about white privilege, talk about white . . . whatever."[55] Bundy's capacity to evade suspicion or capture was certainly a function of his white masculine body's capacity to register as normative—a normativity that tales of his duplicity and other common discourses in the Bundy archive reify.

But the espoused feminist principles that ground alternative renderings of the Bundy saga, such as work by Knoll, Sealey, and Wood, have precious little to say about the whiteness that renders Bundy's victims legible as such. While the fungibility that configures feminine flesh as suitable for violent possession is itself an expression of white supremacy, so too are the rhetorical norms that mark victims such as George Ann Hawkins and Kimberly Dianne Leach as grieveable.[56] The stories of Bundy's victims that feminist writers tell are those of, to borrow from the title of Knoll's novel, itself a critique of Judge Cowart's laments at Bundy's wasted potential, bright young women. As I have argued in previous pages, such notions of futurity presuppose categories of humanity and citizenship that, Ashley R. Hall reminds us, are "informed by and preserved through Black death."[57]

In her powerful commentary regarding white nineteenth-century abolitionist John Rankin, Hartman suggests that his espoused empathy toward the Black slave is only possible to the extent that his white imagination displaces the enslaved. As a result, Hartman writes, "Rankin begins to feel for himself rather than for those whom his exercise in imagination presumably is designed to reach."[58] Each time Bundy kidnapped, raped, and murdered a young white woman or girl, he staged modernity's vast violent enterprise. He expressed sadistic form. Feminist renderings of the Bundy saga function in part to displace the serial killer's perspective, so prominent in artifacts within the Bundy archive, in favor of women and girls whose brightness is legible not only in juxtaposition with Bundy's depravity, but also in relation to other brutalized feminine bodies who figure in public discourse as far less grieveable.[59] While these white women and girls are undeniably also modernity's victims, the empathy they invite obscures the experiences of those whose disposability functions as its anchor.[60]

In her influential critique of white feminist theories of the gaze, hooks describes a Black feminist notion of the oppositional gaze, which, she argues, has the capacity to deconstruct the male-female binary anchoring so many psychoanalytic understandings of cinema and other visual media.[61] While Sealey's young white woman does indeed stare back in ways that invite reappraisals of hegemonic renderings of the Bundy saga, what might a stare that encompasses both white masculinity's sadism and white femininity's normative victimhood entail?[62] It might resemble a meme featuring a Black woman holding back laughter as she drinks from a glass of white wine. Under her is the text, "Someone said not to dress up as a serial killer on Halloween because it's appropriating white culture" (figure 22). The joke, of course, is that, when legions of white people appropriate racial difference to perform genres of monstrosity against which white femininity requires singular protection, the most depraved monsters operate within and in service of white masculinity's vast genealogies.[63] Serial murder is white culture. It is, as I have argued, an expression of a modernist enterprise invested in serially enacting violent possession of bodies, land, and other fungible objects. We are Ted Bundy.

Figure 22. "Somebody said not to dress up as a serial killer on Halloween because it's appropriating white culture." Unknown.

He is our Malcolm X. And even the most progressive elements of the Bundy archive, offering as they do important critical interruptions of stories that center the killer and his sadistic brethren, often invest in white modernist masculinity's broader enterprise.[64] If Ted Bundy will never simply go away, modes of proximity to his archive that refuse sadism's alibis are powerful in their capacity to mobilize anxiety about white masculinity and modernity's many other violent iterations toward fecund critical insights. Alternatives to discourses that render modernist violence normative and joyful are those that center the voices of the fungible bodies and communities whose suffering sustains its sadistic force.

NOTES

Introduction: We Are Ted Bundy

1. Matthew Bright, *Ted Bundy*.
2. Clifton P. Flynn, "Examining the Links between Animal Abuse and Human Violence."
3. Elizabeth Kendall, *The Phantom Prince*; Ann Rule, *The Stranger Beside Me*. To my knowledge, all the women and girls Bundy murdered were white, although one surviving victim, Kathy Kleiner Rubin, is Cuban American. I reference these women and girls' whiteness at several points in this book to underscore the racial politics that animate discourse about Bundy's victims and white womanhood in general—an issue I address in detail in later chapters. See Kathy Kleiner Rubin and Emilie Le Beau Lucchesi, *A Light in the Dark*.
4. Joe Berlinger, *Conversations with a Killer*; Joe Berlinger, *Extremely Wicked, Shockingly Evil, and Vile*.
5. "Ted Bundy," *CineSchlocker*.
6. Spike Lee, *Malcolm X*.
7. "Ted Bundy (2002)."
8. David Sodergren, "Visions from Beyond the Dave #2."
9. Jane Nightshade, "Bundyrama."
10. Nightshade, "Bundyrama."
11. Peter Bradshaw, "*Bundy*."
12. On the relationship between narratives about serial murder and the horror genre, see Philip L. Simpson, *Psycho Paths*.
13. E. Chebrolu, "The Racial Lens of Dylann Roof," 53. Also, Jacques Lacan, *Anxiety*.
14. On violence and modernity, see Tommy J. Curry, *The Man-Not*; Jack D. Forbes, *Columbus and Other Cannibals*; Saidiya V. Hartman, *Scenes of Subjection*; María Lugones, "Toward a Decolonial Feminism"; Walter D. Mignolo, *The Darker Side of Western Modernity*; Sayak Valencia, *Gore Capitalism*. On homology, see Barry Brummett, "The Homology Hypothesis."
15. Dave Kehr, "The Life and Violent Times of a 1970's Serial Killer."

16. Mark Kermode, "Matthew Bright."

17. On January 15, 1978, well before sunrise, Bundy, having recently escaped custody in Colorado, entered the Tallahassee sorority house with a log in hand. He proceeded to bludgeon four sorority sisters as they slept, killing two. He also gnawed at some of them with his teeth and sodomized one with a hairspray bottle. After leaving the Chi Omega house, Bundy attacked another woman in her home. She survived. See Rule, *The Stranger Beside Me*.

18. Peter Vronsky, *Sons of Cain*.

19. David Schmid, *Natural Born Celebrities*.

20. Claire Sisco King, *Mapping the Stars*, 8.

21. For example, Lugones, "Toward a Decolonial Feminism"; Carine M. Mardorossian, *Framing the Rape Victim*; Elizabeth A. Povinelli, *The Empire of Love*; Klaus Theweleit, *Male Fantasies*.

22. On the constitution of publics, see Maurice Charland, "Constitutive Rhetoric"; Christian O. Lundberg, *Lacan in Public*; Michael Warner, "Publics and Counterpublics."

23. Stephen Stiles, *Fatal Addiction*.

24. See Michel Foucault, "Nietzsche, Genealogy, History."

25. Jen Yamato, "'The Ted Bundy Tapes' and 'Shockingly Evil.'"

26. "The Top 50 Report-2019." On *Joker*, see, Joanna Robinson, "This is the *Joker* the Trump Era Deserves."

27. Kendall, *The Phantom Prince*.

28. Stassa Edwards, "*Ted Bundy: Falling for a Killer* Renders the Women Three-Dimensional."

29. Brian Lowry, "With Two New Movies, Ted Bundy is the 'Boogeyman' Who Won't Go Away."

30. Brett A. B. Robinson, "Introduction"; Justin Sayles, "The Bloody Bubble."

31. Jack Z. Bratich, *On Microfascism*; Ijeoma Oluo, *Mediocre*; Jared Yates Sexton, *The Man They Wanted Me to Be*; Jane Ward, *The Tragedy of Heterosexuality*.

32. Casey Ryan Kelly, *Apocalypse Man*; Casey Ryan Kelly, *Caught on Tape*; Paul Elliott Johnson, *I the People*; Michael Kimmel, *Angry White Men*. And as disclosures regarding his predatory behavior imply, Dr. Kimmel is not immune to the trappings of the violent masculinities he critiques. Colleen Flaherty, "More than Rumors."

33. Kelly, *Caught on Tape*; Joshua Gunn, *Political Perversion*.

34. Kelly, *Caught on Tape*.

35. See Paul Johnson, "Owning the Libs."

36. Karma R. Chávez, "Parody, Perversion, and the Violence of 'Normal' Political Culture."

37. Kelly, *Apocalypse Man*; Sexton, *The Man They Wanted Me to Be*.

38. Lugones, "Toward a Decolonial Feminism"; Aileen Moreton-Robinson, *The White Possessive*; Povinelli, *The Empire of Love*; Theweleit, *Male Fantasies*.

39. Phillip Jenkins, *Using Murder*, 122.

40. Mark Seltzer, *Serial Killers*, 21. Also, Robinson, "Introduction."

41. Jon Stratton, "Serial Killing and the Transformation of the Social," 84.

42. Jane Caputi, "The Sexual Politics of Murder."

43. See Kyra Pearson, "The Trouble with Aileen Wuornos, Feminism's 'First Serial Killer.'"

44. Seltzer, *Serial Killers*.

45. Schmid, *Natural Born Celebrities*.

46. Robinson, "Introduction."

47. See Lisa Downing, *The Subject of Murder*; Simpson, *Psycho Paths*; Richard Tithecott, *Of Men and Monsters*.
48. Simpson, *Psycho Paths*.
49. Robert J. Morton, *Serial Murder*.
50. J. C. Macek III, "No Texas, No Chainsaw, No Massacre."
51. Vronsky, *Sons of Cain*.
52. Bryan J. McCann, "Entering the Darkness"; Pearson, "The Trouble with Aileen Wuornos, Feminism's 'First Serial Killer'"; Schmid, *Natural Born Celebrities*, 229–43.
53. Corky Siemaszko, "How Richard Speck's Rampage 50 Years Ago Changes a Nation."
54. "Chicago Massacre"; "Ed Gein"; McCann, "Entering the Darkness."
55. Michael Calvin McGee, "In Search of 'The People,'" 242.
56. Here, I draw from Darrel Wanzer-Serrano's definition of rhetoric. See Darrel Wanzer-Serrano, *The New York Young Lords and the Struggle for Liberation*, 19.
57. Charles E. Morris III, "The Archival Turn in Rhetorical Studies," 113.
58. See Julietta Singh, *No Archive Will Restore You*.
59. Amanda Demeter, "Disgust and Fascination"; Kevin M. Sullivan, *The Bundy Murders*.
60. Barbara A. Biesecker, "Of Historicity, Rhetoric."
61. Jenny Rice (formerly Edbauer), "Unframing Models of Public Distribution," 20. Also, Louis M. Maraj, *Black and Right*.
62. Omedi Ochieng, "Infraconstitutive Rhetoric," 533.
63. Cara A. Finnegan, "What Is This a Picture Of?," 118.
64. Emerson Cram, "Archival Ambience and Sensory Memory," 110–11.
65. See Bernadette Marie Calafell, *Monstrosity, Performance, and Race in Contemporary Culture*; Cram, "Archival Ambience and Sensory Memory"; Leah DeVun and Michael J. McClure, "Archives Behaving Badly"; Charles E. Morris III, "Sunder the Children"; Evan Mitchell Schares, "Witnessing the Archive"; Ann Laura Stoler, "Archival Dis-Ease."
66. Laura Browder, "Dystopian Romance"; Jess Commons, "Why Women Fall in Love with Serial Killers Like Ted Bundy"; Katherine Ramsland, "Girls Who Love Ted Bundy."
67. Diana Taylor, *The Archive and the Repertoire*, 20. Also, Peggy Phelan, *Unmarked*.
68. José Esteban Muñoz, "Ephemera as Evidence." Also, Robert Gutierrez-Perez and Luis Andrade, "Queer of Color Worldmaking"; Schares, "Witnessing the Archive."
69. Hartman, *Scenes of Subjection*. Also Saidiya Hartman, *Wayward Lives, Beautiful Experiments*.
70. Pamela VanHaitsma, *The Erotic as Rhetorical Power*. Also see Aaron D. Gresson, "Minority Epistemology."
71. See Phelan, *Unmarked*.
72. For an example of such thinking, see Leah Ceccarelli, "Temporal Development and Spatial Emplacement in the Dispositional Whole." For a critique thereof, see Bernadette Marie Calafell, "Rhetorics of Possibility"; Ochieng, "Infraconstitutive Rhetoric"; Darrel Wanzer-Serrano, "Delinking Rhetoric."
73. Saidiya Hartman, "Venus in Two Acts," 9.
74. V. Jo Hsu, *Constellating Home*; VanHaitsma, *The Erotic as Rhetorical Power*.
75. Patricia Hill Collins, *Black Feminist Thought*; Audre Lorde, *Sister Outsider*; Cherríe Moraga and Gloria Anzaldúa, *This Bridge Called My Back*.
76. Hsu, *Constellating Home*, 149.
77. Taylor, *The Archive and the Repertoire*.

78. On epistemology and the body, see Bernadette Marie Calafell, "Performance"; Karma R. Chávez, "The Body"; Dwight Conquergood, "Beyond the Text"; Lisa A. Flores, "The Rhetorical 'Realness' of Race"; E. Patrick Johnson, *Appropriating Blackness*; Andrew R. Spieldenner and Shinsuke Eguchi, "Different Sameness."

79. For another example of such an approach, see King, *Mapping the Stars*.

80. Kendall, *The Phantom Prince*.

81. Michael Calvin McGee, "Text, Context, and the Fragmentation of Contemporary Culture," 288 (italics in original).

82. McGee, "Text, Context, and the Fragmentation of Contemporary Culture," 279.

83. For more traditional takes on textuality, see Ceccarelli, "Temporal Development and Spatial Emplacement in the Dispositional Whole"; Roderick P. Hart, "Contemporary Scholarship in Public Address"; Michael Leff, "Things Made By Words."

84. Hsu, *Constellating Home*, 25.

85. See Lisa M. Corrigan and Anjali Vats, "The Structural Whiteness of Academic Patronage"; Wanzer-Serrano, "Delinking Rhetoric." The hegemony of the individual critic as rhetorical studies' idealized figure has deep intellectual roots. See Edwin Black, *Rhetorical Criticism*; James Darsey, "Must We All Be Rhetorical Theorists?"

86. For one variation on this critique, see Julietta Singh, *Unthinking Mastery*.

87. Foundational texts in this regard include: Charland, "Constitutive Rhetoric"; Lisa A. Flores, "Between Abundance and Marginalization"; McGee, "Text, Context, and the Fragmentation of Contemporary Culture"; Raymie E. McKerrow, "Critical Rhetoric"; Kent A. Ono and John M. Sloop, "The Critique of Vernacular Discourse."

88. See Herbert A. Wichelns, "The Literary Criticism of Oratory."

89. Stephen G. Michaud and Hugh Aynesworth, *The Only Living Witness*; Sullivan, *The Bundy Murders*.

90. Calafell, "Performance," 115.

91. Cram, "Archival Ambience and Sensory Memory"; Saidiya Hartman, *Lose Your Mother*; Maggie M. Werner, *Stripped*.

92. Amber Johnson, "Confessions of a Video Vixen"; Charles E. Morris III, "(Self-)Portrait of Prof. R.C."

93. Taylor, *The Archive and the Repertoire*, 24.

94. On similar approaches to rhetorical scholarship, see Brett Lunceford, "Rhetorical Autoethnography"; Hsu, *Constellating Home*; Werner, *Stripped*.

95. Rice, "Unframing Models of Public Distribution."

96. My reference to "conspicuously aesthetic prose" adapts Tracy Stephenson Shaffer's writing on "conspicuous aesthetic performance." Tracy Stephenson Shaffer, "The Place of Performance in Performance Studies." On aesthetic writing and reflexivity in criticism and other scholarship, also see Carolyn Ellis and Arthur P. Bochner, "Autoethnography, Personal Narrative, Reflexivity"; Stephen Benson and Clare Connors, "Introduction"; Hsu, *Constellating Home*; Lunceford, "Rhetorical Autoethnography." For exemplars of such work, see Calafell, *Monstrosity, Performance, and Race in Contemporary Culture*; Eli Clare, *Brilliant Imperfection*; Ann Cvetkovich, *Depression*; D. Soyini Madison, "The Dialogic Performative in Critical Ethnography"; Maraj, *Black or Right*; Aja Y. Martinez, *Counterstory*; Morris, "Sunder the Children"; Maggie Nelson, *Jane*; Werner, *Stripped*.

97. On the use of such artifacts as "auto-archaeology," see Ragan Fox, "Tales of a Fighting Bobcat."

98. Michael S. Bowman, "Killing Dillinger," 349.

99. Sara Baugh-Harris and Darrel Wanzer-Serrano, "Against Canon"; Chela Sandoval, *Methodology of the Oppressed*.
100. Johnson, "Confessions of a Video Vixen"; Morris, "Sunder the Children."
101. Calafell, "Performance." Also see Dwight Conquergood, "Performing as a Moral Act"; María Lugones, *Pilgrimages/Peregrinajes*.
102. On the limits of confessional performance, see David P. Terry, "Once Blind, Now Seeing." On the ways critics of confessional performance themselves reify the violent structures they presume to challenge, see Daniel B. Coleman and Louis Yako, "Personal Is Political."
103. On performance and fidelity, see Mindy Fenske, "The Aesthetic of the Unfinished." I take the language of "custodians" from Annie Hill. See Annie Hill, "SlutWalk as Perifeminist Response to Rape Logic."
104. Maraj, *Black or Right*, 9.

Chapter 1: Serial Killers as Modern Monsters

1. See Bratich, *On Microfascism*; Johnson, *I, the People*; Kelly, *Apocalypse Man*.
2. Calafell, *Monstrosity, Performance, and Race in Contemporary Culture*.
3. Edward J. Ingebretsen, *At Stake*, 47.
4. Kelly, *Caught on Tape*.
5. On anxiety, see Chebrolu, "The Racial Lens of Dylann Roof."
6. On the seams of discourse, see Kendall R. Phillips, "Affective Seams in the Discourses of the Present."
7. Mignolo, *The Darker Side of Western Modernity*. Also, Darrel Wanzer-Serrano, "Decolonizing Imaginaries." On custodians, see Hill, "SlutWalk as Perifeminist Response to Rape Logic."
8. Curry, *The Man-Not*; Hartman, *Scenes of Subjection*; Lugones, "Toward a Decolonial Feminism"; Ashley Noel Mack and Tiara R. Na'puti, "'Our Bodies Are Not *Terra Nullius*'"; Povinelli, *Empire of Love*.
9. Schmid, *Natural Born Celebrities*.
10. On rhetorical form, see Kenneth Burke, *Counter-Statement*; Karlyn Kohrs Campbell and Kathleen Hall Jamieson, "Form and Genre in Rhetorical Criticism: An Introduction"; Erin J. Rand, "An Inflammatory Fag and a Queer Form."
11. On distinctions between rhetorical criticism and empirical modes of inquiry, see Black, *Rhetorical Criticism*; Barry Brummett, "Rhetorical Theory as Heuristic and Moral."
12. On fungibility and rhetorical form, see Ignacio Moreno Segarra and Karrin Vasby Anderson, "Political Pornification Gone Global."
13. Calum Lister Matheson, "Liberal Tears and the Rogue's Yarn of Sadistic Conservatism"; On form and publicity, see Joshua Gunn, "*Maranatha*."
14. "sadism, n."
15. "sadism, n."
16. Matheson, "Liberal Tears and the Rogue's Yarn of Sadistic Conservatism," 343.
17. Matheson, "Liberal Tears and the Rogue's Yarn of Sadistic Conservatism," 342.
18. Arthur Leonoff, "Destruo Ergo Sum," 103.
19. Brummett, "The Homology Hypothesis," 203.
20. Jane Caputi, *The Age of Sex Crime*, 12.

21. See Deborah Cameron and Elizabeth Frazer, *The Lust to Kill*; Wendy Holloway, "'I Just Wanted to Kill a Woman'"; Tithecott, *Of Men and Monsters*; Judith R. Walkowitz, "Jack the Ripper and the Myth of Male Violence."
22. Caputi, *The Age of the Sex Crime*. Also see Schmid, *Natural Born Celebrities*; Tithecott, *Of Men and Monsters*.
23. Mardorossian, *Framing the Rape Victim*, 5. Also see Claire Sisco King and Joshua Gunn, "On a Violence Unseen"; Ashley Noel Mack et al., "Between Bodies and Institutions."
24. Theweleit, *Male Fantasies*, 221–22.
25. Lugones, "Toward a Decolonial Feminism," 743.
26. Lugones, "Toward a Decolonial Feminism, 748–49.
27. Sarah Deer, "Decolonizing Rape Law," 150.
28. King and Gunn, "On a Violence Unseen"; Mack et al., "Between Bodies and Institutions."
29. See Curry, *The Man-Not*; Jenna N. Hanchey, "Catastrophe Colonialism"; Casey Ryan Kelly and Ryan Neville-Shephard, "Virgin Lands"; Mack & Na'puti, "'Our Bodies Are Not Terra Nullius.'"
30. Moreton-Robinson, *The White Possessive*, 20.
31. Brian Jarvis, "Monsters Inc."
32. Achille Mbembe, *Critique of Black Reason*, 4. Also see Maile Arvin, Eve Tuck, and Angie Morrill, "Decolonizing Feminism"; Hartman, *Scenes of Subjection*; Lugones, "Toward a Decolonial Feminism."
33. For social critiques of serial murder, see Cameron and Fraser, *The Lust to Kill*; Caputi, "The Sexual Politics of Murder"; Downing, *The Subject of Murder*; Jarvis, "Monsters Inc."; Alzena MacDonald, "Dissecting the 'Dark Passenger.'"
34. Frank B. Wilderson, III, *Red, White and Black*, 16.
35. Eduardo Subirats, "Totalitarian Lust," 174. Also see Alexander G. Weheliye, *Habeas Viscus*.
36. Jarvis, "Monsters Inc."
37. "Inside the Mind of Jeffrey Dahmer."
38. Del Quentin Wilber, "A Texas Ranger Got a Prolific Serial Killer to Talk."
39. Hartman, *Scenes of Subjection*, 3. Also, Hortense J. Spillers, "Mama's Baby, Papa's Maybe"; Weheliye, *Habeas Viscus*.
40. See Chebrolu, "The Racial Lens of Dylann Roof"; Kelly, *Caught on Tape*.
41. Simpson, *Psycho Paths*, 13.
42. Kelly, *Caught on Tape*. Also, see Ingebretsen, *At Stake*; Schmid, *Natural Born Celebrities*.
43. I offer these descriptions as a composite of Bundy's *modus operandi*. It derives from several sources, including: Michaud and Aynesworth, *The Only Living Witness*; Polly Nelson, *Defending the Devil*; Amber Sealey, *No Man of God*; Sullivan, *The Bundy Murders*; Rubin and Lucchesi, *A Light in the Dark*; *Ted Bundy Multiagency Investigative Team Report*.
44. In some cases, Bundy kept his victim alive for several days before killing her. See Rubin, *A Light in the Dark*.
45. Michaud and Aynesworth, *The Only Living Witness*, 462.
46. Michaud and Aynesworth, *The Only Living Witness*.
47. Michaud and Aynesworth, *The Only Living Witness*, 463.
48. Michaud and Aynesworth, *The Only Living Witness*, 462.
49. Michaud and Aynesworth, *The Only Living Witness*, 462.
50. See Jarvis, "Monsters Inc."

51. Marquis de Sade, "Philosophy in the Bedroom," 344.
52. Sade, "Philosophy in the Bedroom," 344.
53. Matheson, "Liberal Tears and the Rogue's Yarn of Sadistic Conservatism," 347. Also, Johnson, "Owning the Libs."
54. Simone de Beauvoir, "Must We Burn Sade?," 91.
55. Downing, *The Subject of Murder*," 9.
56. Maggie Nelson, *The Art of Cruelty*.
57. Pier Pasolini, *Salò, or the 120 Days of Sodom*. Also, Marquis de Sade, *The 120 Days of Sodom*.
58. See, Richard Warren Perry and Lisa Erin Sanchez, "Transactions in the Flesh."
59. See Downing, *The Subject of Murder*; Mignolo, *The Darker Side of Western Modernity*; Wilderson, *Red, White and Black*.
60. Subirats, "Totalitarian Lust," 174.
61. Subirats, "Totalitarian Lust," 176.
62. Max Horkheimer and Theodor W. Adorno, *Dialectic of Enlightenment*, 88.
63. Wilderson, *Red, White and Black*, 38. Also, Spillers, "Mama's Baby, Papa's Maybe"; Weheliye, *Habeas Viscus*.
64. Hartman, *Scenes of Subjection*.
65. Ashley Noel Mack and Bryan J. McCann, "'Harvey Weinstein, Monster'"; Fred Moten, *Stolen Life*.
66. Hartman, *Scenes of Subjection*; Wilderson, *Red, White and Black*. Also, Weheliye, *Habeas Viscus*.
67. Christina Beltrán, *Cruelty as Citizenship*, 19.
68. Ashley Noel Mack and Bryan J. McCann, "'Strictly an Act of Street Violence.'"
69. Kumarini Silva, "Having the Time of Our Lives," 83. Also, Ersula J. Ore, *Lynching*.
70. Marina Levina, "Whiteness and the Joys of Cruelty," 75.
71. Matheson, "Liberal Tears and the Rogue's Yarn of Sadistic Conservativism," 346.
72. Levina, "Whiteness and the Joys of Cruelty," 75.
73. Johnson, "Owning the Libs," 241.
74. Annalee Newitz, *Pretend We're Dead*, 39. Also, Jarvis, "Monsters Inc."
75. See Petty and Sanchez, "Transactions in the Flesh"; DJ Williams, "Is Serial Sexual Homicide a Compulsion, Deviant Leisure, or Both?"
76. I add this endnote in April 2025, as I review the copyedited version of this manuscript. At this stage in the production process, revisions are supposed to be minimal. Suffice it to say that the US federal government's current administrative and fiscal regimes gleefully express a staggering degree of conspicuous sadism worthy of the Marquis de Sade's proclivities. For example, Rex Huppke, "Musk, Trump Degrade Federal Workers as They Put Them out of Work;" Zak Cheney-Rice, "The Purpose of Trump's Cruel Deportation Theater."
77. Robert Asen, "Neoliberalism, the Public Sphere, and the Public Good," 330.
78. Jodi Dean, *Crowds and Party*.
79. Jennifer McClearen, "Neoliberal Masculinity in the Ultimate Fighting Championship," 436.
80. Robert Asen and Casey Ryan Kelly, "Economizing Whiteness, Rhetoricizing Economy."
81. David Harvey, *A Brief History of Neoliberalism*.
82. Jarvis, "Monsters Inc."
83. On Rand's legacy, see, Jennifer Burns, *Goddess of the Market*; Lisa Duggan, *Mean Girl*.

84. Ceclilia Rasmussen, "Girl's Grisly Killing Had City Residents Up in Arms."
85. Ayn Rand, *The Journals of Ayn Rand*, 27.
86. Also see Burns, *Goddess of the Market*, 24–25.
87. China Miéville, "On Social Sadism."
88. Christopher Burlingame, "Social Identity Crisis?"
89. Kate Maclean, "Gender, Risk, and the Wall Street Alpha Male."
90. Johnson, *I, the People*, 227.
91. Harvey, *A Brief History of Neoliberalism*; Naomi Klein, *Shock Doctrine*.
92. See Curry, *The Man-Not*; Richard Dyer, *White*; Hartman, *Scenes of Subjection*.
93. Theweleit, *Male Fantasies*, 196.
94. Matheson, "Liberal Tears and the Rogue's Yarn of Sadistic Conservatism," 349.
95. Wilderson, *Red, White and Black*, 29.
96. See Forbes, *Columbus and Other Cannibals*, 24–25. Also, Beltrán, *Cruelty as Citizenship*; Silva, "Having the Time of Our Lives."
97. On the uncanny, see Renée L. Bergland, *The National Uncanny*; Sigmund Freud, *The Uncanny*.
98. Dubrofsky, "Monstrous Authenticity."
99. Darrel Wanzer-Serrano, "Rhetoric's Rac(e/ist) Problems."
100. Baugh-Harris and Wanzer, "Against Canon"; Johnson, "My Sanctified Imagination"; Charles E. Morris III, "Introduction."
101. Victor Ray, "The Unbearable Whiteness of Meserach."
102. Rachel E. Dubrofsky, "Monstrous Authenticity."
103. Stella Gaynor, "Better the Devil You Know."
104. See Schmid, *Natural Born Celebrities*.

Chapter 2: Two Teds, One Monster

1. *Alcoholics Anonymous*, 21.
2. *Alcoholics Anonymous*, 64.
3. Bryan J. McCann, "Economies of Misery."
4. Carol J. Clover, *Men, Women, and Chainsaws*.
5. True crime writers and individuals close to the Bundy case agree that Bundy's attacks in Tallahassee were dramatically inconsistent with his usual *modus operandi*. Specifically, they were far less methodical than the other murders. Stephen G. Michaud and Hugh Aynesworth, *Conversations with a Killer*; Rule, *The Stranger Beside Me*; Sullivan, *The Bundy Murders*.
6. Jason Bainbridge, "Soiling Suburbia."
7. Bainbridge, "Soiling Suburbia"; Whitney Crothers Dilley, "Globalization and Cultural Identity in the Films of Ang Lee."
8. Jimmie L. Reeves and Richard Campbell, *Cracked Coverage*.
9. S. Craig Watkins, *Hip Hop Matters*.
10. Kristen Hoerl, "Monstrous Youth in Suburbia."
11. Rule, *The Stranger Beside Me*, 24. Also, Kendall, *The Phantom Prince*.
12. Rule, *The Stranger Beside Me*, 544.
13. Rule, *The Stranger Beside Me*, 544.
14. Edna Cowell Martin and Megan Atkinson, *Dark Tide*, 22.

15. Martin and Atkinson, *Dark Tide*, 22.
16. Nelson, *Defending the Devil*, 281.
17. Nelson, *Defending the Devil*, 282.
18. Nelson, *Defending the Devil*, 282.
19. Nelson, *Defending the Devil*, 288.
20. Nelson, *Defending the Devil*, 288.
21. Martin and Atkinson, *Dark Tide*, 195.
22. Daniel Farrands, *Ted Bundy*.
23. Rule, *The Stranger Beside Me*.
24. Rule, *The Stranger Beside Me*, 536.
25. Justin Coffman, "Ted Bundy Canvas Print."
26. Rule, *The Stranger Beside Me*. Also see Nelson, *Defending the Devil*.
27. Kendall, *The Phantom Prince*.
28. Molly Kendall, "Molly's Story," in Kendall, *The Phantom Prince*, 201.
29. Kendall, "Molly's Story," in Kendall, *The Phantom Prince*, 201.
30. Gabby Raymond, "The 16 Best True Crime Books of All Time."
31. Kendall, *The Phantom Prince*.
32. Michael Kaplan, "Inside Ted Bundy's Life with Girlfriend Elizabeth Kendall and Her Daughter."
33. Curry, *The Man-Not*; Sean Gerrity, "Blinded by the White"; Ronald L. Jackson II, *Scripting the Black Masculine Body*.
34. See Bryan J. McCann, *The Mark of Criminality*.
35. Claire Sisco King, "It Cuts Both Ways," 370.
36. See Dubrofsky, "Monstrous Authenticity."
37. Seltzer, *Serial Killers*, 42.
38. Wendy Lesser, *Pictures at an Execution*, 20
39. Rebecca Gill, "The Evolution of Organizational Archetypes."
40. On how similar archetypes circulate in support of modernist logics, see Mignolo, *The Darker Side of Western Modernity*. On gender and modernity, see Lugones, "Toward a Decolonial Feminism."
41. Clémence Michallon, "Do We Really Need Another Series about Ted Bundy?"
42. Michallon, "Do We Really Need Another Series about Ted Bundy?"
43. The judge in Bundy's trial for the murder of Kimberly Dianne Leach made similar remarks at sentencing. See, Rubin and Lucchesi, *A Light in the Dark*; "'Wasted Life.'"
44. Andrew Rothstein, "Ted Bundy."
45. Marvin J. Chomsky, *The Deliberate Stranger*.
46. See Curry, *The Man-Not*; Ore, *Lynching*.
47. Freud, *The Uncanny*, 153.
48. Avery Gordon, *Ghostly Matters*, 55.
49. Freud, *The Uncanny*, 150.
50. Piotr M. Szpunar, *Homegrown*, 21.
51. Szpunar, *Homegrown*, 2.
52. Simpson, *Psycho Paths*, 4.
53. Jon Nordheimer, "All-American Boy on Trial."
54. Nordheimer, "All-American Boy on Trial."
55. I understand a public in this essay as an assemblage of bodies that exists as a public "by virtue of being addressed." Thus, I am less interested in an empirical viewing public than

in the publics texts such as *Conversations* constitute through the act of address. Michael Warner, *Publics and Counterpublics*, 50; Lundberg, *Lacan in Public*.

56. Grace Gavilanes, "*People*'s 1986 Sexiest Man Alive Mark Harmon Totally Got Teased for the Title."

57. Susan Littwin, "'I Like Walking on the Edge'"; Nancy Mills, "Mark Harmon's Acting Face"; Carol Wallace and James Grant, "Charmin' Harmon."

58. "Lady Killer Nice."

59. Wallace and Grant, "Charmin' Harmon."

60. On celebrity and metonymy, see King, *Mapping the Stars*.

61. See Rule, *The Stranger Beside Me*.

62. Lauren Larson, "Zac Efron Rides Again."

63. Kendall, *The Phantom Prince*.

64. Jen Yamato, "'The Ted Bundy Tapes' and 'Shockingly Evil.'"

65. Sophie Lewis, *Abolish the Family*.

66. See Laura Fries, "*The Stranger Beside Me*"; Tom Jicha, "A Look at Ted Bundy in Stranger."

67. Bright's *Bundy* is, to date, Burke's sole leading role in a feature film. Nemec starred in the popular 1990s television show *Parker Lewis Can't Lose*, but his adult career has been tepid. Since leaving a leading role on the successful show *One Tree Hill*, Murray has secured roles in mostly low-visibility projects. Jon Caramanica, "Hey, Bud, What Comes after Our 15 Minutes?"; "Michael Reilly Burke"; Jon O'Brien and Marika Kazimierska, "Whatever Happened to Chad Michael Murray?"

68. See King, *Mapping the Stars*.

69. On celebrity and serial killers, see Schmid, *Natural Born Celebrities*.

70. Pat J. Gehrke, *The Ethics and Politics of Speech*, 55. Also, Chani Marchiselli, "Masculine Elocution, New Oratory, and the Voice of Elizabeth Holmes."

71. Gina Tron, "Who Was the Real Kathleen McChesney, the Trailblazing Detective Depicted in 'American Boogeyman'?"

72. Berlinger, *Conversations with a Killer*; Bright, *Ted Bundy*.

73. Anne Cohen, "Amber Sealey Didn't Want to Make Another Ted Bundy Movie."

74. Rubin and Lucchesi, *A Light in the Dark*, 34.

75. Rule, *The Stranger Beside Me*, 411.

76. "Carol DaRonch."

77. Moreton-Robinson, *The White Possessive*, 29.

78. Elizabeth Bernstein, "Militarized Humanism Meets Carceral Feminism."

79. See Aya Gruber, *The Feminist War on Crime*; Ashley Noel Mack and Bryan J. McCann, "Critiquing State and Gendered Violence in the Age of #MeToo;" Beth E. Richie, *Arrested Justice*; Andrea J. Ritchie, *Invisible No More*; Emily L. Thuma, *All Our Trials*.

80. Curry, *The Man-Not*. Also, Ore, *Lynching*.

81. See Hill, "SlutWalk as Perifeminist Response to Rape Logic."

82. See Curry, *The Man-Not*.

83. Once again, the pace of academic publishing occurs in the context of shifting family dynamics. As of April 2025, my sister and I have been on generally good terms for over a year. That said, she is not yet aware of this book's content regarding our family. I am still afraid to tell her. I drafted the following during the fall of 2023:

> I have cropped the photograph I include and reference here. It is a mutilated artifact rendered as such to avoid conflict. It is classically alcoholic in

this regard. Not pictured is my sister, three years my junior. Ours is a fraught relationship, in part because we experience our childhood memories in very different ways. We have often-polarized attitudes regarding familial presence and elder care as a result. We have not spoken in six months following an especially intense conflict regarding these issues. Neither she nor my mom are aware that this book contains such confessional content, including unflattering portrayals of my father. One of my chief anxieties regarding the project's publication is how they might react, although I rarely expect family to read my academic work. Suffice it to say, I fear the consequences of including pictures of my estranged sister here. Peace at all costs.

84. Kendall, *The Phantom Prince*.
85. See Patricia Love, *The Emotional Incest Syndrome*.
86. See Tithecott, *Of Men and Monsters*, 45–46.
87. Nelson, *Defending the Devil*, 282.
88. Janet G. Woititz, *Adult Children of Alcoholics*.
89. See Reeves and Campbell, *Cracked Coverage*.
90. Bergland, *The National Uncanny*.
91. Tithecott, *Of Men and Monsters*, 97.
92. Rubin, *A Light in the Dark*.
93. Kendall R. Phillips, *A Place of Darkness*.
94. Robert Louis Stevenson, *The Strange Case of Dr. Jekyll and Mr. Hyde*.
95. Schmid, *Natural Born Celebrities*.

Chapter 3: Ted Bundy, Pornographer

1. *Final Report of the Attorney General's Commission on Pornography*.
2. Stiles, "Fatal Addiction."
3. Al Goldstein, "Ted Bundy's Last Lie"; Sascha Olofson, *Ted Bundy*; Dick Polman, "Bundy's Porn Message Fuels One Final Conflict"; Rule, *The Stranger Beside Me*.
4. Berlinger, *Conversations*.
5. Berlinger, *Conversations*.
6. See Carolyn Bronstein, *Battling Pornography*; Nan D. Hunter, "Contextualizing the Sexuality Debates"; Linda Williams, *Hard Core*.
7. Caputi, *The Age of the Sex Crime*, 166. Also, Karen Boyle and Jenny Reburn, "Portrait of a Serial Killer"; Cameron and Frazer, *The Lust to Kill*; Holloway, "'I Just Wanted to Kill a Woman.'"
8. Andrew Hartman, *A War for the Soul of America*; Rick Perlstein, *Reaganland*.
9. Joel Black, *The Aesthetics of Murder*, 22.
10. Stephanie R. Larson, *What It Feels Like*, 26–27.
11. Lawrence W. Rosenfield, "Politics and Pornography," 418. Also, Laura Kipnis, *Bound and Gagged*.
12. See Augustine Brannigan and Sheldon Goldenberg, "The Study of Aggressive Pornography."
13. Lisa Duggan, "Censorship in the Name of Feminism," 40.
14. Also, Larson, *What It Feels Like*.
15. Caputi, *The Age of the Sex Crime*, 166.
16. Gunn, "*Maranatha*."

17. Catherine Helen Palczewski, "Contesting Pornography."
18. Paul Gewirtz, "On 'I Know It When I See It.'"
19. See, Lisa Duggan, "Sex Panics"; Rosenfield, "Politics and Pornography."
20. Kipnis, *Bound and Gagged*, 182. Also, Williams, *Hard Core*.
21. Brummett, "The Homology Hypothesis."
22. Gunn, "*Maranatha*," 374.
23. Rosenfield, "Politics and Pornography," 414.
24. Norman Mailer, "The White Negro."
25. Gunn, "*Maranatha*," 374.
26. See Dennis Giles, "Pornographic Space."
27. Kipnis, *Bound and Gagged*, 163.
28. Also, Susan Sontag, "The Pornographic Imagination."
29. Brummett, "The Homology Hypothesis"; Gunn, "*Maranatha*"; Kelly, *Caught on Tape*.
30. Audre Lorde, "The Uses of the Erotic," 90.
31. Segarra and Anderson, "Political Pornification Gone Global," 205. Also, Karrin Vasby Anderson, "'Rhymes with Blunt.'"
32. Giles, "Pornographic Space," 56.
33. See Anderson, "'Rhymes with Blunt'"; Ryan Neville-Shepard and Meredith Neville-Shepard, "The Pornified Presidency."
34. Susan Brownmiller, "Excerpt on Pornography from *Against Our Will*," 32.
35. Andrea Dworkin, *Pornography*, 223.
36. Williams, *Hard Core*, 22.
37. Jennifer C. Nash, *The Black Body in Ecstasy*. Also, Ashley R. Hall, "'I Love How That Pussy Talk.'"
38. Hall, "'I Love How That Pussy Talk.'"
39. Dean Lockwood, "All Stripped Down," 46. Also, Sue Tait, "Pornographies of Violence?"
40. Samuel R. Delany, *Times Square Red, Times Square Blue*; Frederick C. Corey and Thomas K. Nakayama, "Sextext."
41. Lorde, "The Uses of the Erotic." Also, Godfried Asante, "Decolonizing the Erotic"; Lore/tta LeMaster, "Felt Sex"; Rowe, "Erotic Pedagogies"; Gloria Steinem, "Erotica and Pornography"; VanHaitsma, *The Erotic as Rhetorical Power*.
42. Ward, *The Tragedy of Heterosexuality*, 155.
43. Also see Williams, *Hard Core*.
44. Stiles, *Fatal Addiction*.
45. Larson, *What It Feels Like*.
46. Kendall, *The Phantom Prince*, 177–78.
47. Rice, *The Stranger Beside Me*; Sullivan, *The Bundy Murders*.
48. Jia Tolentino, "Mike Pence's Marriage and the Beliefs that Keep Women from Power."
49. Olofson, *Ted Bundy*.
50. Empirically, the link between pornography consumption and body insecurities among cis men is not significant. See Chyng Sun et al., "Pornography and the Male Sexual Script."
51. Ward, *The Tragedy of Heterosexuality*. Also, see Eve Kosofsky Sedgwick, *Between Men*.
52. On white masculinity and generational politics, see Sexton, *The Man They Wanted Me to Be*.
53. Catherine R. Squires, "Rethinking the Black Public Sphere." Also, see Karma R. Chávez, "Counter-Public Enclaves and Understanding the Function of Rhetoric in Social

Movement Coalition-Building"; Stefano Harney and Fred Moten, *The Undercommons*; Stacey K. Sowards, "The (Under)Commons across the Américas."

54. Choire Sicha, "The Last Chance to Learn Jeffrey Epstein's Secrets Closes."
55. See David Peace, *Nineteen Eighty-Three*.
56. Cary Joji Fukunaga, *True Detective*.
57. Georges Bataille, *Erotism*. Also, Carl Olson, "Eroticism, Violence, and Sacrifice."
58. Clover, *Men, Women, and Chain Saws*.
59. Bataille, *Erotism*.
60. See Lisi Raskin, "Updating (the) Uses of the Erotic." Importantly, the erotic is politically variable in its own right. See VanHaitsma, *The Erotic as Rhetorical Power*.
61. Bataille, *Erotism*.
62. See Friedrich Nietzsche, *The Genealogy of Morals*.
63. Gunn, *Political Perversion*; Kelly, *Caught on Tape*.
64. See Moreton-Robinson, *The White Possessive*.
65. Hartman, *Scenes of Subjection*; Lugones, "Toward a Decolonial Feminism"; Spillers, "Mama's Baby, Papa's Maybe"; Weheliye, *Habeas Viscus*. Also, Kelly, *Caught on Tape*.
66. Spillers, "Mama's Baby, Papa's Maybe"; Weheliye, *Habeas Viscus*.
67. Hartman, *Scenes of Subjection*.
68. Valencia, *Gore Capitalism*, 22.
69. Lugones, "Toward a Decolonial Feminism"; Povinelli, *The Empire of Love*; Maria Tatar, *Lustmord*; Theweleit, *Male Fantasies*.
70. Mardorossian, *Framing the Rape Victim*, 14. Also Curry, *The Man-Not*; Kelly, *Apocalypse Man*.
71. Pasolini, *Saló, or the 120 Days of Sodom*. Also, Sade, *The 120 Days of Sodom*.
72. Gunn, *Political Perversion*; Kelly, *Caught on Tape*.
73. Roberto Chiesi, "*Saló*."
74. See Horkheimer and Adorno, *Dialectic of Enlightenment*; Theweleit, *Male Fantasies*.
75. Celluloid Liberation Front, "The Lost Pasolini Interview."
76. Stiles, *Fatal Addiction*.
77. Bataille, *Erotism*; René Girard, *Violence and the Sacred*.
78. Nelson, *Defending the Devil*, 254.
79. Nelson, *Defending the Devil*, 254.
80. Nelson, *Defending the Devil*, 254.
81. Olson, "Eroticism, Violence, and Sacrifice," 236.
82. Roger Shattuck, *Forbidden Knowledge*, 269.
83. Mignolo, *The Darker Side of Western Modernity*.
84. On Bundy's alleged psychopathy, Sarah Marshall, "The End of Evil." On the Leach murder, Rule, *The Stranger Beside Me*.
85. Larson, *What It Feels Like*, 51.
86. See Lee Edelman, *No Future*.
87. Larson, *What It Feels Like*, 27.
88. See John R. Thelin, *A History of American Higher Education*. Notably, Bundy did not kidnap Leach from a playground but between buildings at her junior high school. But Dobson situates Bundy's final depraved act in a space, the playground, that functions as a metonym for childhood innocence. See Sullivan, *The Bundy Murders*.
89. Erin J. Rand, "PROTECTing the Figure of Innocence," 258. Also, Bryan J. McCann, "Lonely Young American."

90. Girard, *Violence and the Sacred*.

91. Deer, "Decolonizing Rape Law"; Rachel Alicia Griffin, "Gender Violence and the Black Female Body"; Mack and Na'puti, "'Our Bodies Are Not Terra Nullius'"; Spillers, "Mama's Baby, Papa's Maybe"; Weheliye, *Habeas Viscus*.

92. Larson, *What It Feels Like*.

93. Dick Polman, "Bundy's Porn Message Fuels One Final Conflict."

94. See Matheson, "Liberal Tears and the Rogue's Yarn of Sadistic Conservatism."

95. Nelson, *The Phantom Prince*, 282.

96. Vronsky, *Sons of Cain*, 314.

97. Vronsky, *Sons of Cain*, 315.

98. Adam Parfrey, "From Pulp to Posterity," 29.

99. Barbara A. Biesecker, "Remembering World War II."

100. Vronsky, *Sons of Cain*. Also, Mary Louise Roberts, *What Soldiers Do*.

101. Sheldon Renan, *The Killing of America*.

102. Vronsky, *Sons of Cain*.

103. Ore, *Lynching*, 58.

104. Lisa Downing, *Desiring the Dead*, 8.

105. See Mack and Na'puti, "'Our Bodies Are Not *Terra Nullius*.'"

106. Hartman, *Scenes of Subjection*, 260.

107. Tatar, *Lustmord*, 21.

108. Deer, "Decolonizing Rape Law"; Povinelli, *The Empire of Love*; Weheliye, *Habeas Viscus*.

109. On mannequins as a motif in serial killer discourse, see Jarvis, "Monsters Inc."

110. Sullivan, *The Bundy Murders*, 69.

111. Nelson, *Defending the Devil*.

112. "Ted Bundy Multiagency Investigative Team Report 1992," 5, https://www.santarosa-hitchhikermurders.com/docs/Bundy_Multiagency_Team_Report.pdf.

113. Maldoror, "Peter Sotos Speaking at the Pompidou Centre (2012)." Also, Jean-Paul Sartre, *Saint Genet*.

114. Anderson, "'Rhymes with Blunt';" Ward, *The Tragedy of Heterosexuality*. Also, Neville-Shepard and Neville-Shepard, "The Pornified Presidency."

115. See Schmid, *Natural Born Celebrities*; Tithecott, *Of Men and Monsters*.

116. Peter Sotos, *Pure #2*, 4.

117. Paul Lemos, "Interview with Peter Sotos of *Pure*," 125.

118. See Brandon Stosuy, "Interview with Peter Sotos."

119. Maldoror, "Peter Sotos Speaking at the Pompidou Centre (2012)."

120. Also, Downing, *The Subject of Murder*; Schmid, *Natural Born Celebrities*.

121. VanHaitsma, *The Erotic as Rhetorical Power*.

122. On queer worldmaking, see Lauren Berlant and Michael Warner, "Sex in Public"; José Esteban Muñoz, *Cruising Utopia*.

123. Kipnis, *Bound and Gagged*; Lorde, "The Uses of the Erotic"; Williams, *Hard Core*.

124. James Dobson, "A Christian Response to Homosexuality."

125. Edelman, *No Future*.

126. See Jaclyn Diaz, "At Least 9 GOP-led State Legislatures Want to Restrict or Criminalize Drag Shows."

127. Edelman, *No Future*; Jasbir K. Puar, *Terrorist Assemblages*.

128. See Jarvis, "Monsters Inc."

129. Muñoz, *Cruising Utopia*.

130. Berlant and Warner, "Sex in Public"; Corey and Nakayama, "SexText"; LeMaster, "Felt Sex"; Charles E. Morris III and John M. Sloop, "'What Lips Have These Lips Kissed"; Tavia Nyong'o, *Afro-Fabulations*.
131. Karma R. Chávez, *Queer Migration Politics*.
132. Ward, *The Tragedy of Heterosexuality*. Also, LeMaster, "Felt Sex."
133. See Brian Masters, "Dahmer's Inferno."
134. Which is not to say that such spaces are unproblematic. See Luis M. Andrade and Deven Cooper, "Defending Whiteness."
135. Corey and Nakayama, "SexText"; LeMaster, "Felt Sex."
136. On Bundy's childhood, see Nelson, *Defending the Devil*.
137. Stephanie Coontz, *The Way We Never Were*; Lewis, *Abolish the Family*.
138. Myra MacPherson, "The Roots of Evil."
139. MacPherson, "The Roots of Evil," 143.
140. For example, Michaud and Aynesworth, *The Only Living Witness*; Rule, *The Stranger Beside Me*.
141. Rule, *The Stranger Beside Me*.
142. Michaud and Aynesworth, *Conversations with a Killer*, 28.
143. @caroldaronch1974, "Ted Bundy Trial Louise Bundy Takes the Stand July 1979." Also, MacPherson, "The Roots of Evil"; Rule, *The Stranger Beside Me*.
144. Kendall, *The Phantom Prince*.
145. MacPherson, "The Roots of Evil," 192.
146. MacPherson, "The Roots of Evil," 192. In her memoir, Bundy's cousin makes a similar speculation. Martin and Atkinson, *Dark Tide*, 49.
147. Ochieng, "Infraconstitutive Rhetoric."

Chapter 4: Student Bodies, Campus Rituals

1. For example, Rule, *The Stranger Beside Me*.
2. A dean whose own responses to sexual violence, at least for some, have left much to be desired. *Doe #1, et al. v. Board of Supervisors of Louisiana State University and Agricultural and Mechanical College, et al.*
3. See Tithecott, *Of Men and Monsters*.
4. On the gaze and possession, see, Laura Mulvey, "Visual Pleasure and Narrative Cinema."
5. Allen's character, Marion Ravenwood, was a teenager when she and Professor Jones first slept together. In an early scene, Ravenwood confronts Jones about the relationship, exclaiming, "I was a child!" Jones replies, "You knew what you were doing." Steven Spielberg, *Indiana Jones and the Raiders of the Lost Ark*.
6. Carol Stabile, "Confronting Sexual Harassment and Hostile Climates in Higher Education."
7. Annie Hill and Carol A. Stabile, "Rhetoric and Sexual Violence."
8. Kenny Jacoby, Nancy Armour, and Jessica Luther, "LSU Mishandled Sexual Misconduct Complaints against Students, Including Top Athletes."
9. Matt Buedel, "Director of Bradley's Star Speech Program Resigns after Allegations of Sexual Assault"; Caroline Kitchener, "A #MeToo Nightmare in the World of Competitive College Speech."

10. For example, Zoe Greenberg, "What Happens to #MeToo When a Feminist Is the Accused?"
11. See Michael Tristano Jr., "For My Students Considering Abolition in *Communication and Gender*."
12. Michaud and Aynesworth, *The Only Living Witness*.
13. On youth and futurity, see Edelman, *No Future*.
14. Bryan J. McCann, "Lonely Young American."
15. See Jacob Breslow, "Adolescent Citizenship, or Temporality and the Negation of Black Childhood in Two Eras"; Edelman, *No Future*; McCann, "Lonely Young American"; Erica R. Meiners, *For the Children?*
16. Rule, *The Stranger Beside Me*, 69.
17. For example, Kendall, *The Phantom Prince*; Jessica Knoll, *Bright Young Women*; Rubin and Lucchesi, *A Light in the Dark*; Sullivan, *The Bundy Murders*.
18. See Boyle and Reburn, "Portrait of a Serial Killer."
19. See Judith Butler, *Precarious Life*; Ashley Noel Mack and Bryan J. McCann, "'Strictly an Act of Street Violence.'"
20. Wood, *Ted Bundy*. Also, Edwards, "*Ted Bundy*"; Kendall, *Phantom Prince*; Knoll, *Bright Young Women*.
21. Rubin and Lucchesi, *A Light in the Dark*, 160.
22. Caputi, "The Sexual Politics of Murder." Also, Boyle and Reburn, "Portrait of a Serial Killer"; Holloway, "'I Just Wanted to Kill a Woman'"; Walkowitz, "Jack the Ripper and the Myth of Male Violence."
23. See Audre Lorde, "The Uses of Anger"; Lugones, *Pilgrimages/Peregrinajes*. Also, Richie, *Arrested Justice*.
24. See Kristiana L. Báez and Ersula Ore, "The Moral Imperative of Race for Rhetorical Studies"; Calafell, *Monstrosity, Performance, and Race in Contemporary Culture*.
25. Chomsky, *The Deliberate Stranger*.
26. Rule, *The Stranger Beside Me*, 2.
27. Michael Daly, "Who Is the Real Ted Bundy?"; Mark Pinsky, "Just an Excitable Boy?"
28. For example, Kendall, *The Phantom Prince*; Nelson, *Defending the Devil*; Rule, *The Stranger Beside Me*.
29. Downing, *The Subject of Murder*. Also, Simpson, *Psycho Paths*.
30. Thomas de Quincey, *On Murder Considered as One of the Fine Arts*.
31. Of these three, the subject of Lars von Trier's *The House That Jack Built* expresses the most ironic self-awareness. Such awareness itself is in the service of von Trier's reflections on his own status as an artist whose oeuvre is notorious regarding violence and gender. Thus, serial murder remains a modality for making claims about creativity and genius. Lecter and Carroll, while quite sardonic, remain ultimately sincere. See Andrew Lapin, "In Grisly, Sadistic 'The House That Jack Built,' Lars von Trier Deconstructs Himself."
32. Harney and Moten, *The Undercommons*.
33. Jessica Hatrick, "How to Outlive the University?"; Matthew Houdek, "In the Aftertimes, Breath"; la paperson, *A Third University Is Possible*.
34. Singh, *Unthinking Mastery*.
35. Jennifer S. Hirsch and Shamus Khan, *Sexual Citizens*; Mack et al., "Between Bodies and Institutions."
36. See kristen bain, "Rape Culture on Campus"; Jacoby, Armour, and Luther, "LSU Mishandled Sexual Misconduct Complaints against Students, Including Top Athletes"; Wagatwe Wanjuki, "Dear Tufts Administrators Who Expelled Me after My Sexual Assaults."

37. Brittney McNamara, "Sexual Assault Activism and the #MeToo Era."
38. Griffin, "Gender Violence and the Black Female Body"; Joshua Daniel Phillips and Rachel Alicia Griffin, "Crystal Mangum as Hypervisible Object and Invisible Subject."
39. See Greenberg, "What Happens to #MeToo When a Feminist Is the Accused?"; Hill, "Reporting Sexual Harassment"; Stabile, "Confronting Sexual Harassment and Hostile Climates in Higher Education."
40. Mack et al., "Between Bodies and Institutions," 96–97. Also, Hirsch and Khan, *Sexual Citizens*.
41. See Curry, *The Man-Not*; Lugones, "Toward a Decolonial Feminism"; Povinelli, *Empire of Love*.
42. See Báez and Ore, "The Moral Imperative of Race for Rhetorical Studies"; Calafell, *Monstrosity, Performance, and Race in Contemporary Culture*; Lisa B. Y. Calvente, Bernadette Marie Calafell, and Karma R. Chávez, "Here Is Something You Can't Understand"; Olga Idriss Davis, "In the Kitchen"; Hatrick, "How to Outlive the University?"; Maraj, *Black or Right*; Gabriella Gutiérez y Muhs et al., *Presumed Incompetent*.
43. Hill and Stabile, "Rhetoric and Sexual Violence."
44. For example, Jacoby, Armour, and Luther, "LSU Mishandled Sexual Misconduct Complaints against Students, Including Top Athletes."
45. la paperson, *A Third University Is Possible*.
46. See Báez and Ore, "The Moral Imperative of Race for Rhetorical Studies"; Calafell, *Monstrosity, Performance, and Race in Contemporary Culture*; Calvente, Calafell, and Chávez, "Here Is Something You Can't Understand"; Davis, "In the Kitchen"; Gutiérez y Muhs et al., *Presumed Incompetent*.
47. John Landis, *National Lampoon's Animal House*. Also, Rule, *The Stranger Beside Me*.
48. Gregory A. Waller, "An Annotated Filmography of R-Rated Sexploitation Films Released during the 1970s."
49. Bob Clark, *Black Christmas*.
50. Clover, *Men, Women, and Chain Saws*.
51. Jean Baudrillard, *The Spirit of Terrorism*. Also see Caputi, "The Sexual Politics of Murder"; Clover, *Men, Women, and Chainsaws*.
52. See John R. Thelin, *A History of American Higher Education*.
53. Karen Thorsen, "An Intimate Revolution in Campus Life," 32.
54. For example, Coontz, *The Way We Never Were*.
55. Molly Peterson, "*National Lampoon's Animal House*."
56. For analysis along these lines, see Eric Hoover, "'Animal House' at 30."
57. "Business: Bed Sheets Bonanza"; Hoover, "'Animal House' at 30."
58. Mack et al., "Between Bodies and Institutions," 98.
59. Stephen Bishop, "Animal House."
60. Krista M. Tucciarone, "Cinematic College."
61. Stacie Seifrit-Griffin, "On the Film Registry."
62. Michaud and Aynesworth, *The Only Living Witness*.
63. Nelson, *Defending the Devil*.
64. See Jackson, *Scripting the Black Masculine Body*.
65. Gregory Forter, *Murdering Masculinities*. Also, Clover, *Men, Women, and Chain Saws*.
66. King and Gunn, "On a Violence Unseen," 202. Also, Todd McGowan, "Looking for the Gaze."
67. Sandra Y. L. Korn, "When No Means Yes."

68. Kendall, *The Phantom Prince*; Rule, *The Stranger Beside Me*; Sullivan, *The Ted Bundy Murders*.
69. James Cramer and Deanna Thompson, "Fear Reigns on Campus, But No Panic," 1A.
70. Robert D. Keppel, *The Riverman*; Michaud and Aynesworth, *The Only Living Witness*.
71. Dwight Conquergood, "Lethal Theatre," 360. Also, Michel Foucault, *Discipline and Punish*; Austin Sarat, *When the State Kills*.
72. "Butch Pierce, Left, of Starke, and Bob Reeves, of Gainesville, Light up Bundy Effigy at Prison."
73. Dave von Drehle, "Execution Ends Bundy Horror Macabre Carnival," 1A.
74. "55th Annual Sugar Bowl Classic."
75. von Drehle, "Execution Ends Bundy Horror Macabre Carnival," 1A.
76. David Gelman and David L. Gonzalez, "The Bundy Carnival," 66.
77. Gelman and Gonzalez, "The Bundy Carnival," 66.
78. Gelman and Gonzalez, "The Bundy Carnival," 66.
79. Rubin and Lucchesi, *A Light in the Dark*, 200.
80. Rule, *The Stranger Beside Me*, 534.
81. Conquergood, "Lethal Theatre," 361–62. Also, Foucault, *Discipline and Punish*; Peter Linebaugh, *The London Hanged*; Michael Meranze, *Laboratories of Virtue*.
82. Conquergood, "Lethal Theatre."
83. See Curry, *The Man-Not*; Peter Ehrenhaus and A. Susan Owen, "Race Lynching and Christian Evangelicalism"; Ore, *Lynching*.
84. Timothy R. Steffensmeier, "Sacred Sundays," 219. Also, Tonya Williams Bradford and John F. Sherry Jr., "Domesticating Public Space through Ritual."
85. Schmid, *Natural Born Celebrities*, 215.
86. Susan Sontag, *Regarding the Pain of Others*, 7.
87. Also, Butler, *Precarious Life*; Mack and McCann, "'Strictly an Act of Street Violence.'"
88. Ore, *Lynching*.
89. Rule, *The Stranger Beside Me*, 73.
90. See Tatiana Tenreyro, "Olivia Newton-John Responds to Recent *Grease* Discourse, Says People Need to 'Relax.'"
91. See William F. Lewis, "Telling America's Story"; Rick Perlstein, *Reaganland*; Janice Hocker Rushing, "The Rhetoric of the American Western Myth"; Craig R. Smith, "Ronald Reagan's Rhetorical Re-Invention of Conservatism."
92. See Michelle Alexander, *The New Jim Crow*; Mike Davis, *City of Quartz*; Angie-Marie Hancock, *The Politics of Disgust*; Perlstein, *Reaganland*.
93. On controlling images of Black women, see Patricia Hill Collins, *Black Sexual Politics*. On BIPOC women in the academy, see Báez and Ore, "The Moral Imperative of Race for Rhetorical Studies"; Calvente, Calafell, and Chávez, "Here Is Something You Can't Understand."
94. "*Animal House*'s Sarah Holcomb Had Three Horrible Years of Fame."
95. Richard Johnson, "Sad Ending to Frat Flick."
96. Johnson, "Sad Ending to Frat Flick."
97. Johnson, "Sad Ending to Frat Flick."
98. See Butler, *Precarious Life*; Herman Gray, "Race, Media, and the Cultivation of Concern."
99. Mack and McCann, "'Strictly an Act of Street Violence.'"
100. Hirsch and Khan, *Sexual Citizens*.

101. See Báez and Ore, "The Moral Imperative of Race for Rhetorical Studies"; Calafell, *Monstrosity, Performance, and Race in Contemporary Culture*; Calvente, Calafell, and Chávez, "Here Is Something You Can't Understand"; Davis, "In the Kitchen"; Hatrick, "How to Outlive the University?"; Maraj, *Black or Right*; Gutiérrez y Muhs et al., *Presumed Incompetent*; Wanzer-Serrano, "Rhetoric's Rac(e/ist) Problems."

Chapter 5: My Art Shall Be My Revenge

1. Rule, *The Stranger Beside Me*.
2. Keppel, *The Riverman*; Sullivan, *The Bundy Murders*.
3. Clover, *Men, Women, and Chain Saws*.
4. On vengeance and serial murder typologies, see, Arnon Edelstein, "Revenge."
5. Donovan O. Schaefer, "Whiteness and Civilization," 5.
6. On shame's critical potential, see Sarah Ahmed, *The Cultural Politics of Emotion*; Joe Edward Hatfield, "Moments of Shame in the Figural History of Trans Suicide."
7. Barry Brummett, "Burkean Scapegoating, Mortification, and Transcendence in Presidential Campaign Rhetoric."
8. Schaefer, "Whiteness and Civilization," 5. Also, Barbara A. Biesecker, "No Time for Mourning."
9. See Anderson, "'Rhymes with Blunt.'"
10. Kelly, *Apocalypse Man*; Schaefer, "Whiteness and Civilization."
11. Adam Nagourney et al., "Before Brief, Deadly Spree, Trouble Since Age 8."
12. Elliot Rodger, "My Twisted World." Also, Andrew Springer, "The Secret Life of Elliot Rodger."
13. Robert Hariman, "Political Parody and Public Culture," 251.
14. "YouTube Video: Retribution."
15. Rodger, "My Twisted World," 53.
16. Mulvey, "Visual Pleasure and Narrative Cinema," 835–36.
17. Mulvey, "Visual Pleasure and Narrative Cinema," 836.
18. See Hatfield, "Moments of Shame in the Figural History of Trans Suicide," 820.
19. "Elliot Rodger"; Kelly, *Apocalypse Man*; Jessica Wildfire, "Ted Bundy."
20. Kelly, *Apocalypse Man*.
21. The Airborne Toxic Event, "Sometime Around Midnight."
22. The Airborne Toxic Event, "Sometime Around Midnight."
23. The Airborne Toxic Event, "Sometime Around Midnight."
24. As in music of the global West (North America and Western Europe), not country and western music—although country undoubtedly produces its share of this kind of music. Rhian E. Jones and Eli Davies, "Introduction."
25. Andy Greenwald, *Nothing Feels Good*.
26. Emily Ryalls, "Emo Angst, Masochism, and Masculinity in Crisis," 91.
27. Jessica Hopper, "Emo," 100.
28. Illustrative songs include Afghan Whigs, "Debonair"; My Chemical Romance, "Famous Last Words"; Nine Inch Nails, "Something I Can Never Have"; Panic! At the Disco, "Lying Is the Most Fun a Girl Can Have without Taking Her Clothes Off"; Weezer, "Across the Sea." For critical engagements with such work, see Daphne Carr, *Nine Inch Nails' 'Pretty*

Hate Machine"; Marissa Chen, "I've Got Your Letter, You've Got My Song"; Bob Gendron, *The Afghan Whigs' "Gentlemen"*; Greenwald, *Nothing Feels Good*.

29. See Megan Garber, "How Rom-Coms Undermine Women."
30. On rhetorical genre, see, Campbell and Jamieson, "Form and Genre in Rhetorical Criticism"; Gunn, "*Maranatha*"; Carolyn R. Miller, Amy J. Devitt, and Victoria J. Gallagher, "Genre."
31. Rule, *The Stranger Beside Me*.
32. Michaud and Aynesworth, *The Only Living Witness*.
33. Sullivan, *The Bundy Murders*, 61.
34. Rule, *The Stranger Beside Me*; Sullivan, *The Bundy Murders*.
35. MacPherson, "The Roots of Evil."
36. Berlinger, *Conversations with a Killer*.
37. Berlinger, *Conversations with a Killer*.
38. Berlinger, *Conversations with a Killer*.
39. Tori Telfer, "Ted Bundy's Living Victim Tells Her Story."
40. MacPherson, "The Roots of Evil," 190.
41. Michael Feifer, *Bundy: A Legacy of Evil*.
42. Foywonder, "Bundy: A Legacy of Evil."
43. For a critique of representations of victims in mass mediated texts on Bundy, see Rubin and Lucchesi, *A Light in the Dark*.
44. Paul Shapiro, *Ann Rule Presents: The Stranger Beside Me*.
45. Rodger, "My Twisted World."
46. Wildfire, "Ted Bundy."
47. See Allison L. Rowland, "Small Dick Problems."
48. Rule, *The Stranger Beside Me*, 12.
49. Rule, *The Stranger Beside Me*.
50. Michaud and Aynesworth, *The Only Living Witness*.
51. Also, Sullivan, *The Bundy Murders*.
52. See King, *Mapping the Stars*.
53. In his work on sadism, Matheson explains that, in the Lacanian lexicon, this fusion of hatred and love is *hainamoration*. See, Matheson, "Liberal Tears and the Rogue's Yarn of Sadistic Conservatism," 348.
54. Ryalls, "Emo Angst, Masochism, and Masculinity in Crisis," 92.
55. Kelly, *Apocalypse Man*.
56. Afghan Whigs, "Debonair," track 4 on *Gentlemen*, Sub Pop, 1993.
57. Joshua Gunn and Mirko M. Hall, "Stick It in Your Ear."
58. Bob Gendron, *The Afghan Whigs' "Gentlemen,"* 73.
59. "YouTube Video."
60. Greenwald, *Nothing Feels Good*.
61. Bruna Horvath, "Nick Fuentes Confronted at His Home after 'Your Body, My Choice' Refrain Goes Viral"; Nilofer Khan, "Andrew Tate and Jordan Peterson."
62. Silvan Tomkins, *Shame and Its Sisters*, 136.
63. Casey Ryan Kelly, "White Pain," 212.
64. Elaine Scarry, *The Body in Pain*.
65. On personae in rhetoric, see Philip Wander, "The Third Persona."
66. On the scholarly use of such artifacts, see Fox, "Tales of a Fighting Bobcat."

67. Joyce Johnson, *Minor Characters*; Whitney Kimball, "Mary Karr Reminds the World That David Foster Wallace Abused and Stalked Her, and Nobody Cared."
68. See Ryalls, "Emo Angst, Masochism, and Masculinity in Crisis."
69. Tom Breihan, "Nine Inch Nails: *Pretty Hate Machine*."
70. Kelly, "White Pain"; Ryalls, "Emo Angst, Masochism, and Masculinity in Crisis."
71. Emily L. King, *Civil Vengeance*.
72. See William E. Connolly, "The Ethos of Revenge"; Johnson, "Owning the Libs"; Kelly, "Donald J. Trump and the Rhetoric of *Ressentiment*"; Kyle Wiggins, "Introduction."
73. Kelly, *Apocalypse Man*. Also, Nina Maria Lozano, *Not One More!*
74. Rule, *The Stranger Beside Me*, 43.
75. Rule, *The Stranger Beside Me*, 45. Also, Sullivan, *The Bundy Murders*.
76. Rule, *The Stranger Beside Me*, 46.
77. Rule, *The Stranger Beside Me*, 17.
78. Rule, *The Stranger Beside Me*, 425.
79. MacPherson, "The Roots of Evil," 192.
80. Rule, *The Stranger Beside Me*, 425–26.
81. MacPherson, "The Roots of Evil," 192.
82. Hanif Abdurraquib, *They Can't Kill Us Until They Kill Us*, 72.
83. See Joshua Atkinson and Bernadette Marie Calafell, "Darth Vader Made Me Do It!"
84. Eli Davies, "Knowing Him Now After Only Guessing," 119.
85. Rodger, "My Twisted World," 136.
86. Rodger, "My Twisted World," 136.
87. Kelly, *Apocalypse Man*. Also, Theleweit, *Male Fantasies*.
88. Bratich, *On Microfascism*; Jack Z. Bratich and Sarah Banet-Weiser, "From Pick-Up Artists to Incels."
89. Bryan McCann, "12/31/95," 72.
90. McCann, "12/31/95," 72.
91. McCann, "12/31/95," 72.
92. For example, Lionel Trilling, "Art and Neuroses."
93. Julissa O. Muñiz, "Exclusionary Discipline Policies, School-Police Partnerships, Surveillance Technologies and Disproportionality."
94. Mark Paxton, "Student Free Expression Rights and the Columbine Shootings"; Ryalls, "Emo Angst, Masochism, and Masculinity in Crisis," 90.
95. Keppel, *The Riverman*; Michaud and Aynesworth, *Conversations with a Killer*.
96. I am indebted to Stephanie R. Larson for this line of reasoning.
97. Lugones, "Toward a Decolonial Feminism"; Mack et al., "Between Bodies and Institutions."
98. Marshall, "The End of Evil."
99. See Downing, *Desiring the Dead*.
100. Michaud and Aynesworth, *The Only Living Witness*.
101. Keppel, *The Riverman*; Michaud and Aynesworth, *Conversations with a Killer*.
102. Keppel, *The Riverman*, 344.
103. Rubin and Lucchesi, *A Light in the Dark*, 81.
104. Bill Eagles, *The Riverman*.
105. Michaud and Aynesworth, *The Only Living Witness*, 462.
106. For a similar argument, see Armond R. Towns, "Toward a Black Media Philosophy."

Conclusion

1. Knoll, *Bright Young Women*, 257.
2. Rubin and Lucchesi, *A Light in the Dark*, 243.
3. Samuel Argyle, "Ted Bundy Would Be Thrilled to Know We're Still Talking about Him."
4. Schmid, *Natural Born Celebrities*.
5. The nine films are *The Deliberate Stranger* (1986), *Ted Bundy* (2002), *The Stranger Beside Me* (2003), *The Riverman* (2004), *Bundy: An American Icon* (2008), *The Capture of the Green River Killer* (2008), *Extremely Wicked, Shockingly Evil, and Vile* (2019), *No Man of God* (2021), and *Ted Bundy: American Boogeyman* (2021). Documentaries include *Conversations with a Killer: The Ted Bundy Tapes* (2019) and *Ted Bundy: Falling for a Killer* (2020). I have referenced several books about Bundy throughout this book. Podcasts such as *My Favorite Murder* address Bundy, whereas the podcast *Interview with Evil: Ted Bundy's FBI Confessions* deals exclusively with Bundy. On social media fandom, see Brittany Spanos, "Ted Bundy and Charles Manson Fans Are Deep in a Twitter Feud."
6. Vronsky, *Sons of Cain*.
7. For example, Rule, *The Stranger Beside Me*. On executions as rituals, see, Conquergood, "Lethal Theatre."
8. Rubin and Lucchesi, *A Light in the Dark*, 197.
9. In fact, Bundy's final death row lawyers tried in vain to prove their client's mental illness precluded a fair trial or execution. See Marshall, "The End of Evil"; Nelson, *Defending the Devil*.
10. Purple Mountains, "Nights That Won't Happen"; David Foster Wallace, *Infinite Jest*.
11. On the logics of suicidality, see Alexandre Baril, "Suicidism"; Emily Krebs, "Queering the Desire to Die"; Lore/tta LeMaster, "Suicidal"; McCann, "Economies of Misery."
12. See Anne Case and Angus Deaton, *Deaths of Despair and the Future of Capitalism*; Sexton, *The Man They Wanted Me to Be*.
13. Rowland, "Small Dick Problems."
14. On bare life, see Giorgio Agamben, *Homo Sacer*.
15. bell hooks, *The Will to Change*. Also, Sexton, *The Man They Wanted Me to Be*.
16. Adrian T. Peperzak, Simon Critchley, and Robert Bernasconi, *Emmanuel Levinas*.
17. See Bratich and Banet-Weiser, "From Pick-Up Artists to Incels"; Case and Deaton, *Deaths of Despair and the Future of Capitalism*; Sexton, *The Man They Wanted Me to Be*.
18. Marshall, "The End of Evil."
19. Marshall, "The End of Evil."
20. McCann, "Economies of Misery."
21. Michaud and Aynesworth, *Conversations with a Killer*; Michaud and Aynesworth, *The Only Living Witness*.
22. Keppel, *The Riverman*.
23. Rule, *The Stranger Beside Me*.
24. Kendall, *The Phantom Prince*.
25. Alex Gibney, *Crazy, Not Insane*.
26. Portions of this interview appear in *Conversations with a Killer* and *Falling for a Killer*. Efron reenacts it in *Extremely Wicked*.
27. Marshall, "The End of Evil."
28. Kendall, *The Phantom Prince*.

29. Marshall, "The End of Evil"; Nelson, *Defending the Devil*.
30. Frantz Fanon, *Black Skin, White Masks*.
31. David R. Roediger, *The Wages of Whiteness*.
32. For a summary of Baldwin's thinking in this area, see Eddie S. Glaude Jr., *Begin Again*.
33. Beltrán, *Cruelty as Citizenship*; Levina, "Whiteness and the Joys of Cruelty"; Silva, "Having the Time of Our Lives"; Eric King Watts, "A Monstrous Genre."
34. Greg Wohead, *The Ted Bundy Project*, 2.
35. Wohead, *The Ted Bundy Project*, 2. Throughout the text's technical prose, Wohead refers to himself in the third person.
36. Rule, *The Stranger Beside Me*.
37. Lyn Gardner, "The Ted Bundy Project Review."
38. Tracy Clark-Flory, "Let's Watch a Murder."
39. Matheson, "Liberal Tears and the Rogue's Yarn of Sadistic Conservativism."
40. "Britain's Most Notorious Serial Killers."
41. See, for example, Lisa M. Corrigan, "Beyond Grievance Masculinity."
42. Ruth Whippman, "We Can Do Better than 'Positive Masculinity.'"
43. Amnesty International, "'You Feel Like You Are Subhuman'"; Peter Beinart, "Democrats Ignored Gaza and Brought Down Their Party"; "Tim Walz"; University Network for Human Rights, "Genocide in Gaza."
44. See Hartman, *Wayward Lives, Beautiful Experiments*; Hsu, *Constellating Home*; Morris, "The Archival Turn in Rhetorical Studies"; Muñoz, "Ephemera as Evidence." On alternative performances of masculinity, see hooks, *The Will to Change*.
45. Matheson, "Liberal Tears and the Rogue's Yarn of Sadistic Conservatism," 347.
46. Also, Chebrolu, "The Racial Lens of Dylan Roof."
47. Cohen, "Amber Sealey Didn't Want to Make Another Ted Bundy Movie."
48. Cohen, "Amber Sealey Didn't Want to Make Another Ted Bundy Movie."
49. Chebrolu, "The Racial Lens of Dylann Roof."
50. Bryan J. McCann, "Therapeutic and Material <Victim>hood"; Richie, *Arrested Justice*.
51. Also, Rubin and Lucchesi, *A Light in the Dark*; Telfer, "Ted Bundy's Living Victim Tells Her Story."
52. Knoll, *Bright Young Women*, 57.
53. Rule, *The Stranger Beside Me*, 411.
54. See Thomas K. Nakayama and Robert L. Krizek, "Whiteness."
55. Jessica Napoli and Tyler McCarthy, "Zac Efron Says White Privilege Allowed Ted Bundy to Kill People for So Long before Being Captured." Also, Dorian Geiger, "Want an Example of White Privilege?"; Sean Gerrity, "Blinded by the White."
56. See Gray, "Race, Media, and the Cultivation of Concern"; Mack and McCann, "'Strictly an Act of Street Violence.'"
57. Ashley R. Hall, "Slippin' in and out of Frame," 343. Also, Wilderson, *Red, White, and Black*.
58. Hartman, *Scenes of Subjection*, 19.
59. See, for example, Kelly Macías, "'Sisters in the Collective Struggle'"; Phillips and Griffin, "Crystal Mangum as Hypervisible Object and Invisible Subject."
60. See Chandan Reddy, *Freedom with Violence*.
61. bell hooks, *Black Looks*. Also, King and Gunn, "On a Violence Unseen."
62. Similarly, Chávez theorizes the textual stare. See Chávez, "The Body."

63. See Calafell, *Monstrosity, Performance, and Race in Contemporary Culture*; Jackson, *Scripting the Black Masculine Body*; Johnson, *Appropriating Blackness*; Ore, *Lynching*; Watts, "A Monstrous Genre."

64. See Phaedra C. Pezzullo, "Performing Critical Interruptions."

BIBLIOGRAPHY

@caroldaronch. "Ted Bundy Trial Louise Bundy Takes the Stand July 1979." *YouTube*, January 6, 2023, https://www.youtube.com/watch?v=tPGybWra4rQ.
Abdurraqib, Hanif. *They Can't Kill Us Until They Kill Us: Essays*. Two Dollar Radio, 2017.
Afghan Whigs. "Debonair." *Gentlemen*. Sub Pop, 1993.
Agamben, Giorgio. *Homo Sacer: Sovereign Power and Bare Life*. Translated by Daniel Heller-Roazen. Stanford University Press, 1998.
Ahmed, Sara. *The Cultural Politics of Emotion*, 2nd ed. Edinburgh University Press, 2014.
Alcoholics Anonymous. 4th ed. Alcoholics Anonymous World Services, 2001.
Alexander, Michelle. *The New Jim Crow: Mass Incarceration in the Age of Colorblindness*. New Press, 2012.
Amnesty International. "'You Feel Like You Are Subhuman': Israel's Genocide Against Palestinians in Gaza." 2024. https://www.amnesty.org/en/documents/mde15/8668/2024/en/.
Anderson, Karrin Vasby. "'Rhymes with Blunt': Pornification and U.S. Political Culture." *Rhetoric and Public Affairs* 14, no. 2 (2011): 327–68.
Andrade, Luis M., and Deven Cooper. "Defending Whiteness: The Psychic Life of Anti-Blackness on Grindr." *Contemporary Argumentation and Debate* 38, no. 1 (2023). https://commons.lib.jmu.edu/cad/vol38/iss1/10.
"Animal House's Sarah Holcomb Had Three Horrible Years of Fame." *80s Kids*. https://www.eightieskids.com/animal-houses-sarah-holcomb-had-three-horrible-years-of-fame/.
Argyle, Samuel. "Ted Bundy Would Be Thrilled to Know We're Still Talking about Him." *The Outline*, February 4, 2019. https://theoutline.com/post/7040/ted-bundy-tapes-zac-efron-essay.
Arvin, Maile, Eve Tuck, and Angie Morrill. "Decolonizing Feminism: Challenging Connections Between Settler Colonialism and Heteropatriarchy." *Feminist Formations* 25 (2013): 8–34.
Asante, Godfried. "Decolonizing the Erotic: Building Alliances of (Queer) African Eros." *Women's Studies in Communication* 43, no. 2 (2020): 113–18.
Asen, Robert. "Neoliberalism, the Public Sphere, and the Public Good." *Quarterly Journal of Speech* 103, no. 4 (2017): 329–49.

Asen, Robert, and Casey Ryan Kelly. "Economizing Whiteness, Rhetoricizing Economy: Investigating Discourses of Whiteness and the Production of Racial and Economic Inequality." In *Rhetorical Economies of Whiteness: Exploring the Intersections of Power, Privilege, and Race*, edited by Robert Asen and Casey Ryan Kelly, 1–28. Ohio State University Press, 2024.

Atkinson, Joshua, and Bernadette Calafell. "Darth Vader Made Me Do It! Anakin Skywalker's Avoidance of Responsibility and the Gray Areas of Hegemonic Masculinity in the Star Wars Universe." *Communication, Culture, and Critique* 2, no. 1 (2009): 1–20.

Báez, Kristiana L., and Ersula Ore. "The Moral Imperative of Race for Rhetorical Studies: On Civility and Walking-in-White in Academe." *Communication and Critical/Cultural Studies* 15, no. 4 (2018): 331–36.

bain, kristen. "Rape Culture on Campus." *Off Our Backs* 32, no. 9/10 (2002): 26–27.

Bainbridge, Jason. "Soiling Suburbia: Lynch, Solondz and the Power of Dirt." *M/C Journal* 9, no. 5 (2006). https://doi.org/10.5204/mcj.2675.

Baril, Alexandre. "Suicidism: A New Theoretical Framework to Conceptualize Suicide from an Anti-Oppressive Perspective." *Disability Studies Quarterly* 40, no. 3 (2020). https://doi-org.libezp.lib.lsu.edu/10.18061/dsq.v40i3.7053.

Bataille, Georges. *Erotism: Death and Sensuality*. Translated by Mary Dalwood. 1957; City Lights, 1986.

Baudrillard, Jean. *The Spirit of Terrorism*. Verso, 2002.

Baugh-Harris, Sara, and Darrel Wanzer-Serrano. "Against Canon: Engaging the Imperative of Race in Rhetoric." *Communication and Critical/Cultural Studies* 15, no. 4 (2018): 337–42.

Beauvoir, Simone de. "Must We Burn Sade?" In *Political Writings*, edited by Margaret A. Simons and Marybeth Timmermann, 44–101. University of Illinois Press, 2014.

Beinart, Peter. "Democrats Ignored Gaza and Brought Down Their Party." *The New York Times*, November 7, 2024. https://www.nytimes.com/2024/11/07/opinion/democrats-israel-gaza-war.html.

Beltrán, Christina. *Cruelty as Citizenship: How Migrant Suffering Sustains White Democracy*. University of Minnesota Press, 2020.

Benson, Stephen, and Clare Connors. "Introduction." In *Creative Criticism: An Anthology and Guide*, 1–47. Edinburgh University Press, 2014.

Bergland, Renée L. *The National Uncanny: Indian Ghosts and American Subjects*. Dartmouth College Press, 2000.

Berlant, Lauren, and Michael Warner. "Sex in Public." *Critical Inquiry* 24, no. 2 (1998): 547–66.

Berlinger, Joe. *Conversations with a Killer: The Ted Bundy Tapes*. Netflix, 2019.

Berlinger, Joe. *Extremely Wicked, Shockingly Evil, and Vile*. Netflix, 2019.

Berman, David. "Nights That Won't Happen." *Purple Mountains*. Drag City, 2019.

Bernstein, Elizabeth. "Militarized Humanitarianism Meets Carceral Feminism: The Politics of Sex, Rights, and Freedom in Contemporary Antitrafficking Campaigns." *Signs* 36, no. 1 (2010): 45–71.

Bey, Marquis. *Black Trans Feminism*. Duke University Press, 2022.

Biesecker, Barbara A. "No Time for Mourning: The Rhetorical Production of the Melancholic Citizen-Subject in the War on Terror." *Philosophy and Rhetoric* 40, no. 1 (2007): 147–69.

Biesecker, Barbara A. "Of Historicity, Rhetoric: The Archive as Scene of Invention." *Rhetoric and Public Affairs* 9, no. 1 (2006): 124–31.

Biesecker, Barbara A. "Remembering World War II: The Rhetoric and Politics of National Commemoration at the Turn of the 21st Century." *Quarterly Journal of Speech* 88, no. 4 (2002): 393–409.
Bishop, Stephen. "Animal House." Recorded 1978. Track 10 on *On and On: The Hits of Stephen Bishop*. MCA, compact disc, 1994.
Black, Edwin. *Rhetorical Criticism: A Study in Method*. University of Wisconsin Press, 1965.
Black, Joel. *The Aesthetics of Murder: A Study in Romantic Literature and Contemporary Culture*. Johns Hopkins University Press, 1991.
Bowman, Michael S. "Killing Dillinger: A Mystory." *Text and Performance Quarterly* 20, no. 4 (2000): 342–74.
Boyle, Karen, and Jenny Reburn. "Portrait of a Serial Killer." *Feminist Media Studies* 15, no. 2 (2014): 192–207. https://doi.org/10.1080/14680777.2014.946943.
Bradford, Tonya Williams, and John F. Sherry Jr. "Domesticating Public Space Through Ritual: Tailgating as Vestaval." *Journal of Consumer Research* 42 (2015): 130–51.
Bradshaw, Peter. "*Bundy*." *The Guardian*, November 21, 2002. https://www.theguardian.com/culture/2002/nov/22/artsfeatures13.
Brand, Amanda N. "White Masculine Abjection, Victimhood, and Disavowal in Rape Culture: Reconstituting Brock Turner." *Quarterly Journal of Speech* 108, no. 2 (2022): 148–71.
Brannigan, Augustine, and Sheldon Goldenberg. "The Study of Aggressive Pornography: The Vicissitudes of Relevance." *Critical Studies in Mass Communication* 4, no. 3 (1987): 262–83.
Bratich, Jack Z. *On Microfascism: Gender, War, and Death*. Common Notions, 2022.
Bratich, Jack Z., and Sarah Banet-Weiser. "From Pick-Up Artists to Incels: Con(fidence) Games, Networked Misogyny, and the Failure of Neoliberalism." *International Journal of Communication* 13 (2019): 5003–27.
Breihan, Tom. "Nine Inch Nails: Pretty Hate Machine." *Pitchfork*, November 24, 2010. https://pitchfork.com/reviews/albums/14890-pretty-hate-machine/.
Breslow, Jacob. "Adolescent Citizenship, or Temporality and the Negation of Black Childhood in Two Eras." *American Quarterly* 71 (2019): 473–94.
Bright, Matthew. "Ted Bundy." First Look International, 2002.
"Britain's Most Notorious Serial Killers." *Reuters*, January 20, 2007. https://www.reuters.com/article/uk-britain-killers/britains-most-notorious-serial-killers-idUKL1315230120061221.
Bronstein, Carolyn. *Battling Pornography: The American Feminist Anti-Pornography Movement, 1976–1986*. Cambridge University Press, 2011.
Browder, Laura. "Dystopian Romance: True Crime and the Female Reader." *Journal of Popular Culture* 39, no. 6 (2006): 928–53.
Brownmiller, Susan. "Excerpt on Pornography from *Against Our Will: Men, Women, and Rape*." In *Take Back the Night: Women on Pornography*, edited by Laura Lederer, 30–34. William Morrow, 1980.
Brummett, Barry. "Burkean Scapegoating, Mortification, and Transcendence in Presidential Campaign Rhetoric." *Central States Speech Journal* 32, no. 4 (1981): 254–64.
Brummett, Barry. "The Homology Hypothesis: Pornography on the VCR." *Critical Studies in Mass Communication* 5, no. 3 (1988): 202–16.
Brummett, Barry. "Rhetorical Theory as Heuristic and Moral: A Pedagogical Justification. *Communication Education* 33, no. 2 (1984): 97–107.

Buedel, Matt. "Director of Bradley's Star Speech Program Resigns after Allegations of Sexual Assault." *Peoria Journal Star*, October 26, 2018. https://www.pjstar.com/news/20181026/director-of-bradleys-star-speech-program-resigns-after-allegations-of-sexual-assault.

Burke, Kenneth. *Counter-Statement*. Rev. ed. University of California Press, 1968.

Burlingame, Christopher. "Social Identity Crisis? Patrick Bateman, Donald Trump, and the Hermeneutic Maelstrom." *Journal of Popular Culture* 52, no. 2 (2019): 330–50.

Burns, Jennifer. *Goddess of the Market: Ayn Rand and the American Right*. Oxford University Press, 2009.

"Business: Bed Sheets Bonanza." *Time*, October 23, 1978. http://content.time.com/time/subscriber/article/0,33009,946118,00.html.

"Butch Pierce, Left, of Starke, and Bob Reeves, of Gainesville, Light up Bundy Effigy at Prison." Photo caption, *Tallahassee Democrat*, January 25, 1989, 1A.

Butler, Judith. *Precarious Life: The Powers of Mourning and Violence*. Verso, 2004.

Calafell, Bernadette Marie. *Monstrosity, Performance, and Race in Contemporary Culture*. Peter Lang, 2015.

Calafell, Bernadette Marie. "Performance: Keeping Rhetoric Honest." *Text and Performance Quarterly* 34, no. 1 (2014): 115–17.

Calafell, Bernadette Marie. "Rhetorics of Possibility: Challenging the Textual Bias of Rhetoric Through the Theory of the Flesh." In *Rhetorica in Motion: Feminist Rhetorical Methods and Methodologies*, edited by Eileen E. Schell and K. J. Rawson, 104–17. University of Pittsburgh Press, 2010.

Calvente, Lisa B. Y., Bernadette Marie Calafell, and Karma R. Chávez. "Here Is Something You Can't Understand: The Suffocating Whiteness of Communication Studies." *Communication and Critical/Cultural Studies* 17 (2020): 202–9.

Cameron, Deborah, and Elizabeth Frazer. *The Lust to Kill: A Feminist Investigation of Sexual Murder*. New York University Press, 1987.

Campbell, Karlyn Kohrs, and Kathleen Hall Jamieson. "Form and Genre in Rhetorical Criticism: An Introduction." In *Form and Genre: Shaping Rhetorical Action*, edited by Karlyn Kohrs Campbell, and Kathleen Hall Jamieson, 9–32. Speech Communication Association, 1978.

Caputi, Jane. *The Age of the Sex Crime*. Bowling Green State University Popular Press, 1987.

Caputi, Jane. "The Sexual Politics of Murder." *Gender and Society* 3, no. 4 (1989): 437–56.

Caramanica, Jon. "Hey, Bud, What Comes After Our 15 Minutes?" *The New York Times*, June 24, 2009. https://www.nytimes.com/2009/06/28/arts/television/28cara.html.

"Carol DaRonch." Internet Movie Database. https://www.imdb.com/name/nm10485695/.

Carr, Daphne. *Nine Inch Nails' Pretty Hate Machine*. Continuum, 2011.

Case, Anne, and Angus Deaton. *Deaths of Despair and the Future of Capitalism*. Princeton University Press, 2020).

Ceccarelli, Leah. "Temporal Development and Spatial Emplacement in the Dispositional Whole: The (Con)Text of Hillary Clinton's 'Basket of Deplorables' Speech." In *The Conceit of Context: Resituating Domains in Rhetorical Studies*, edited by Charles E. Morris III and Kendall R. Phillips, 47–54. Peter Lang, 2020.

Charland, Maurice. "Constitutive Rhetoric: The Case of the *Peuple Québécois*." *Quarterly Journal of Speech* 73 (1987): 133–50.

Chávez, Karma R. "The Body: An Abstract and Actual Rhetorical Concept." *Rhetoric Society Quarterly* 48, no. 3 (2018): 242–50.

Chávez, Karma R. "Counter-Public Enclaves and Understanding the Function of Rhetoric in Social Movement Coalition-Building." *Communication Quarterly* 59, no. 1 (2011): 1–18. https://Doi.org/10.1080/01463373.2010.541333.

Chávez, Karma R. "Parody, Perversion, and the Violence of 'Normal' Political Culture." In *The Conceit of Context: Resituating Domains in Rhetorical Studies*, edited by Charles E. Morris III and Kendall R. Phillips, 157–64. Peter Lang, 2020.

Chávez, Karma R. *Queer Migration Politics: Activist Rhetoric and Coalitional Possibilities*. University of Illinois Press, 2013.

Chebrolu, E. "The Racial Lens of Dylann Roof: Racial Anxiety and White Nationalist Rhetoric on New Media." *Review of Communication* 20, no. 1 (2020): 47–68.

Chen, Marissa. "I've Got Your Letter, You've Got My Song: On *Pinkerton*." In *Under My Thumb: Songs that Hate Women and the Women Who Love Them*, edited by Rhian Jones Eli Davies, 185–200. Repeater Books, 2017.

Cheney-Rice, Zak. "The Purpose of Trump's Cruel Deportation Theater." *MSN*, 4 April 2025. https://www.msn.com/en-us/news/opinion/the-purpose-of-trump-s-cruel-deportation-theater/ar-AA1Cjcze.

"Chicago Massacre: Richard Speck." *Rotten Tomatoes*. https://www.rottentomatoes.com/m/chicago_massacre_richard_speck.

Chiesi, Roberto. "*Salò*: The Present as Hell." *Criterion*, October 4, 2011. https://www.criterion.com/current/posts/513-sal-the-present-as-hell.

Chomsky, Marvin J. *The Deliberate Stranger*. Warner Bros. Television, 1986.

Clare, Eli. *Brilliant Imperfection: Grappling with Cure*. Duke University Press, 2017.

Clark, Bob. *Black Christmas*. Warner Brothers, 1974.

Clark-Flory, Tracy. "Let's Watch a Murder." *Salon*, June 10, 2012. https://www.salon.com/2012/06/10/lets_watch_a_murder/.

Clover, Carol J. *Men, Women, and Chain Saws: Gender in the Modern Horror Film*. 1992. Princeton University Press, 2015.

Coffman, Justin. "Ted Bundy Canvas Print." https://fineartamerica.com/featured/ted-bundy-justin-coffman.html?product=canvas-print.

Cohen, Anne. "Amber Sealey Didn't Want to Make Another Ted Bundy Movie. That's Why She Had To." *Refinery 29*, June 10, 2021. https://www.refinery29.com/en-us/2021/06/10517086/no-man-of-god-ted-bundy-movie-amber-sealey.

Coleman, Daniel B. (formerly Brittany Chávez), and Louis Yako. "Personal Is Political: The Myth of Diversity and Critical Thinking in American Academia." *Feminist Wire*, October 7, 2014. https://thefeministwire.com/2014/10/academia/

Collins, Patricia Hill. *Black Feminist Thought: Knowledge, Consciousness, and the Politics of Empowerment*. Routledge, 2008.

Collins, Patricia Hill. *Black Sexual Politics: African Americans, Gender, and the New Racism*. Routledge, 2004.

Combahee River Collective. "The Combahee River Collective Statement." 1974. https://americanstudies.yale.edu/sites/default/files/files/Keyword%20Coalition_Readings.pdf.

Commons, Jess. "Why Women Fall in Love with Serial Killers Like Ted Bundy." *Refinery 29*, January 24, 2019. https://www.refinery29.com/en-us/what-is-hybristophilia.

Connolly, William E. "The Ethos of Revenge." *Communication and Critical/Cultural Studies* 4, no. 1 (2007): 93–97.

Conquergood, Dwight. "Beyond the Text: Toward a Performative Cultural Politics." In *Cultural Struggles: Performance, Ethnography, Praxis*, edited by E. Patrick Johnson, 47–63. University of Michigan Press, 2013.

Conquergood, Dwight. "Lethal Theatre: Performance, Punishment, and the Death Penalty." *Theatre Journal* 54, no. 3 (2002): 339–67.

Conquergood, Dwight. "Performing as a Moral Act: Ethical Dimensions of the Ethnography of Performance." *Text and Performance Quarterly* 5, no. 2 (1985): 1–13.

Coontz, Stephanie. *The Way We Never Were: American Families and the Nostalgia Trap*. Basic Books, 1993.

Corey, Frederick C., and Thomas K. Nakayama. "Sextext." *Text and Performance Quarterly* 17, no. 1 (1997): 58–68.

Corrigan, Lisa M. "Beyond Grievance Masculinity: Tim Walz and White Male Joy." *Clio and the Contemporary*, September 4, 2024. https://clioandthecontemporary.com/2024/09/04/beyond-grievance-masculinity/?fbclid=IwY2xjawFHNx9lehRua2FlbQIxMQABH WveDffjn_xrABa5_9uW7onsAX9QGed7onIcsNZgDKNVYnaYeT-osJW1mQ_aem_ CiWF1_Yu8CxSUGtrBFq-g.

Corrigan, Lisa M., and Anjali Vats. "The Structural Whiteness of Academic Patronage." *Communication and Critical/Cultural Studies* 17, no. 2 (2020): 220–27.

Cram, Emerson. "Archival Ambience and Sensory Memory: Generating Queer Intimacies in the Settler Colonial Archive." *Communication and Critical/Cultural Studies* 13, no. 2 (2016): 109–29.

Cramer, James, and Deanna Thompson. "Fear Reigns on Campus, but No Panic." *Tallahassee Democrat*, January 16, 1978, 1A.

Curry, Tommy J. *The Man-Not: Race, Class, Genre, and the Dilemmas of Black Manhood*. Temple University Press, 2017.

Cvetkovich, Ann. *Depression: A Public Feeling*. Duke University Press, 2012.

Daly, Michael. "Who Is the Real Ted Bundy?" *Floridian*, January 21, 1978, 18–27.

Darsey, James. "Must We All Be Rhetorical Theorists? An Anti-Democratic Inquiry." *Western Journal of Communication* 58 (1994): 164–81.

Davies, Eli. "Knowing Him Now After Only Guessing." In *Under My Thumb: Songs That Hate Women and the Women Who Love Them*, edited by Rhian E. Jones and Eli Davies, 116–25. Repeater, 2017.

Davis, Mike. *City of Quartz: Excavating the Future in Los Angeles*. Verso, 1990.

Davis, Olga Idriss. "In the Kitchen: Transforming the Academy through Safe Spaces of Resistance." *Western Journal of Communication* 63 (1999): 364–81.

Dean, Jodi. *Crowds and Party*. Verso, 2018.

Deer, Sarah. "Decolonizing Rape Law: A Native Feminist Synthesis of Safety and Sovereignty." *Wicazo Sa Review* 24, no. 2 (2009): 149–67.

Delany, Samuel R. *Times Square Red, Times Square Blue*. 1999. New York University Press, 2019.

Demeter, Amanda. "Disgust and Fascination: Feminist Ethics of Care and the Ted Bundy Investigative Files." *Journal of Critical Library and Information Studies* 30, no. 2 (2021). https://journals.litwinbooks.com/index.php/jclis/article/view/124/99.

DeVun, Leah, and Michael Jay McClure. "Archives Behaving Badly." *Radical History Review* 120 (2014): 121–30.

Diaz, Jaclyn. "At Least 9 Gop-Led State Legislatures Want to Restrict or Criminalize Drag Shows." *NPR*, February 8, 2023. https://www.npr.org/2023/02/08/1151731736/at-least-10-state-legislatures-trying-restrict-criminalize-drag-shows.
Dilley, Whitney Crothers. "Globalization and Cultural Identity in the Films of Ang Lee." *Film and Globalization* 43, no. 1 (2009): 45–64.
Dobson, James. "A Christian Response to Homosexuality—Part 1." *Dr. James Dobson Family Institute*, May 23, 2022. https://www.drjamesdobson.org/broadcasts/a-christian-response-to-homosexuality-part-1.
Doe #1, et al. v. Board of Supervisors of Louisiana State University and Agricultural and Mechanical College, et al., 3:21-cv-00564-SDD-EWD (USDC-Middle District of Louisiana 2021). https://www.insidehighered.com/sites/default/files/media/lsu_suit.pdf.
Downing, Lisa. *Desiring the Dead: Necrophilia and Nineteenth-Century French Literature*. Legenda, 2003.
Downing, Lisa. *The Subject of Murder: Gender, Exceptionality, and the Modern Killer*. University of Chicago Press, 2013.
Dubrofsky, Rachel E. "Monstrous Authenticity: Trump's Whiteness." In *Interrogating the Communicative Power of Whiteness*, edited by Dawn Marie D. McIntosh, Dreama G. Moon, and Thomas K. Nakayama, 155–75. Routledge, 2019.
Duggan, Lisa. "Censorship in the Name of Feminism." In *Sex Wars: Sexual Dissent and Political Culture*, edited by Lisa Duggan and Nan D. Hunter, 29–39. Routledge, 2006.
Duggan, Lisa. *Mean Girl: Ayn Rand and the Culture of Greed*. University of California Press, 2019.
Dworkin, Andrea. *Pornography: Men Possessing Women*. 1979. Plume, 1989.
Dyer, Richard. *White*. Routledge, 1997.
Eagles, Bill. *The Riverman*. Starz!, 2017.
"Ed Gein." *Rotten Tomatoes*. https://www.rottentomatoes.com/m/ed_gein.
Edelman, Lee. *No Future: Queer Theory and the Death Drive*. Duke University Press, 2004.
Edelstein, Arnon. "Revenge: The Missing Category in Serial Murder Typologies." *Psychology* 15 (2024): 1086–91.
Edwards, Stassa. "Ted Bundy: Falling for a Killer Renders the Women Three-Dimensional." *Jezebel*, February 6, 2020. https://jezebel.com/ted-bundy-falling-for-a-killer-renders-the-women-three-1841453387.
Ehrenhaus, Peter, and A. Susan Owen. "Race Lynching and Christian Evangelicalism: Performances of Faith." *Text and Performance Quarterly* 24, no. 3–4 (2004): 276–301.
"Elliot Rodger: How Misogynist Killer Became 'Incel Hero.'" *BBC News*, April 26, 2018. https://www.bbc.com/news/world-us-canada-43892189.
Ellis, Carolyn, and Arthur P. Bochner. "Autoethnography, Personal Narrative, Reflexivity: Researcher as Subject." In *Handbook of Qualitative Research*, edited by Norman K. Denzin and Yvonna S. Lincoln, 733–68. SAGE, 2000.
Fanon, Frantz. *Black Skin, White Masks*. Translated by Richard Philcox. New York: Grove Press, 2008.
Farrands, Daniel. *Ted Bundy: American Boogeyman*. Fathom Events/Voltage Pictures, 2021.
Feifer, Michael. *Bundy: A Legacy of Evil*. Accent, 2009.
Fenske, Mindy. "The Aesthetic of the Unfinished: Ethics and Performance." *Text and Performance Quarterly* 24, no. 1 (2004): 1–19.
"55th Annual Sugar Bowl Classic ~ January 1, 1989." Allstate Sugar Bowl. Accessed February 1, 2021. https://allstatesugarbowl.org/classic/1989-game-recap/.

Final Report of the Attorney General's Commission on Pornography. Rutlidge Hill Press, 1986.
Finnegan, Cara A. "What Is This a Picture Of? Some Thoughts on Images and Archives." *Rhetoric and Public Affairs* 9, no. 1 (2006): 116–23.
Flaherty, Colleen. "More Than Rumors." *Inside Higher Ed*, August 10, 2018. https://www.insidehighered.com/news/2018/08/10/michael-kimmels-former-student-putting-name-and-details-those-harassment-rumors.
Flores, Lisa A. "Between Abundance and Marginalization: The Imperative of Racial Rhetorical Criticism." *Review of Communication* 16 (2016): 4024.
Flores, Lisa A. "The Rhetorical 'Realness' of Race, or Why Critical Race Rhetoricians Need Performance Studies." *Text and Performance Quarterly* 34, no. 1 (2014): 94–96.
Flynn, Clifton P. "Examining the Links between Animal Abuse and Human Violence." *Crime, Law and Social Change* 55 (2011): 453–68.
Forbes, Jack D. *Columbus and Other Cannibals: The Wétiko Disease of Exploitation, Imperialism, and Terrorism*. Seven Stories, 2008.
Forter, Gregory. *Murdering Masculinities: Fantasies of Gender and Violence in the American Crime Novel*. New York University Press, 2000.
Foucault, Michel. *Discipline and Punish: The Birth of the Prison*. Translated by Alan Sheridan. Vintage Books, 1975.
Foucault, Michel. "Nietzsche, Genealogy, History." In *Language, Counter-Memory, Practice: Selected Essays and Interviews*, edited by D. F. Bouchard, 139–64. Cornell University Press, 1977.
Fox, Ragan. "Tales of a Fighting Bobcat: An 'Auto-Archaeology' of Gay Identity Formation and Maintenance." *Text and Performance Quarterly* 30, no. 2 (2010): 122–42.
Foywonder. "Bundy: A Legacy of Evil." *Dread Central*, June 11, 2009. https://www.dreadcentral.com/reviews/12044/bundy-a-legacy-of-evil-2009/
Freud, Sigmund. *The Uncanny*. Translated by David McLintock. Penguin, 2003.
Fries, Laura. "*The Stranger Beside Me*." *Variety*, March 20, 2003. https://variety.com/2003/tv/reviews/the-stranger-beside-me-1200542669/.
Fukunaga, Cary Joji. *True Detective*. HBO, 2014.
Garber, Megan. "How Rom-Coms Undermine Women." *The Atlantic*, November 1, 2016. https://www.theatlantic.com/entertainment/archive/2016/11/its-rom-coms-fault-too/505928/.
Gardner, Lyn. "*The Ted Bundy Project* Review—Gripping One-Man Show about Violence." *The Guardian*, June 19, 2014. https://www.theguardian.com/stage/2014/jun/19/the-ted-bundy-project-review
Gavilanes, Grace. "People's 1986 Sexiest Man Alive Mark Harmon Totally Got Teased for the Title." *People*, October 22, 2015. https://people.com/celebrity/mark-harmon-peoples-sexiest-man-alive-1986/.
Gaynor, Stella. "Better the Devil You Know: Nostalgia for the Captured Killer in Netflix's *Conversations with a Killer: The Ted Bundy Tapes*." In *Serial Killers in Contemporary Television: Familiar Monsters in Post-9/11 Culture*, edited by Bret A. B. Robinson and Christine Daigle, 135–51. Routledge, 2022.
Gehrke, Pat J. *The Ethics and Politics of Speech: Communication and Rhetoric in the Twentieth Century*. Southern Illinois University Press, 2009.
Geiger, Dorian. "Want an Example of White Privilege? Just Look at Ted Bundy." *Oxygen*, May 3, 2019. https://www.oxygen.com/martinis-murder/white-privilege-ted-bundy-shockingly-evil.

Gelman, David, and David L. Gonzalez. "The Bundy Carnival." *Newsweek*, February 6, 1989, 66.
Gendron, Bob. *The Afghan Whigs' "Gentlemen."* Continuum, 2008.
Gerrity, Sean. "Blinded by the White: Race and the Exceptionalizing of Ted Bundy." *Nursing Clio*, July 18, 2019. https://nursingclio.org/2019/07/18/blinded-by-the-white-race-and-the-exceptionalizing-of-ted-bundy/.
Gewirtz, Paul. "On 'I Know It When I See It.'" *Yale Law Journal* 105, no. 4 (1996): 1023–47.
Gibney, Alex. *Crazy, Not Insane*. Max, 2020.
Giles, Dennis. "Pornographic Space: The Other Place." In *Film: Historical-Theoretical Speculations*, edited by Ben Lawton, and Janet Staiger, 52–66. Routledge, 1977.
Gill, Rebecca. "The Evolution of Organizational Archetypes: From the American to the Entrepreneurial Dream." *Communication Monographs* 80, no. 3 (2013): 331–53.
Girard, René. *Violence and the Sacred*. Translated by Patrick Gregory. Johns Hopkins University Press, 1979. 1972.
Glaude, Eddie S., Jr. *Begin Again: James Baldwin's America and Its Urgent Lessons for Our Own*. Crown, 2020.
Goldstein, Al. "Ted Bundy's Last Lie." *The New York Times*, February 18, 1989. https://www.nytimes.com/1989/02/18/opinion/ted-bundys-last-lie.html.
Gordon, Avery. *Ghostly Matters: Haunting and the Sociological Imagination*. University of Minnesota Press, 2008.
Gray, Herman. "Race, Media, and the Cultivation of Concern." *Communication and Critical/Cultural Studies* 10, no. 2-3 (2013): 253–58.
Greenberg, Zoe. "What Happens to #Metoo When a Feminist Is the Accused?" *The New York Times*, August 13, 2018. https://www.nytimes.com/2018/08/13/nyregion/sexual-harassment-nyu-female-professor.html.
Greenwald, Andy. *Nothing Feels Good: Punk Rock, Teenagers, and Emo*. St. Martin's Griffin, 2003.
Gresson, Aaron D. "Minority Epistemology and the Rhetoric of Creation." *Philosophy and Rhetoric* 10, no. 4 (1977): 244–62.
Griffin, Rachel Alicia. "Gender Violence and the Black Female Body: The Enduring Significance of 'Crazy' Mike Tyson." *Howard Journal of Communication* 24 (2013): 71–94.
Gruber, Aya. *The Feminist War on Crime: The Unexpected Role of Women's Liberation in Mass Incarceration*. University of California Press, 2021.
Gutierrez-Perez, Robert, and Luis Andrade. "Queer of Color Worldmaking: <Marriage> in the Rhetorical Archive and the Embodied Repertoire." *Text and Performance Quarterly* 38, nos. 1-2 (2018): 1–18.
Gunn, Joshua. "Maranatha." *Quarterly Journal of Speech* 98, no. 4 (2012): 359–85.
Gunn, Joshua. *Political Perversion: Rhetorical Aberration in the Time of Trumpeteering*. University of Chicago Press, 2020.
Gunn, Joshua, and Mirko M. Hall. "Stick It in Your Ear: The Psychodynamics of iPod Enjoyment." *Communication and Critical/Cultural Studies* 5, no. 2 (2008): 135–57.
Gutiérrez y Muhs, Gabriella, Yolanda Flores Niemann, Carmen G. González, and Angela P. Harris, eds. *Presumed Incompetent: The Intersections of Race and Class for Women in Academia*. Utah State University Press, 2012.
Halberstam, Jack. *Female Masculinity*. Duke University Press, 2018.
Hall, Ashley R. "'I Love How That Pussy Talk': Black Women, Subversive Reclamation, and the Rhetorical Power of Black Pussy Talk." *Quarterly Journal of Speech* 110, no. 4 (2024): 556–75.

Hall, Ashley R. "Slippin' in and out of Frame: An Afrafuturist Feminist Orientation to Black Women and American Citizenship." *Quarterly Journal of Speech* 106, no. 3 (2020): 341–51.

Hanchey, Jenna N. "Catastrophe Colonialism: Global Disaster Films and the White Right to Migrate." *Journal of International and Intercultural Communication* 16, no. 4 (2023): 300–316.

Hancock, Angie-Marie. *The Politics of Disgust: The Public Identity of the Welfare Queen.* New York University Press, 2004.

Hariman, Robert. "Political Parody and Public Culture." *Quarterly Journal of Speech* 94, no. 3 (2008): 247–72.

Harney, Stefano, and Fred Moten. *The Undercommons: Fugitive Planning and Black Study.* Minor Compositions, 2013.

Hart, Roderick P. "Contemporary Scholarship in Public Address: A Research Editorial." *Western Journal of Speech Communication* 50 (1986): 283–95.

Hartman, Andrew. *A War for the Soul of America, Second Edition: A History of the Culture Wars.* University of Chicago Press, 2019.

Hartman, Saidiya. *Lose Your Mother: A Journey Along the Atlantic Slave Route.* Farrar, Straus and Giroux, 2008.

Hartman, Saidiya. "Venus in Two Acts." *Small Axe: A Caribbean Journal of Criticism* 12, no. 2 (2008): 1–14.

Hartman, Saidiya. *Wayward Lives, Beautiful Experiments: Intimate Histories of Social Upheaval.* W. W. Norton, 2019.

Hartman, Saidiya V. *Scenes of Subjection: Terror, Slavery, and Self-Making in Nineteenth-Century America.* Oxford University Press, 1997.

Harvey, David. *A Brief History of Neoliberalism.* Oxford University Press, 2007.

Hatfield, Joe Edward. "Moments of Shame in the Figural History of Trans Suicide." *Cultural Studies* 37, no. 6 (2023): 813–45.

Hatrick, Jessica. "How to Outlive the University?" *Communication and Critical/Cultural Studies* 17 (2020): 410–17.

Hill, Annie. "Reporting Sexual Harassment: Toward Accountability and Action." *Gender Policy Report*, July 19, 2018. https://genderpolicyreport.umn.edu/reporting-sexual-harassment-towards-accountability-and-action/.

Hill, Annie. "Slutwalk as Perifeminist Response to Rape Logic: The Politics of Reclaiming a Name." *Communication and Critical/Cultural Studies* 13, no. 1 (2016): 23–39.

Hill, Annie, and Carol A. Stabile. "Rhetoric and Sexual Violence: A Conversation with Annie Hill and Carol A. Stabile." *Rhetoric and Public Affairs* 24, no. 1–2 (2021): 149–68.

Hirsch, Jennifer S., and Shamus Khan. *Sexual Citizens: A Landmark Study of Sex, Power, and Assault on Campus.* National Geographic Books, 2020.

Hoerl, Kristen. "Monstrous Youth in Suburbia: Disruption and Recovery of the American Dream." *Southern Communication Journal* 67, no. 3 (2002): 259–75.

Holloway, Wendy. "'I Just Wanted to Kill a Woman.' Why? The Ripper and Male Sexuality." *Feminist Review* 9 (1981): 33–40.

hooks, bell. *Black Looks: Race and Representation.* South End Press, 1992.

hooks, bell. *The Will to Change: Men, Masculinity, and Love.* Washington Square Press, 2004.

Hoover, Eric. "'Animal House' at 30: O Bluto, Where Art Thou?" *Chronicle of Higher Education* 55, no. 2 (2008). https://search.ebscohost.com/login.aspx?direct=true&db=mzh&AN=2008301854&site=eds-live&scope=site&profile=eds-main.

Hopper, Jessica. "Emo: Where the Girls Aren't." *Punk Planet*, July–August 2003, 100–102.

Horkheimer, Max, and Theodor W. Adorno. *Dialectic of Enlightenment: Philosophical Fragments*. Translated by Edmund Jephcott. Stanford University Press, 2002. 1947.

Horvath, Bruna. "Nick Fuentes Confronted at His Home after 'Your Body, My Choice' Refrain Goes Viral." *NBC News*, November 14, 2024. https://www.nbcnews.com/tech/internet/nick-fuentes-confronted-home-body-choice-refrain-goes-viral-rcna179865.

Houdek, Matthew. "In the Aftertimes, Breathe: Rhetorical Technologies of Suffocation and an Abolitionist Praxis of (Breathing in) Relation." *Quarterly Journal of Speech* 108, no. 1 (2022): 48–74.

Hsu, V. Jo. *Constellating Home: Trans and Queer Asian American Rhetorics*. Ohio State University Press, 2022.

Hunter, Nan D. "Contextualizing the Sexuality Debates: A Chronology." In *Sex Wars: Sexual Dissent and Political Culture*, edited by Lisa Duggan and Nan D. Hunter, 16–29. Routledge, 1995.

Huppke, Rex. "Musk, Trump Degrade Federal Workers as They Put Them out of Work. It's Sadistic." *USA Today*, February 12, 2025. https://www.usatoday.com/story/opinion/columnist/2025/02/12/elon-musk-donald-trump-federal-workers-jobs-cruelty/78428472007/.

Ingebretsen, Edward J. *At Stake: Monsters and the Rhetoric of Fear in Public Culture*. University of Chicago Press, 2001.

"Inside the Mind of Jeffrey Dahmer: Serial Killer's Chilling Jailhouse Interview." *Inside Edition*, 1993. https://www.youtube.com/watch?v=iWjYsxaBjBI.

Jackson, Ronald L., II. *Scripting the Black Masculine Body: Identity, Discourse, and Racial Politics in Popular Media*. State University of New York Press, 2006.

Jacoby, Kenny, Nancy Armour, and Jessica Luther. "LSU Mishandled Sexual Misconduct Complaints against Students, Including Top Athletes." *USA Today*, November 16, 2020. https://www.usatoday.com/in-depth/sports/ncaaf/2020/11/16/lsu-ignored-campus-sexual-assault-allegations-against-derrius-guice-drake-davis-other-students/6056388002/.

Jarvis, Brian. "Monsters Inc.: Serial Killers and Consumer Culture." *Crime, Media, Culture* 3, no. 3 (2007): 326–44.

Jenkins, Phillip. *Using Murder: The Social Construction of Serial Homicide*. Aldine de Gruyter, 1994.

Jicha, Tom. "A Look at Ted Bundy in *Stranger*." *South Florida Sun-Sentinel*, March 15, 2003. https://www.sun-sentinel.com/news/fl-xpm-2003-03-16-0304020293-story.html.

Johnson, Amber. "Confessions of a Video Vixen: My Autocritography of Sexuality, Desire, and Memory." *Text and Performance Quarterly* 34, no. 2 (2014): 182–200.

Johnson, Andre W. "My Sanctified Imagination: Carter G. Woodson and a Speculative (Rhetorical) History of African American Public Address, 1925–1960." *Rhetoric and Public Affairs* 24, no. 1–2 (2021): 15–50.

Johnson, E. Patrick. *Appropriating Blackness: Performance and the Politics of Authenticity*. Duke University Press, 2003.

Johnson, Joyce. *Minor Characters: A Beat Memoir*. Methuen, 1999.

Johnson, Paul. "Owning the Libs: The Contemporary Politics of Envy." *Theory and Event* 27, no. 2 (2024): 233–57.

Johnson, Paul Elliott. *I the People: The Rhetoric of Conservative Populism in the United States*. University of Alabama Press, 2022.

Johnson, Richard. "Sad Ending to Frat Flick." *The New York Post*, December 29, 2006. https://web.archive.org/web/20090116162346/http://www.nypost.com/seven/12292006/gossip/pagesix/sad_ending_to_frat_flick_pagesix_.htm.

Jones, Rhian E., and Eli Davies. "Introduction." In *Under My Thumb: Songs That Hate Women and the Women Who Love Them*, edited by Rhian E. Jones and Eli Davies, 1–9. Repeater, 2017.

Kaplan, Michael. "Inside Ted Bundy's Life with Girlfriend Elizabeth Kendall and Her Daughter." *New York Post*, January 4, 2020. https://nypost.com/2020/01/04/inside-ted-bundys-life-with-girlfriend-elizabeth-kendall-and-her-daughter/.

Kehr, Dave. "The Life and Violent Times of a 1970's Serial Killer." *The New York Times*, September 13, 2002. https://www.nytimes.com/2002/09/13/movies/film-review-the-life-and-violent-times-of-a-1970-s-serial-killer.html.

Kelly, Casey Ryan. *Apocalypse Man: The Death Drive and the Rhetoric of White Masculine Victimhood*. Ohio State University Press, 2020.

Kelly, Casey Ryan. *Caught on Tape: White Masculinity and Obscene Enjoyment*. Oxford University Press, 2023.

Kelly, Casey Ryan. "Donald J. Trump and the Rhetoric of *Ressentiment*." *Quarterly Journal of Speech* 106, no. 1 (2020): 2–24.

Kelly, Casey Ryan. "White Pain." *Quarterly Journal of Speech* 107, no. 2 (2021): 209–33.

Kelly, Casey Ryan, and Ryan Neville-Shephard. "Virgin Lands: Gender, Nature, and the Frontier Myth in David Magnusson's *Purity*." *Women's Studies in Communication* 43 (2020): 1–22.

Kendall, Elizabeth. *The Phantom Prince: My Life with Ted Bundy*. Abrams Press, 2020.

Keppel, Robert D., with William J. Birnes. *The Riverman: Ted Bundy and I Hunt for the Green River Killer*. Pocket Books, 2005.

Kermode, Mark. "Matthew Bright: Peculiar Passions." *Independent*, November 9, 2002. https://www.independent.co.uk/arts-entertainment/films/features/matthew-bright-peculiar-passions-126740.html.

Khan, Nilofer. "Andrew Tate and Jordan Peterson: The Far-Reaching Effects of Toxic Internet Father Figures." *Mashable Middle East*, August 23, 2022. https://me.mashable.com/culture/19087/andrew-tate-and-jordan-peterson-the-far-reaching-effects-of-toxic-internet-father-figures.

Kimball, Whitney. "Mary Karr Reminds the World That David Foster Wallace Abused and Stalked Her, and Nobody Cared." *Jezebel*, May 25, 2018. https://jezebel.com/mary-karr-reminds-the-world-that-david-foster-wallace-a-1825799769.

Kimmel, Michael. *Angry White Men: American Masculinity at the End of an Era*. Nation, 2013.

King, Claire Sisco. "It Cuts Both Ways: Fight Club, Masculinity, and Abject Hegemony." *Communication and Critical/Cultural Studies* 6, no. 4 (2009): 366–85.

King, Claire Sisco. *Mapping the Stars: Celebrity, Metonymy, and the Networked Politics of Identity*. Ohio State University Press, 2023.

King, Claire Sisco, and Joshua Gunn. "On a Violence Unseen: The Womanly Object and Sacrificed Man." *Quarterly Journal of Speech* 99, no. 2 (2013): 200–208.

King, Emily L. *Civil Vengeance: Literature, Culture, and Early Modern Revenge*. Cornell University Press, 2019.

Kipnis, Laura. *Bound and Gagged: Pornography and the Politics of Fantasy in America*. Duke University Press, 1996.

Kitchener, Caroline. "A #Metoo Nightmare in the World of Competitive College Speech." *The Atlantic*, March 26, 2019. https://www.theatlantic.com/education/archive/2019/03/students-accuse-gmu-forensics-coach-sexual-harassment/585211/.

Klein, Naomi. *The Shock Doctrine: The Rise of Disaster Capitalism*. Picador, 2008.

Knoll, Jessica. *Bright Young Women*. Marysue Rucci, 2023.
Korn, Sandra Y. L. "When No Means Yes." *The Harvard Crimson*, November 12, 2010. https://www.thecrimson.com/article/2010/11/12/yale-dke-harvard-womens/.
Krebs, Emily. "Queering the Desire to Die: Access Intimacy as Worldmaking for Survival." *Journal of Homosexuality* 70, no. 1 (2023): 168–91.
Kubrick, Stanley. *A Clockwork Orange*. Warner Brothers, 1974.
la paperson. *A Third University Is Possible*. University of Minnesota Press, 2017.
"Lady Killer Nice." *Providence Journal*, May 2, 1986.
Landis, John. *National Lampoon's Animal House*. Universal Pictures, 1978.
Lapin, Andrew. "In Grisly, Sadistic 'The House That Jack Built,' Lars Von Trier Deconstructs Himself." *NPR*, December 13, 2018. https://www.npr.org/2018/12/13/675254118/in-grisly-sadistic-the-house-that-jack-built-lars-von-trier-deconstructs-himself.
Larson, Lauren. "Zac Efron Rides Again." *Men's Health*, October 2022, 54–61.
Larson, Stephanie R. *What It Feels Like: Visceral Rhetoric and the Politics of Rape Culture*. Penn State University Press, 2021.
Lee, Spike. *Malcolm X*. Warner Bros., 1992.
Leff, Michael. "Things Made by Words: Reflections on Textual Criticism." *Quarterly Journal of Speech* 78 (1992): 223–31.
LeMaster, Lore/tta. "Felt Sex: Erotic Affects and a Case for Critical Erotic/a." *Departures in Critical Qualitative Research* 9, no. 3 (2020): 105–11.
LeMaster, Lore/tta. "Suicidal." *Cultural Studies ↔ Critical Methodologies* 22, no. 4 (2022): 391–95.
Lemos, Paul. "Interview with Peter Sotos of Pure." In *Apocalypse Culture*, edited by Adam Parfrey, 125–27. Amok Press, 1987.
Leonoff, Arthur. "Destruo Ergo Sum: Towards a Psychoanalytic Understanding of Sadism." *Canadian Journal of Psychoanalysis* 5, no. 1 (1997): 95–112.
Lesser, Wendy. *Pictures at an Execution: An Inquiry into the Subject of Murder*. Harvard University Press, 1993.
Levina, Marina. "Whiteness and the Joys of Cruelty." *Communication and Critical/Cultural Studies* 15, no. 1 (2018): 73–78.
Levine, Judith. *Harmful to Minors: The Perils of Protecting Children from Sex*. University of Minnesota Press, 2002.
Lewis, Sophie. *Abolish the Family: A Manifesto for Care and Liberation*. Verso, 2022.
Lewis, William F. "Telling America's Story: Narrative Form and the Reagan Presidency." *Quarterly Journal of Speech* 73, no. 3 (1987): 280–302.
Linebaugh, Peter. *The London Hanged: Crime and Civil Society in the Eighteenth Century*. Cambridge University Press, 1992.
Littwin, Susan. "Charmin' Harmon." *TV Guide*, May 3, 1986, 12–15.
Lockwood, Dean. "All Stripped Down: The Spectacle of 'Torture Porn.'" *Popular Communication* 7, no. 1 (2009): 40–48.
Lorde, Audre. *Sister Outsider: Essays and Speeches*. Crossing, 2007.
Lorde, Audre. "The Uses of Anger: Women Responding to Racism." Keynote address, 1981. Accessed July 24, 2019. https://www.blackpast.org/african-american-history/1981-audre-lorde-uses-anger-women-responding-racism/.
Lorde, Audre. "The Uses of the Erotic: The Erotic as Power." In *Sexualities and Communication in Everyday Life: A Reader*, edited by Karen E. Lovaas and Mercilee M. Jenkins, 87–91. SAGE, 2007.

Love, Patricia. *The Emotional Incest Syndrome: What to Do When a Parent's Love Rules Your Life*. Bantam, 1991.
Lowry, Brian. "With Two New Movies, Ted Bundy Is the 'Boogeyman' Who Won't Go Away." *CNN*, August 27, 2021. https://www.cnn.com/2021/08/27/entertainment/ted-bundy-movies/index.html.
Lozano, Nina Maria. *Not One More! Feminicido on the Border*. Ohio State University Press, 2019.
Lugones, María. *Pilgrimages/Peregrinajes: Theorizing Coalition against Multiple Oppressions*. Rowman and Littlefield, 2003.
Lugones, María. "Toward a Decolonial Feminism." *Hypatia*, no. 4 (2010): 742–59.
Lunceford, Brett. "Rhetorical Autoethnography." *Journal of Contemporary Rhetoric* 5, no. 1/2 (2015): 1–20.
Lundberg, Christian O. *Lacan in Public: Psychoanalysis and the Science of Rhetoric*. University of Alabama Press, 2012.
MacDonald, Alzena. "Dissecting the 'Dark Passenger': Reading Representations of Serial Killers." In *Murders and Acquisitions: Representations of the Serial Killer in Popular Culture*, edited by Alzena MacDonald, 1–13. Bloomsbury, 2013.
Macek, J. C., III. "No Texas, No Chainsaw, No Massacre: The True Links in the Chain." *PopMatters*, February 4, 2013. https://www.popmatters.com/167248-no-texas-no-chainsaw-no-massacre-the-true-links-in-the-chain-2495785410.html.
Macías, Kelly. "'Sisters in the Collective Struggle': Sounds of Silence on the Unspoken Assault on Black Females in Modern America." *Cultural Studies ⇔ Critical Methodologies* 15, no. 4 (2015): 260–64.
Mack, Ashley Noel, and Bryan J. McCann. "Critiquing State and Gendered Violence in the Age of #Metoo." *Quarterly Journal of Speech* 104, no. 3 (2018): 329–44.
Mack, Ashley Noel, and Bryan J. McCann. "'Harvey Weinstein, Monster': Antiblackness and the Myth of the Monstrous Rapist." *Communication and Critical/Cultural Studies* (2021). https://doi.org/10.1080/14791420.2020.1854802.
Mack, Ashley Noel, and Bryan J. McCann. "'Strictly an Act of Street Violence': Intimate Publicity and Affective Divestment in the New Orleans Mother's Day Shooting." *Communication and Critical/Cultural Studies* 14, no. 4 (2017): 334–50.
Mack, Ashley Noel, Carli Bershon, Douglas D. Laiche, and Melissa Navarro. "Between Bodies and Institutions: Gendered Violence as Co-Constitutive." *Women's Studies in Communication* 41, no. 2 (2018): 95–99.
Mack, Ashley Noel, and Tiara R. Na'puti. "'Our Bodies Are Not Terra Nullius': Building a Decolonial Feminist Resistance to Gendered Violence." *Women's Studies in Communication* 42, no. 3 (2019): 347–70.
Maclean, Kate. "Gender, Risk, and the Wall Street Alpha Male." *Journal of Gender Studies* 25, no. 4 (2016): 427–44.
MacPherson, Myra. "The Roots of Evil." *Vanity Fair*, May 1989, 140–49, 188–98.
Madison, D. Soyini. "The Dialogic Performative in Critical Ethnography." *Text and Performance Quarterly* 26, no. 4 (2006): 320–24.
Mailer, Norman. "The White Negro." In *The Portable Beat Reader*, edited by Ann Charters, 582–606. Penguin, 1992.
Maldoror. "Peter Sotos Speaking at the Pompidou Centre (2012)." *YouTube*, February 26, 2012. https://www.youtube.com/watch?v=WpJVnQMk1RQ.

Maraj, Louis M. *Black or Right: Anti/Racist Campus Rhetorics*. Utah State University Press, 2020.

Marchiselli, Chani. "Masculine Elocution, New Oratory, and the Voice of Elizabeth Holmes." *Communication and Critical/Cultural Studies* (2024). https://doi.org/10.1080/14791420.2024.2415647.

Mardorossian, Carine M. *Framing the Rape Victim: Gender and Agency Reconsidered*. Rutgers University Press, 2014.

Marshall, Sarah. "The End of Evil." *The Believer*, February 1, 2018. https://www.thebeliever.net/the-end-of-evil/.

Martin, Edna Cowell, and Megan Atkinson. *Dark Tide: Growing Up with Ted Bundy*. Permuted Press, 2024.

Martinez, Aja Y. *Counterstory: The Rhetoric and Writing of Critical Race Theory*. National Council of Teachers of English, 2020.

Masters, Brian. "Dahmer's Inferno." *Vanity Fair*, November 1991. https://archive.vanityfair.com/article/1991/11/dahmers-inferno.

Matheson, Calum Lister. "Liberal Tears and the Rogue's Yarn of Sadistic Conservativism." *Rhetoric Society Quarterly* 52, no. 4 (2022): 341–55.

Mbembe, Achille. *Critique of Black Reason*. Duke University Press, 2017.

McCann, Bryan. "12/31/95." *Edda* 35 (1997): 72.

McCann, Bryan J. "Economies of Misery: Success and Surplus in the Research University." *Communication and Critical/Cultural Studies* 20, no. 1 (2023): 54–71.

McCann, Bryan J. "Entering the Darkness: Rhetorics of Transformation and Gendered Violence in Patty Jenkins's Monster." *Women's Studies in Communication* 37, no. 1 (2014): 1–21. https://doi.org/10.1080/07491409.2013.867914.

McCann, Bryan J. "Lonely Young American: Queer Terrorist Recruitment and the Trope of the Child." *QED: A Journal in GLBTQ Worldmaking* 7, no. 2 (2020): 25–47.

McCann, Bryan J. "Therapeutic and Material <Victim>hood: Ideology and the Struggle for Meaning in the Illinois Death Penalty Controversy." *Communication and Critical/Cultural Studies* 4, no. 4 (2007): 382–401.

McClearen, Jennifer. "Neoliberal Masculinity in the Ultimate Fighting Championship." *Communication and Critical/Cultural Studies* 20, no. 4 (2023): 435–52.

McCune, Jeffrey Q., Jr. *Sexual Discretion: Black Masculinity and the Politics of Passing*. University of Chicago Press, 2014.

McGee, Michael Calvin. "'In Search of 'the People': A Rhetorical Alternative." *Quarterly Journal of Speech* 61, no. 3 (1975): 235–49.

McGee, Michael Calvin. "Text, Context, and the Fragmentation of Contemporary Culture." *Western Journal of Communication* 54 (1990): 274–89.

McGowan, Todd. "Looking for the Gaze: Lacanian Film Theory and Its Vicissitudes." *Cinema Journal* 42, no. 3 (2003): 27–47.

McKerrow, Raymie E. "Critical Rhetoric: Theory and Praxis." *Communication Monographs* 56 (1989): 91–111.

McNamara, Brittney. "Sexual Assault Activism and the #Metoo Era: Four Activists on How the World Has Changed." *Teen Vogue*, December 19, 2019. https://www.teenvogue.com/story/sexual-assault-activism-20teens.

Meiners, Erica R. *For the Children? Protecting Innocence in a Carceral State*. University of Minnesota Press, 2016.

Meranze, Michael. *Laboratories of Virtue: Punishment, Revolution, and Authority in Philadelphia, 1760–1835.* University of North Carolina Press, 1996.
Michallon, Clémence. "Do We Really Need Another Series About Ted Bundy? The Answer Is Yes—Because We Still Haven't Admitted His Misogyny." *Independent*, October 18, 2019. https://www.independent.co.uk/voices/ted-bundy-series-amazon-falling-for-a-killer-elizabeth-kendall-girlfiriend-daughter-molly-a9162411.html.
Michaud, Stephen G., and Hugh Aynesworth. *Conversations with a Killer: The Ted Bundy Tapes.* Sterling, 2019.
Michaud, Stephen G., and Hugh Aynesworth. *The Only Living Witness: The True Story of Serial Sex Killer Ted Bundy.* Authorlink, 1999.
"Michael Reilly Burke." Internet Movie Database. https://www.imdb.com/name/nm0121805/.
Miéville, China. "On Social Sadism." *Salvage*, December 17, 2015. https://salvage.zone/on-social-sadism/.
Mignolo, Walter D. *The Darker Side of Western Modernity: Global Futures, Decolonial Options.* Duke University Press, 2011.
Miller, Carolyn R., Amy J. Devitt, and Victoria J. Gallagher. "Genre: Permanence and Change." *Rhetoric Society Quarterly* 48, no. 3 (2018): 269–77.
Mills, Nancy. "Mark Harmon's Acting Face." *Los Angeles Times*, April 28, 1986. ProQuest.
Moraga, Cherríe, and Gloria Anzaldúa, ed. *This Bridge Called My Back: Writings by Radical Women of Color.* 4th ed. State University of New York Press, 2015.
Moreton-Robinson, Aileen. *The White Possessive: Property, Power, and Indigenous Sovereignty.* University of Minnesota Press, 2015.
Morris, Charles E., III. "The Archival Turn in Rhetorical Studies; or, the Archive's Rhetorical (Re)Turn." *Rhetoric and Public Affairs* 9, no. 1 (2006): 113–15.
Morris, Charles E., III. "Introduction: Portrait of a Queer Rhetorical/Historical Critic." In *Queering Public Address: Sexualities in American Historical Discourse*, edited by Charles E. Morris III, 1–19. University of South Carolina Press, 2007.
Morris, Charles E., III. "(Self-)Portrait of Prof. R.C.: A Retrospective." *Western Journal of Communication* 74, no. 1 (2010): 4–42.
Morris, Charles E., III. "Sunder the Children: Abraham Lincoln's Queer Rhetorical Pedagogy." *Quarterly Journal of Speech* 99, no. 4 (2013): 395–422.
Morris, Charles E., III, and John M. Sloop. "'What Lips These Lips Have Kissed': Refiguring the Politics of Queer Public Kissing." *Communication and Critical/Cultural Studies* 3, no. 1 (2006): 1–26.
Morton, Robert J., ed. *Serial Murder: Multi-Disciplinary Perspectives for Investigators.* US Department of Justice, 2005.
Moten, Fred. *Stolen Life.* Duke University Press, 2018.
Mulvey, Laura. "Visual Pleasure and Narrative Cinema." *Screen* 16, no. 3 (1975): 6–18.
Muñiz, Julissa O. "Exclusionary Discipline Policies, School-Police Partnerships, Surveillance Technologies and Disproportionality: A Review of the School to Prison Pipeline Literature." *Urban Review* 53 (2021): 735–60.
Muñoz, José Esteban. *Cruising Utopia: The Then and There of Queer Futurity.* New York University Press, 2019.
Muñoz, José Esteban. "Ephemera as Evidence: Introductory Notes to Queer Acts." *Women and Performance: A Journal of Feminist Theory* 8, no. 2 (1996): 5–16.

Nagourney, Adam, Michael Cieply, Alan Feuer, and Ian Lovett. "Before Brief, Deadly Spree, Trouble Since Age 8." *The New York Times*, June 1, 2014. https://www.nytimes.com/2014/06/02/us/elliot-rodger-killings-in-california-followed-years-of-withdrawal.html.

Nakayama, Thomas K., and Robert L. Krizek. "Whiteness: A Strategic Rhetoric." *Quarterly Journal of Speech* 81, no. 3 (1995): 291–309.

Napoli, Jessica, and Tyler McCarthy. "Zac Efron Says White Privilege Allowed Ted Bundy to Kill for So Long Before Being Captured." *Fox News*, May 3, 2019. https://www.foxnews.com/entertainment/zac-efron-ted-bundy-white-privilege.

Nash, Jennifer C. *The Black Body in Ecstasy: Reading Race, Reading Pornography*. Duke University Press, 2014.

"National Lampoon's Animal House." NPR, July 29, 2002. https://web.archive.org/web/20100128032723/http://www.npr.org/programs/morning/features/patc/animalhouse/.

Nelson, Maggie. *The Art of Cruelty: A Reckoning*. W. W. Norton, 2011.

Nelson, Maggie. *Jane: A Murder*. Soft Skull Press, 2005.

Nelson, Polly. *Defending the Devil: My Story as Ted Bundy's Last Lawyer*. Echo Point, 1994.

Neville-Shepard, Ryan, and Meredith Neville-Shepard. "The Pornified Presidency: Hyper-Masculinity and the Pornographic Style in U.S. Political Rhetoric." *Feminist Media Studies* 21, no. 7 (2021): 1193–208.

Newitz, Annalee. *Pretend We're Dead: Capitalist Monsters in American Pop Culture*. Duke University Press, 2006.

Nietzsche, Friedrich. *The Genealogy of Morals*. 1887. Project Gutenberg, 2016. https://www.gutenberg.org/files/52319/52319-h/52319-h.htm.

Nightshade, Jane. "Bundyrama: Five Actors Who Played Ted Bundy before Zac Efron." *HorrorNews.Net*, July 29, 2019. https://horrornews.net/127875/bundyrama-five-actors-played-ted-bundy-zac-efron/.

Nine Inch Nails. "Something I Can Never Have." *Pretty Hate Machine*. TVT, 1989.

Nordheimer, Jon. "All-American Boy on Trial." *The New York Times*, December 10, 1978. https://www.nytimes.com/1978/12/10/archives/allamerican-boy-on-trial-ted-bundy.html.

Nyong'o, Tavia. *Afro-Fabulations: The Queer Drama of Black Life*. New York University Press, 2018.

O'Brien, Jon, and Marika Kazimierska. "Whatever Happened to Chad Michael Murray?" *Nicki Swift*, May 10, 2022. https://www.nickiswift.com/339444/whatever-happened-to-chad-michael-murray/.

Ochieng, Omedi. "Infraconstitutive Rhetoric: Insurgent Abolition and the Black Radical Imagination." *Quarterly Journal of Speech* 110, no. 4 (2024): 530–55.

OED Online. Oxford University Press, 2021.

Olofson, Sascha. *Ted Bundy: Natural Porn Killer*. Channel 4, 2006.

Olson, Carl. "Eroticism, Violence, and Sacrifice: A Postmodern Theory of Religion and Ritual." *Method and Theory in the Study of Religion* 6, no. 3 (1994): 231–50.

Oluo, Ijeoma. *Mediocre: The Dangerous Legacy of White Male America*. Seal Press, 2021.

Ono, Kent A., and John M. Sloop. "The Critique of Vernacular Discourse." *Communication Monographs* 62 (1995): 19–46.

Ore, Ersula J. *Lynching: Violence, Rhetoric, and American Identity*. University Press of Mississippi, 2019.

Palczewski, Catherine Helen. "Contesting Pornography: Terministic Catharsis and Definitional Argument." *Argumentation and Advocacy* 38, no. 1 (2001): 1–17.

Panic! At the Disco. "Lying Is the Most Fun a Girl Can Have without Taking Her Clothes Off." *A Fever You Can't Sweat Out*. Fueled by Ramen, 2005.
Parfrey, Adam. "From Pulp to Posterity: The Origins of Men's Adventure Magazines." In *It's a Man's World: Men's Adventure Magazines, the Postwar Pulps*, edited by Adam Parfrey, 29–34. Feral House, 2015.
Pasolini, Pier. *Salò, or the 120 Days of Sodom*. United Artists, 1975.
Paxton, Mark. "Student Free Expression Rights and the Columbine Shootings." *Free Speech Yearbook* 37, no. 1 (1999): 135–43.
Peace, David. *Nineteen Eighty-Three: The Red Riding Quartet, Book Four*. Vintage Crime/Black Lizard, 2010.
Pearson, Kyra. "The Trouble with Aileen Wuornos, Feminism's 'First Serial Killer.'" *Communication and Critical/Cultural Studies* 4, no. 3 (2007): 256–75.
Peperzak, Adriaan T., Simon Critchley, and Robert Bernasconi, editors. *Emmanuel Levinas: Basic Philosophical Writings*. Indiana University Press, 1996.
Perlstein, Rick. *Reaganland: America's Right Turn 1976–1980*. Simon and Schuster, 2020.
Peterson, Molly. "National Lampoon's Animal House." NPR, July 29, 2002. https://web.archive.org/web/20100128032723/http://www.npr.org/programs/morning/features/patc/animalhouse/.
Petty, Richard Warren, and Lisa Erin Sanchez. "Transactions in the Flesh: Toward an Ethnography of Embodied Sexual Reason." *Studies in Law, Politics, and Society* 18 (1998): 29–76.
Pezzullo, Phaedra C. "Performing Critical Interruptions: Stories, Rhetorical Invention, and the Environmental Justice Movement." *Western Journal of Communication* 65, no. 1 (2001): 1–25.
Phelan, Peggy. *Unmarked: The Politics of Performance*. Routledge, 1996.
Phillips, Joshua Daniel, and Rachel Alicia Griffin. "Crystal Mangum as Hypervisible Object and Invisible Subject: Black Feminist Thought, Sexual Violence, and the Pedagogical Repercussions of the Duke Lacrosse Rape Case." *Women's Studies in Communication* 38, no. 1 (2015): 36–56.
Phillips, Kendall R. "Affective Seams in the Discourses of the Present." *Critical Studies in Media Communication* 29, no. 1 (2012): 1–6.
Phillips, Kendall R. *A Place of Darkness: The Rhetoric of Horror in Early American Cinema*. University of Texas Press, 2018.
Pinsky, Mark. "Just an Excitable Boy?" *New Times*, November 27, 1978, 53–64.
Polman, Dick. "Bundy's Porn Message Fuels One Final Conflict." *Orlando Sentinel*, February 21, 1989. NewsBank.
Povinelli, Elizabeth A. *The Empire of Love: Toward a Theory of Intimacy, Genealogy, and Carnality*. Duke University Press, 2006.
Puar, Jasbir K. *Terrorist Assemblages: Homonationalism in Queer Times*. Duke University Press, 2017.
Quincey, Thomas de. *On Murder Considered as One of the Fine Arts: Being an Address Made to a Gentlemen's Club Concerning its Aesthetic Appreciation*. 1827. CreateSpace, 2014.
Ramsland, Katherine. "Girls Who Love Ted Bundy." *Psychology Today*, October 21, 2019. https://www.psychologytoday.com/us/blog/shadow-boxing/201910/girls-who-love-ted-bundy.
Rand, Ayn. *The Journals of Ayn Rand*. Edited by David Harriman. Dutton, 1997.

Rand, Erin J. "An Inflammatory Fag and a Queer Form: Larry Kramer, Polemics, and Rhetorical Agency." *Quarterly Journal of Speech* 94, no. 3 (2008): 297–319.
Rand, Erin J. "Protecting the Figure of Innocence: Child Pornography Legislation and the Queerness of Childhood." *Quarterly Journal of Speech* 105, no. 3 (2019): 251–72.
Raskin, Lisi. "Updating (the) Uses of the Erotic." *Brooklyn Rail*, September 2014. https://brooklynrail.org/2014/09/criticspage/updating-the-uses-of-the-erotic-from-georges-bataille-and-jean-genet-to-audre-lorde-and-bell-hooks.
Rasmussen, Cecilia. "Girl's Grisly Killing Had City Residents up in Arms." *Los Angeles Times*, February 5, 2001, VCB7.
Ray, Victor. "The Unbearable Whiteness of Mesearch." *Inside Higher Ed*, October 21, 2016. https://www.insidehighered.com/advice/2016/10/21/me-studies-are-not-just-conducted-people-color-essay.
Raymond, Gabby. "The 16 Best True Crime Books of All Time." *Time*, November 20, 2019. https://time.com/5355643/best-true-crime-books-of-all-time/.
Reddy, Chandan. *Freedom with Violence: Race, Sexuality, and the US State*. Duke University Press, 2011.
Reeves, Jimmie L., and Richard Campbell. *Cracked Coverage: Television News, the Anti-Cocaine Crusade, and the Reagan Legacy*. Duke University Press, 1994.
Reeves, Richard. *President Kennedy: Profile of Power*. Simon & Schuster, 1993.
Renan, Sheldon. *The Killing of America*. Toho-Towa, 1982.
Rice, Jenny. "Unframing Models of Public Distribution: From Rhetorical Situation to Rhetorical Ecologies." *Rhetoric Society Quarterly* 35, no. 4 (2005): 5–24.
Richie, Beth E. *Arrested Justice: Black Women, Violence, and America's Prison Nation*. New York University Press, 2012.
Ritchie, Andrea J. *Invisible No More: Police Violence Against Black Women and Women of Color*. Beacon, 2017.
Roberts, Mary Louise. *What Soldiers Do: Sex and the American GI in World War II France*. University of Chicago Press, 2013.
Robinson, Brett A. B. "Introduction—From the Shadows to Our Living Rooms: Serial Killers on Popular TV after 9/11." In *Serial Killers in Contemporary Television: Familiar Monsters in Post-9/11 Culture*, edited by Brett A. B. Robinson and Christine Daigle, 1–16. Routledge, 2021.
Robinson, Joanna. "This Is the *Joker* the Trump Era Deserves—but Not the One We Need Right Now." *Vanity Fair*, October 4, 2019. https://www.vanityfair.com/hollywood/2019/10/joker-joaquin-phoenix-trump-era.
Rodger, Elliot. "My Twisted World: The Story of Elliot Rodger." https://www.documentcloud.org/documents/1173808-elliot-rodger-manifesto/.
Roediger, David R. *The Wages of Whiteness: Race and the Making of the American Working Class*. Verso, 1999.
Rosenfield, Lawrence W. "Politics and Pornography." *Quarterly Journal of Speech* 59, no. 4 (1973): 413–22.
Rothstein, Andrew. "Ted Bundy: The Mind of a Killer." *Biography*, September 12, 1995. https://www.youtube.com/watch?v=k-X6U87wrg4.
Rowe, Aimee Carrillo. "Erotic Pedagogies." *Journal of Homosexuality* 59 (2012): 1031–56.
Rowland, Allison L. "Small Dick Problems: Masculine Entitlement as Rhetorical Strategy." *Quarterly Journal of Speech* 109, no. 1 (2023): 26–47.

Rubin, Kathy Kleiner, and Emilie Le Beau Lucchesi. *A Light in the Dark: Surviving More Than Ted Bundy*. Chicago Review Press, 2024.
Rule, Ann. *The Stranger Beside Me*. Gallery Books, 2009.
Rushing, Janice Hocker. "The Rhetoric of the American Western Myth." *Communication Monographs* 50, no. 1 (1983): 14–32.
Ryalls, Emily. "Emo Angst, Masochism, and Masculinity in Crisis." *Text and Performance Quarterly* 33, no. 2 (2013): 83–97.
Sade, Marquis de. "Philosophy in the Bedroom." Edited and translated by Richard Seaver and Austryn Wainhouse. In *Justine, Philosophy in the Bedroom, and Other Writings*, 178–367. Grove Press, 1965.
Sade, Marquis de. *The 120 Days of Sodom, or the School of Libertinage*. Translated by Will McMorran and Thomas Wynn. 1904. Penguin, 2016.
Sandoval, Chela. *Methodology of the Oppressed*. University of Minnesota Press, 2000.
Sarat, Austin. *When the State Kills: Capital Punishment and the American Condition*. Princeton University Press, 2002.
Sartre, Jean-Paul. *Saint Genet: Actor and Martyr*. University of Minnesota Press, 2012.
Sayles, Justin. "The Bloody Bubble." *The Ringer*, July 9, 2021. https://www.theringer.com/tv/2021/7/9/22567381/true-crime-documentaries-boom-bubble-netflix-hbo.
Scarry, Elaine. *The Body in Pain: The Making and Unmaking of the World*. Oxford University Press, 1985.
Schaefer, Donovan O. "Whiteness and Civilization: Shame, Race, and the Rhetoric of Donald Trump." *Communication and Critical/Cultural Studies* 17, no. 1 (2020): 1–18.
Schares, Evan Mitchell. "Witnessing the Archive: Stormé Delarverie and Queer Performance Historicity." *Text and Performance Quarterly* 40, no. 3 (2020): 250–67.
Schmid, David. *Natural Born Celebrities: Serial Killers in American Culture*. University of Chicago Press, 2005.
Sealey, Amber. *No Man of God*. RLJE Films, 2021.
Sedgwick, Eve Kosofsky. *Between Men: English Literature and Male Homosocial Desire*. Columbia University Press, 1985.
Segarra, Ignacio Moreno, and Karrin Vasby Anderson. "Political Pornification Gone Global: Teresa Rodríguez as Fungible Object in the 2015 Spanish Regional Elections." *Quarterly Journal of Speech* 105, no. 2 (2019): 204–28.
Seifrit-Griffin, Stacie. "On the Film Registry: 'National Lampoon's Animal House' (1978): An Interview with Tim Matheson." *Library of Congress*, August 2, 2021. https://blogs.loc.gov/now-see-hear/2021/08/national-lampoons-animal-house-1978-an-interview-with-tim-matheson/.
Seltzer, Mark. *Serial Killers: Death and Life in America's Wound Culture*. Routledge, 1998.
Sexton, Jared Yates. *The Man They Wanted Me to Be: Toxic Masculinity and a Crisis of Our Own Making*. Counterpoint, 2020.
Shaffer, Tracy Stephenson. "The Place of Performance in Performance Studies." *Text and Performance Quarterly* 40, no. 1 (2020): 49–71.
Shapiro, Paul. *Ann Rule Presents: The Stranger Beside Me*. Sonar, 2003.
Shattuck, Roger. *Forbidden Knowledge: From Prometheus to Pornography*. Harvest, 1996.
Sicha, Choire. "The Last Chance to Learn Jeffrey Epstein's Secrets Closes." *Intelligencer*, 2022. https://nymag.com/intelligencer/2022/02/exasd-epstein-prince-andrew.html.
Siemaszko, Corky. "How Richard Speck's Rampage 50 Years Ago Changed a Nation." *NBC News*, July 13, 2016. https://www.nbcnews.com/news/crime-courts/how-richard-speck-s-rampage-50-years-ago-changed-nation-n606211.

Silva, Kumarini. "Having the Time of Our Lives: Love-Cruelty as Patriotic Impulse." *Communication and Critical/Cultural Studies* 15, no. 1 (2018): 79–84.
Simpson, Philip L. *Psycho Paths: Tracking the Serial Killer through Contemporary American Film and Fiction*. Southern Illinois University Press, 2000.
Singh, Julietta. *No Archive Will Restore You*. Punctum Books, 2018.
Singh, Julietta. *Unthinking Mastery: Dehumanism and Decolonial Entanglements*. Duke University Press, 2018.
Smith, Craig R. "Ronald Reagan's Rhetorical Re-Invention of Conservatism." *Quarterly Journal of Speech* 103, nos. 1–2 (2017): 33–65.
Sodergren, David. "Visions from Beyond the Dave #2—Ted Bundy (2002)." *Kendall Reviews*, March 1, 2019. http://kendallreviews.com/visions-from-beyond-the-dave-2-ted-bundy-2002-matthew-bright/.
"Sometime Around Midnight." *Genius*, August 5, 2008. https://genius.com/2233217.
Sontag, Susan. "The Pornographic Imagination." *Partisan Review* 34, no. 2 (1967): 181–212.
Sontag, Susan. *Regarding the Pain of Others*. Picador, 2003.
Sotos, Peter. *Pure*. 1984.
Sotos, Peter. *Pure #2*. 1984.
Sowards, Stacey K. "The (Under)Commons across the Américas: Connecting Spaces for Fugitivity and Futurity." *Rhetoric Society Quarterly* 53, no. 3 (2023): 301–15.
Spanos, Brittany. "Ted Bundy and Charles Manson Fans Are Deep in a Twitter Feud." *Rolling Stone*, August 15, 2019. https://www.rollingstone.com/culture/culture-news/ted-bundy-charles-manson-stan-twitter-war-871495/.
Spielberg, Steven. *Indiana Jones and the Raiders of the Lost Ark*. Paramount, 1981.
Spieldenner, Andrew R., and Shinsuke Eguichi. "Different Sameness: Queer Autoethnography and Coalition Politics." *Cultural Studies ⇔ Critical Methodologies* 20, no. 2 (2020): 134–43.
Spillers, Hortense J. "Mama's Baby, Papa's Maybe: An American Grammar Book." *Diacritics* 17, no. 2 (1987): 65–81. https://doi.org/10.2307/464747. http://www.jstor.org/stable/464747.
Springer, Andrew. "The Secret Life of Elliot Rodger." *ABC News*, June 27, 2014. https://abcnews.go.com/US/fullpage/secret-life-elliot-rodger-24322227.
Squires, Catherine R. "Rethinking the Black Public Sphere: An Alternative Vocabulary for Multiple Public Spheres." *Communication Theory* 12, no. 4 (2002): 446–68.
Stabile, Carol. "Confronting Sexual Harassment and Hostile Climates in Higher Education." *Ms.*, December 13, 2017. https://msmagazine.com/2017/12/13/confronting-sexual-harassment-hostile-climates-higher-education/.
Steffensmeier, Timothy R. "Sacred Saturdays: College Football and Local Identity." In *Sporting Rhetoric: Performance, Games, and Politics*, edited by Barry Brummett, 218–34. Peter Lang, 2009.
Steinem, Gloria. "Erotica and Pornography: A Clear and Present Difference." In *Take Back the Night: Women on Pornography*, edited by Laura Lederer, 35–39. William Morrow, 1980.
Stevenson, Robert Louis. *The Strange Case of Dr. Jekyll and Mr. Hyde*. Reader's Library Classics, 1886.
Stiles, Stephen. "Fatal Addiction: Ted Bundy's Final Interview." Focus on the Family, 1989.
Stoler, Ann Laura. "Archival Dis-Ease: Thinking through Colonial Ontologies." *Communication and Critical/Cultural Studies* 7, no. 2 (2010): 215–19.
Stosuy, Brandon. "Interview with Peter Sotos." *Fanziine*, January 19, 2006. http://thefanzine.com/interview-with-peter-sotos-2/.

Stratton, Jon. "Serial Killing and the Transformation of the Social." *Theory, Culture and Society* 13, no. 1 (1996): 77–98.
Subirats, Eduardo. "Totalitarian Lust: From *Salò* to Abu Ghraib." *South Central Review* 24, no. 1 (2007): 174–82.
Sullivan, Kevin M. *The Bundy Murders: A Comprehensive History*. 2nd ed. McFarland, 2020.
Sun, Chyng, Ana Bridges, Jennifer A. Johnson, and Matthew B. Ezzell. "Pornography and the Male Sexual Script: An Analysis of Consumption and Sexual Relations." *Archives of Sexual Behavior* 45 (2016): 983–94.
Szpunar, Piotr M. *Homegrown: Identity and Difference in the American War on Terror*. New York University Press, 2018.
Tait, Sue. "Pornographies of Violence? Internet Spectatorship on Body Horror." *Critical Studies in Media Communication* 25, no. 1 (2008): 91–111.
Tatar, Maria. *Lustmord: Sexual Murder in Weimar Germany*. Princeton University Press, 1995.
Taylor, Diana. *The Archive and the Repertoire: Performing Cultural Memory in the Americas*. Duke University Press, 2007.
"Ted Bundy." *CineSchlocker*, 2002. https://cineschlocker.net/ted-bundy/.
"Ted Bundy (2002)." *Rotten Tomatoes*. https://www.rottentomatoes.com/m/ted_bundy.
Ted Bundy Multiagency Investigative Team Report. Federal Bureau of Investigation (1992). http://www.santarosahitchhikermurders.com/docs/Bundy_Multiagency_Team_Report.pdf.
Telfer, Tori. "Ted Bundy's Living Victim Tells Her Story." *Rolling Stone*, January 27, 2019. https://www.rollingstone.com/culture/culture-features/ted-bundy-kathy-kleiner-living-victim-serial-killer-784780/.
Tenreyro, Tatiana. "Olivia Newton-John Responds to Recent Grease Discourse, Says People Need to 'Relax.'" AV Club, February 5, 2021. https://www.avclub.com/olivia-newton-john-responds-to-recent-grease-discourse-1846205175.
Terry, David P. "Once Blind, Now Seeing: Problematics of Confessional Performance." *Text and Performance Quarterly* 26, no. 3 (2006): 209–28.
Thelin, John R. *A History of American Higher Education*. 3rd ed. Johns Hopkins University Press, 2019.
Theweleit, Klaus. *Male Fantasies, Volume 1: Women, Floods, Bodies, History*. Translated by Stephen Conway. University of Minnesota Press, 1987.
Thorsen, Karen. "An Intimate Revolution in Campus Life." *Life*, November 20, 1970, 32–39.
Thuma, Emily L. *All Our Trials: Prisons, Policing, and the Feminist Fight to End Violence*. University of Illinois Press, 2019.
"Tim Walz: How Does Kamala Harris's VP Pick View Israel, Palestine, China?" *Al Jazeera*, August 7, 2024. https://www.aljazeera.com/features/2024/8/7/tim-walz-how-does-harriss-vp-pick-view-israel-palestine-and-china.
Tithecott, Richard. *Of Men and Monsters: Jeffrey Dahmer and the Construction of the Serial Killer*. University of Wisconsin Press, 1998.
Tolentino, Jia. "Mike Pence's Marriage and the Beliefs That Keep Women from Power." *The New Yorker*, March 31, 2017. https://www.newyorker.com/culture/jia-tolentino/mike-pences-marriage-and-the-beliefs-that-keep-women-from-power.
Tomkins, Silvan. *Shame and Its Sisters: A Silvan Tomkins Reader*, edited by Eve Kosofsky Sedgwick and Adam Frank. Duke University Press, 1995.

"The Top 50 Report-2019." Wikipedia, 2019. https://en.wikipedia.org/wiki/Wikipedia:2019_Top_50_Report.
Towns, Armond R. "Toward a Black Media Philosophy." *Cultural Studies* 34, no. 6 (2020): 851–73.
Tron, Gina. "Who Was the Real Kathleen McChesney, the Trailblazing Detective Depicted in 'American Boogeyman'?" *Oxygen*, December 13, 2021. https://www.oxygen.com/true-crime-buzz/who-was-the-real-detective-kathleen-mcchesney-from-ted-bundy-american-boogeyman.
Tucciarone, Krista M. "Cinematic College: *National Lampoon's Animal House* Teaches Theories of Student Development." *College Student Journal* 41, no. 4 (2007).
Trilling, Lionel. "Art and Neuroses." In *The Liberal Imagination*, 160–80. New York Review of Books, 2008.
Tristano, Michael, Jr. "For ~~My~~ Students Considering Abolition in *Communication and Gender*." *Women's Studies in Communication* 47, no. 2 (2024): 109–14.
University Network for Human Rights. "Genocide in Gaza: Analysis of International Law and Its Application to Israel's Military Actions Since October 7, 2023," May 15, 2024. https://static1.squarespace.com/static/66a134337e960f229da81434/t/66fb05bb0497da472 6e125d8/1727727037094/Genocide+in+Gaza+-+Final+version+051524.pdf.
Valencia, Sayak. *Gore Capitalism*. Translated by John Pluecker. South Pasadena, CA: Semiotext(e), 2018.
VanHaitsma, Pamela. *The Erotic as Rhetorical Power: Archives of Romantic Friendship Between Women Teachers*. Ohio State University Press, 2024.
Von Drehle, Dave. "Execution Ends Bundy Horror Macabre Carnival." *Miami Herald*, January 25, 1989, 1A.
Vronsky, Peter. *Sons of Cain: A History of Serial Killers from the Stone Age to the Present*. Penguin Random House, 2018.
Walkowitz, Judith R. "Jack the Ripper and the Myth of Male Violence." *Feminist Studies* 8, no. 3 (1982): 542–74.
Wallace, Carol, and James Grant. "Charmin' Harmon." *People*, January 27, 1986, 46–52.
Wallace, David Foster. *Infinite Jest*. Back Bay Books, 1996.
Waller, Gregory A. "An Annotated Filmography of R-Rated Sexploitation Films Released During the 1970s." *Journal of Popular Film and Television* 9, no. 2 (1981): 98–112.
Wander, Philip. "The Third Persona: An Ideological Turn in Rhetorical Theory." *Central States Speech Journal* 35 (1984): 197–216.
Wanjuki, Wagatwe. "Dear Tufts Administrators Who Expelled Me after My Sexual Assaults." *Medium*, April 21, 2016. https://medium.com/the-establishment/dear-tufts-administrators-who-expelled-me-after-my-sexual-assaults-25d109c464f6.
Wanzer-Serrano, Darrel. "Decolonizing Imaginaries: Rethinking 'the People' in the Young Lords' Church Offensive." *Quarterly Journal of Speech* 98, no. 1 (2012): 1–23.
Wanzer-Serrano, Darrel. "Delinking Rhetoric, or Revisiting McGee's Fragmentation Thesis Through Decoloniality." *Rhetoric and Public Affairs* 15, no. 4 (2012): 647–58.
Wanzer-Serrano, Darrel. *The New York Young Lords and the Struggle for Liberation*. Temple University Press, 2015.
Wanzer-Serrano, Darrel. "Rhetoric's Rac(e/ist) Problems." *Quarterly Journal of Speech* 105, no. 4 (2019): 465–76.
Ward, Jane. *The Tragedy of Heterosexuality*. New York University Press, 2020.

Warner, Michael. *Publics and Counterpublics*. Zone Books, 2002.
"'Wasted Life'; Bundy Gets 3rd Death Sentence." *Spokesman-Review*, February 13, 1980, A11.
Watkins, S. Craig. *Hip Hop Matters: Politics, Pop Culture, and the Struggle for the Soul of a Movement*. Beacon Press, 2006.
Watts, Eric King. "A Monstrous Genre—Violent 'Man.'" *Quarterly Journal of Speech* 107, no. 2 (2021): 235–38.
Weezer. "Across the Sea." *Pinkerton*. DGC and Geffen, 1996.
Weheliye, Alexander G. *Habeas Viscus: Racializing Assemblages, Biopolitics, and the Black Feminist Theories of the Human*. Duke University Press, 2014.
Werner, Maggie M. *Stripped: Reading the Erotic Body*. Pennsylvania State University Press, 2020.
Whippman, Ruth. "We Can Do Better than 'Positive Masculinity.'" *The New York Times*, October 8, 2024. https://www.nytimes.com/2024/10/08/opinion/positive-masculinity.html?smid=nytcore-ios-share&referringSource=articleshare.
Wichelns, Herbert A. "The Literary Criticism of Oratory." In *Studies in Rhetoric and Public Speaking: In Honor of James Albert Winans*, 181–216. Century, 1925.
Wiggins, Kyle. "Introduction." In *American Revenge Narratives: A Collection of Critical Essays*, edited by Kyle Wiggins, 1–18. Cham, Switzerland: Palgrave Macmillan, 2018.
Wilber, Del Quentin. "A Texas Ranger Got a Prolific Serial Killer to Talk. This Is How." *Los Angeles Times*, September 26, 2019. https://www.latimes.com/world-nation/story/2019-09-25/exas-ranger-got-one-of-the-nations-worst-serial-killers-to-talk-this-is-how.
Wilderson, Frank B., III. *Red, White and Black*. Duke University Press, 2010.
Wildfire, Jessica. "Ted Bundy: The First Incel." *Pulp*, January 24, 2019. https://www.thepulpmag.com/articles/ted-bundy-the-first-incel.
Williams, DJ. "Is Serial Sexual Homicide a Compulsion, Deviant Leisure, or Both? Revisiting the Case of Ted Bundy." *Leisure Sciences* 42, no. 2 (2020): 205–23.
Williams, Linda. *Hard Core: Power, Pleasure, and the "Frenzy of the Visible."* University of California Press, 1989.
Wohead, Greg. *The Ted Bundy Project*. https://gregwohead.files.wordpress.com/2014/08/the-ted-bundy-project-info-pack.pdf.
Woititz, Janet G. *Adult Children of Alcoholics*. Health Communications, 1990.
Wood, Trish. *Ted Bundy: Falling for a Killer*. Amazon, 2020.
Yamato, Jen. "'The Ted Bundy Tapes' and 'Shockingly Evil': Why Joe Berlinger Doubled Down on the Serial Killer." *Los Angeles Times*, February 7, 2019. https://www.latimes.com/entertainment/movies/la-ca-mn-Sunday-conversation-joe-berlinger-ted-bundy-20190207-story.html.
"YouTube Video: Retribution." *The New York Times*, May 24, 2014. https://www.nytimes.com/video/us/100000002900707/youtube-video-retribution.html.

INDEX

Abdurraqib, Hanif, 142
abject hegemony, 47. *See also* King, Claire Sisco
addiction, 8, 14, 18, 19, 20, 37–39, 54, 59–63, 65–66, 68–69, 77, 80, 84, 92, 96, 125, 139, 152, 153, 154, 157, 158
Adorno, Theodor, 31
affect, 7, 24, 25, 28, 32, 50, 53, 82, 90, 122, 127, 135–36, 138, 150, 164
affective investment and divestment. *See* affect
Afghan Whigs, 130, 134, 139
aggrieved entitlement, 8, 134. *See also* white masculinity
Ahmed, Sara, 127
Aime, Laura Ann, 39
Airborne Toxic Event, 129, 130
Alcoholics Anonymous, 37. *See also* addiction
alcoholism. *See* addiction
Allen, Karen, 100, 121
American Beauty (1999), 40
American Psycho (1991), 34
American Psycho (2000). See *American Psycho* (1991)
Anderson, Jesse, 47
Anderson, Karrin Vasby, 75, 92
"Animal House" (song), 109, 121. See also *National Lampoon's Animal House* (1979)

anti-Blackness, 27, 28, 31–32, 81, 102, 104, 117, 159, 166
anxiety, 5, 102, 119, 127, 137, 139, 144, 148, 151, 158, 163, 164, 166
Anzaldúa, Gloria, 14
archives, 11–16, 17, 19, 34, 35, 37, 65, 94, 128, 136, 142, 148, 161, 162. *See also* Bundy archive
Asen, Robert, 33
Aynesworth, Hugh, 29, 56, 119, 131, 133, 140, 144, 147, 154

Bacon, Kevin. See *National Lampoon's Animal House* (1978)
Baldwin, James, 159
Ball, Brenda Carol, 39, 101
bare life, 152
Bataille, Georges, 80–81, 83
Bateman, Patrick. See *American Psycho* (1991)
Baudrillard, Jean, 106
Baugh-Harris, Sarah, 35
Beauvoir, Simone de, 30
Beltrán, Cristina, 32
Belushi, John. See *National Lampoon's Animal House* (1978)
Bergland, Renée L., 67
Berlinger, Joe, 7, 45, 46, 48, 49, 52–53, 63–64, 119, 145, 165. *See also* *Conversations*

217

with a Killer (2019); *Extremely Wicked, Shockingly Evil, and Vile* (2019)
Berman, David, 150
Bernstein, Elizabeth, 58. *See also* feminism: carceral
Bishop, Stephen, 109
Black, Joel, 72
Black Christmas (1974), 106
Black masculinity, 47, 58, 111. *See also* anti-Blackness
Black public sphere, 79–80
Bowman, Margaret Elizabeth, 101, 112
Bowman, Michael, 18
Brady, Ian, 161
Breihan, Tom, 139
Bright, Matthew, 4–6, 55, 149, 155. *See also* *Ted Bundy* (2002)
Bright Young Women (2023), 147, 163, 164–65, 166
Brownmiller, Susan, 75
Brummett, Barry, 25
Buchanan, Pat, 72
Bundy (2008), 55, 97, 131–33, 140, 155
Bundy, Louise, 96
Bundy, Richard, 158
Bundy, Theodore Robert: childhood, 76–77, 96, 131, 155, 158; confessions, 41, 83, 114, 144–45, 157–58; duplicity and, 38–39, 40–51, 52, 53, 57–59, 62–65, 66–68, 157, 162, 163; education, 103, 115, 133, 139; execution, 36, 41–42, 56, 57, 114–20, 147, 149–50, 152–53, 157, 158, 160; family of origin, 60, 95–97, 126, 131, 141, 155; mental illness, 153–56, 158; *modus operandi*, 28–30, 40–41, 67, 79, 80, 84, 90, 99, 111, 114, 120, 130, 133–34, 144–45, 152, 153, 156, 166; political activity, 120, 139–40; pornography and, 7, 71–72, 73, 76–77, 82–83, 84, 87–88, 90–92, 97, 133, 155, 163; ubiquity of, 6, 7, 146, 147–48; victims, 39, 67, 84–85, 99, 101, 102, 134, 141–42, 163, 165–66, 169n3
Bundy archive, 5, 6–7, 11–14, 16–19, 23–24, 30, 36, 42, 46, 51, 56–58, 73, 82, 90–91, 94, 97, 102, 103, 105, 112, 118, 126, 127, 130, 131, 134, 136, 140–42, 146, 147–49, 154–55, 158, 161, 162–67. *See also* archives
Burke, Kenneth, 127

Burke, Michael Reilly, 4, 55, 149–50, 155. *See also* *Ted Bundy* (2002)
Burlington, Vermont, 96, 97
Burr, Ann Marie, 154
Burroughs, William S., 86

Caddyshack (1980), 121
Calafell, Bernadette Marie, 16–17, 19, 23, 105
Campbell, Billy, 55, 133, 149. *See also* *Stranger Beside Me, The* (2002)
Campbell, Caryn Eileen, 39, 61
capital punishment. *See* death penalty
Caputi, Jane, 9, 25–26, 72, 102–3
carcerality, 3, 47, 56–59, 160, 164
Cascade Mountains, 29, 126
celebrity, 6, 9, 51, 53–55, 67, 87, 102, 130, 148
Chandler, Karen, 112
Chávez, Karma R., 8, 95
Chebrolu, E., 5. *See also* anxiety
Chi Omega sorority, 5, 48, 49, 54, 57, 91, 101, 102, 106, 107, 112–15, 117, 119, 120, 149, 164–65. *See also* Florida State University
Chicago suburbs/Chicagoland, 13, 63, 85, 92, 126, 138, 143, 152. *See also* suburbia
Chiesi, Roberto, 82
children and childhood, 40, 85–86, 101, 106–7, 109, 112, 123, 150
"Chirpy Chirpy Cheep Cheep" (song), 160
Chomsky, Marvin J. *See* *Deliberate Stranger, The* (1986)
Christianity, 70, 72, 85, 86, 95, 96
citizenship, 95, 112, 166
Clover, Carol J. *See* Terrible Place
Cohen, Ann, 164
Collins, Lily, 52
Collins, Patricia Hill, 14
colonialism and colonization, 14, 15, 24–27, 31, 32, 67, 90, 95, 102, 104–5, 112, 159, 162
Colorado, 3, 11, 19, 39, 41, 52, 61, 87, 114, 143–44, 155
Columbine High School shooting, 143–44
Connolly, William E., 141
Conquergood, Dwight, 114, 117, 119
Conversations with a Killer (2019), 7, 46–47, 48, 49, 51, 52, 56, 57, 63–64, 71–72, 119, 131, 132, 133, 140–41, 145, 147, 152–53
Cowart, Edward, 48–49, 69, 102, 166

Cowell, Samuel, 96
Cram, Emerson, 12
Cramer, James, 114
Crazy, Not Insane (2020), 155
culture war, 20, 72, 85, 155, 163
Culver, Lynette Dawn, 39
Cunningham, Julie, 39
Curry, Tommy J. *See* Black masculinity
Curtis, Susan, 39

Dahmer, Jeffrey, 13, 21, 27, 47–48, 95, 102
DaRonch, Carol, 57
Dashboard Confessional. *See* emo
Davies, Eli, 142
Davis, Olga Idriss, 105
death penalty, 3, 36, 50, 114, 117, 147
"Debonair" (song), 134
decapitation, 30, 53, 55, 89, 99, 145. *See also* necrophilia
Deckle, Bob, 56, 57–59, 152–53
Deer, Sarah, 26, 86
Defending the Devil (1994). *See* Nelson, Polly
Deliberate Stranger, The (1986), 49, 51–52, 54, 55, 67, 84, 85, 103, 155–56
Democratic Party, 161–62
detective magazines, 88–89, 92, 133
Dobson, James, 7, 20, 71–72, 76–77, 82–83, 84, 85–86, 88, 90, 91, 94, 95, 97, 155, 163–64. *See also* pornography
double, 20, 50–51. *See also* uncanny
Downing, George. *See Massage Book, The* (1972)
Downing, Lisa, 30, 90, 104
Dread Central (website), 131–32
Du Bois, W. E. B., 159
Duggan, Lisa, 73
Dulli, Greg, 134, 135, 139, 142
Dworkin, Andrea, 75

Eagles, Bill. *See Riverman, The* (2004)
Edelman, Lee, 94–95
Edwards, Diane, 130–34, 135, 136–37, 139–42
Efron, Zac, 12, 52, 53, 55, 56, 155, 165. *See also Extremely Wicked, Shockingly Evil, and Vile* (2019)
Elizabeth Lund Home for Unwed Mothers, 96

Ellis, Brett Easton. *See American Psycho* (1991)
Elwes, Cary, 145
emo, 129–30, 134, 135, 138, 139, 142, 146
empathy, 162–63, 166
enclaves, 79–80, 94, 126
ephemera, 6, 7, 13–14, 15
Epstein, Jeffrey, 80, 81
eroticism, 20, 74–75, 76, 79, 80, 94–95, 97, 100, 136
Extremely Wicked, Shockingly Evil, and Vile (2019), 7, 45, 46, 52–55, 67, 85, 155, 165. *See also* Berlinger, Joe; Efron, Zac

Falwell, Jerry, 72
family, 44, 46, 52–53, 59–66, 80, 85, 95–97, 151–53, 154, 156–57
Fanon, Frantz, 159
Farrands, Daniel. *See Ted Bundy: American Boogeyman* (2021)
fascism, 8, 31, 82, 83, 90, 139, 142
Federal Bureau of Investigation (FBI), 29, 42, 56, 90, 92, 114, 145
Feifer, Michael. *See Bundy* (2008)
feminism, 9, 10, 13, 20, 56, 58, 72, 94, 102, 106, 162; Black, 14, 86, 166; carceral, 56, 58; decolonial, 14, 20, 26, 86; "sex wars," 72; white, 76, 103, 165–66. *See also* intersectionality; pornography
Finnegan, Cara A., 12
Florida, 3, 9, 11, 19, 39, 41, 49, 57, 60, 62, 77, 84, 87, 110, 114–15, 119–20, 149
Florida State Prison, 114–15, 117, 118, 119, 147
Florida State University, 5, 48, 106, 112–13, 115, 164–65; Seminoles, 115
Focus on the Family. *See* Dobson, James
forensics (speech and debate), 100, 125
form, rhetorical, 17, 24, 27, 73, 74–75, 76, 101, 130, 136, 146, 161. *See also* pornography; rhetorical criticism; sadistic form
Forter, Greg, 111
Freud, Sigmund, 37, 50. *See also* uncanny
Fuentes, Nick, 135
Fugazi. *See* emo
fugitive planning, 104. *See also* university
fungibility, 6, 21, 24, 26, 31, 32, 59, 75, 80, 81, 90, 92, 103, 127, 133–34, 136, 139, 146, 153, 157, 161, 163, 165, 166–67

Furst, Stephen. See *National Lampoon's Animal House* (1978)
futurity, 20, 32, 54, 64–65, 85, 87–88, 94–95, 101, 102, 103, 105, 114, 115, 166

Gacy, John Wayne, 13, 95
Gainesville, Florida. *See* Florida
Gardner, Lyn, 160
gaze, 99–100, 109, 111–12, 120–21, 133, 157, 161, 163–64, 166
Gehrke, Pat J., 55–56
Gein, Ed, 10
Gekko, Gordon. See *Wall Street* (1987)
gendered violence, 5, 6, 9, 18–19, 23, 25, 26, 42, 48, 58–59, 68, 75–76, 81–82, 95, 101, 103–5, 106–8, 118, 122–23, 162, 163–64
Gendron, Bob, 134
genealogy, 7, 14, 28, 166
Genet, Jean, 92
genre, rhetorical, 23, 130, 166. *See also* form, rhetorical
Gentlemen (1993), 134
Ginsberg, Allen, 86, 138, 143
Girard, René, 83
Giles, Dennis, 75
Gordon, Avery, 50. *See also* uncanny
Grant, Cary, 49
Grease (1978), 120
Greenwood, Bruce, 145
Griffin, Rachel Alicia, 86, 104
Grizzard, George. See *Deliberate Stranger, The* (1986)
Gunn, Joshua, 8, 74, 82, 111

Hagmaier, Bill, 29, 30, 56, 57–59, 71–72, 145, 146, 150, 157–58
Hall, Ashley R., 166
Harmon, Mark, 49, 51–52, 54, 55, 56, 84, 103, 155. See also *Deliberate Stranger, The* (1986)
Harney, Stefano, 104
Harris, Kamala, 161
Harris, Thomas, 104
Hartman, Saidiya V., 13–14, 28, 81, 166
Hawkins, Georgeann, 39, 102, 119, 145, 159, 165
Healy, Lynda Ann, 39, 101
Hershey, Barbara, 97

Hickman, William Edward, 33
higher education. *See* university
Hitler, Adolf, 55–56, 88
Holcomb, Sarah, 112, 121–22
Holt, Sandi, 131
homology, 5, 17, 25, 32, 34, 68, 117, 118, 121, 146, 152, 157, 163, 165. *See also* form, rhetorical
homosociality, 79
hooks, bell, 152, 166
Hopper, Jessica, 130
Horkheimer, Max, 31
House That Jack Built, The (2018), 184n31
Hsu, V. Jo, 14, 15
Hulce, Tom. See *National Lampoon's Animal House* (1978)

Ice Storm (1997), 40
Illinois, 125–26, 134, 135, 143
incels, 21, 23, 128–29, 132
incest, 96, 155
Infinite Jest (1996), 150
Indiana Jones and the Raiders of the Lost Arc (1981), 100
Ingebretsen, Edward J., 23
intersectionality, 102
Interview (magazine), 87
Isla Vista, California, 128

Jacobellis v. Ohio (1964), 74. *See also* pornography
Jekyll and Hyde. See *Strange Case of Dr. Jekyll and Mr. Hyde, The* (1886)
Jenkins, Philip, 9
Jimmy Eat World, 129. *See also* emo
Johnson, Andre E., 35
Johnson, Paul Elliot, 8, 32, 34
Joker (2019), 7
Jollet, Mikel, 129, 142. *See also* Airborne Toxic Event
Joy of Sex, The (1972), 87

Kaufman, Andy, 93
Kelly, Casey Ryan, 8, 28, 33, 82, 136, 142
Kemper, Edmund, 27, 47–48, 89–90
Kendall, Elizabeth "Liz," 7–8, 14, 44–46, 52, 53, 54, 59, 62, 63, 77, 97, 147, 154, 156, 158, 163, 165

Kendall, Molly, 44–46, 52, 53, 68, 69, 156, 158, 163
Kennedy, John F., 49, 51
Kenney, Douglas, 107
Kent, Debra Jean, 39
Keppel, Bob, 56, 145–46, 154
Kerouac, Jack, 138
Kimmel, Michael, 8
King, Claire Sisco, 6, 47, 111, 148. See also abject hegemony; celebrity
King, Emily L., 139
Kipnis, Laura, 72, 74, 94
Kirby, Luke, 150. See also *No Man of God* (2021)
Kleiner, Kathy. See Rubin, Kathy Kleiner
Knoll, Jessica. See *Bright Young Women* (2023)
Kubrick, Stanley, 86
Kynard, Carmen, 105

Lacan, Jacques, 111, 188n53
Lake Sammamish State Park, 5, 159, 165
Landis, John. See *National Lampoon's Animal House* (1978)
Larsen, Richard. See *Deliberate Stranger, The* (1986)
Larson, Stephanie R., 72, 85
Leach, Kimberly Dianne, 14, 39, 42, 57, 77, 84–86, 88, 95, 101, 108, 114, 165
Lee, Spike. See *Malcolm X* (1992)
Leon County, Florida. See Florida
Leonoff, Arthur, 25
Lesser, Wendy, 48
Levina, Marina, 32
Levinas, Emmanuel, 153
Levy, Lisa, 101, 112
Lewis, Dorothy Otnow, 155
Lewis, Sophie. See family
libertine, 30, 31, 81, 83, 125
Life (magazine), 88, 106–7
Lin, Jun. See *1 Lunatic, 1 Ice Pick* (video)
Little, Samuel, 27, 102
Littleton, Colorado, 143–44
Lockwood, Dean, 76
Lorde, Audre, 14, 20, 74, 76, 94, 103
Lugones, María, 26, 81, 103
Lynch, David, 40, 134
lynching, 47, 50, 58, 89, 117, 118

Mack, Ashley Noel, 86, 104–5, 108–9, 122
MacPherson, Myra, 96, 97, 131, 141
Magnotta, Luka. See *1 Lunatic, 1 Ice Pick* (video)
Mailer, Norman, 74
"Make America Great Again," 9. See also Trump, Donald J.
Malcolm X (1992), 3–4
Manson, Donna Gail, 39
Maraj, Louis M., 19
Mardorossian, Carine M., 26, 81–82
Marshall, Sarah, 144, 153–54, 156, 157, 158
Martin, Edna Cowell, 41, 42
masculinity, 3, 9, 24–26, 33, 34, 41, 45, 48, 50, 51, 55–59, 66, 85, 86, 94, 99, 100, 104, 109–11, 119, 128, 130, 134, 150–52, 154, 162–67. See also Black masculinity; white masculinity
Massage Book, The (1972), 87
masturbation, 5, 29, 79, 86–87, 90–92, 119, 145, 152
Matheson, Calum Lister, 25, 30, 32, 35, 162
Matheson, Tim. See *National Lampoon's Animal House* (1978)
Mbembe, Achille, 26–27
McChesney, Kathleen, 56
McClearen, Jennifer, 33
McGee, Michael Calvin, 10, 15, 16
McGill, Bruce. See *National Lampoon's Animal House* (1978)
Meese Commission, 71, 72, 85. See also pornography
memoir (as method), 7, 16–19
men's adventure magazines. See detective magazines
#MeToo, 8, 104
Michaud, Stephen G., 29, 46–47, 48, 49, 56, 77, 96, 131, 132, 133, 140, 144, 147, 154
Miami Herald (newspaper), 115
Miéville, China, 34
Mignolo, Walter, 24
Miller, Chanel, 104
Miller, Chris, 107, 122
misogyny, 9, 10, 19, 23, 26, 72, 75–76, 83, 85, 96, 103, 127, 128, 135, 138, 142, 146, 148, 155, 157, 165
modernity, 5, 7, 8, 11, 13–15, 17–18, 19, 23–27, 28, 30–32, 35–36, 56, 68, 73, 81–82, 84, 95,

104–5, 109, 119, 120, 144, 145, 148, 149, 153, 154, 159, 161, 163, 164, 166–67
monsters and monstrosity, 18–19, 23–24, 27, 31, 35–36, 39, 40–42, 44–48, 49, 51–52, 55, 59, 62–63, 64–65, 66–69, 73, 81, 83–84, 90, 97, 115, 118–19, 120, 123, 127, 131, 133, 135, 139, 142, 145–46, 154, 156, 157, 158, 159, 166
Moore, Thomas, 24
Moraga, Cherríe, 14
Moreton-Robinson, Aileen, 26, 58
Mormon Church, 59
Morris, Charles E., III, 11, 35
Moten, Fred, 104
Mr. Skin (website), 122
Mulvey, Lauren, 99–100, 128
Muñoz, José Esteban, 13, 95
Murray, Chad Michael, 55. See also *Ted Bundy: American Boogeyman* (2021)
My Chemical Romance, 129, 130. See also emo

Na'puti, Tiara R., 86
Nash, Jennifer C., 76
Naslund, Denise Marie, 5, 39, 159
National Lampoon (magazine), 107
National Lampoon's Animal House (1978), 100, 106, 107–12, 119, 120–22
necrophilia, 4, 30, 48, 53, 55, 63, 64, 89, 90, 92, 99, 110, 122, 131, 144–46, 158, 160
Nelson, Maggie, 30
Nelson, Polly, 41, 42, 56, 83, 91–92, 155, 158
Nemec, Corin, 55, 132. See also *Bundy* (2008)
neoliberalism, 33–34, 81, 90, 120
New York Post (newspaper), 122
Newitz, Analee, 32
Newsweek (magazine), 115, 117
Nietzsche, Frederick, 33, 81, 92
Nikolaisen, Jen, 132
Nilsen, Dennis, 161
Nine Inch Nails, 130, 138–39, 144
No Man of God (2021), 8, 56, 57, 85, 150, 157–58, 163–64, 165, 166
nostalgia, 107, 119, 120

Ochieng, Omedi, 12
Oliverson, Denise Lynn, 39
Olson, Carl, 83

On Murder Considered as One of the Fine Arts (1827), 104
onanism. *See* masturbation
1 Lunatic, 1 Ice Pick (video), 160
Ore, Ersula J., 89
Ott, Janice Ann, 5, 39, 159
Our Bodies, Our Selves (1970), 87

Pacific Northwest, 3, 19, 39, 41, 52, 83, 96, 114, 126
pain, 25, 66, 90–91, 118, 125, 126, 129, 134–36, 139, 142–43, 150–51, 153
Palczewski, Catherine Helen, 73–74
Parfrey, Adam, 88
Parker, Marion. *See* Hickman, William Edward
Parks, Roberta Kathleen, 39, 101
parody, 104, 110, 115, 128
Pasolini, Pierre. *See Saló, or the 120 Days of Sodom* (1975)
Peace, David, 80
pedophilia, 80, 81, 87–88, 92–93. *See also* children and childhood
Pence, Mike, 77
People (magazine), 51
Peterson, Jordan, 135
Phantom Prince, The (2020). *See* Kendall, Elizabeth "Liz"
Phelan, Peggy, 13
Philadelphia, Pennsylvania, 96
Phillips, Kendall, 67
Pierce, Butch, 115
Pizzolatto, Nic, 80
PornHub, 81, 87, 93
pornification, 75
pornography, 7, 71, 77–79, 82–83, 86–87, 90, 151, 164; culture war and, 7, 71–72, 85, 94, 95, 155; definitional politics, 73–74, 75–76; desire and, 74, 75; feminism and, 72, 75, 76; as rhetorical form, 72–76, 79, 85–86, 92–93, 99, 122
pornotroping, 81. *See also* anti-Blackness
Pretty Hate Machine (1989), 138–39
psychoanalysis, 166
Puar, Jasbir K., 94–95
public, 177n55
Pulp Magazine (magazine), 132

queerness, 13, 72, 76, 82, 86, 93–95, 97, 102, 162
Quincey, Thomas de, 104

Ramirez, Richard, 21
Ramis, Harold, 107
Rancourt, Susan Elaine, 39
Rand, Ayn, 33
Rand, Erin J., 86
Rankin, John, 166
rape, 4, 7, 10, 26, 53, 57, 58, 72–73, 75, 80, 85, 86, 88–89, 94, 95, 103, 108–9, 120, 122, 128, 144, 146; on campus, 12, 100, 104–5, 106–7, 109–10
Reagan, Ronald Wilson, 33, 71, 72, 85, 120, 121. *See also* neoliberalism
Red Riding novels, 80
Reeves, Bob, 115
reflexive sadomasochism, 134
Republican Party, 49, 72, 120, 139, 140, 162
Reznor, Trent, 139, 142. *See also* Nine Inch Nails
rhetorical criticism and studies, 10–11, 15, 16, 18, 24, 25, 35, 55–56, 73–76, 86, 100, 105, 162; personal artifacts and, 18
rhetorical ecologies, 12, 17, 148
rhetorical formations, 12, 96, 161
Rice, Jenny, 12
Ridgway, Gary, 47–48, 102, 146
Riegert, Peter. See *National Lampoon's Animal House* (1978)
Rites of Spring, 129. *See also* emo
ritual, 25, 27–30, 44, 65, 66, 79, 83, 86, 89–90, 91, 101, 109, 114, 117–18, 122, 127, 145, 146, 149, 161
Riverman, The (2004), 145–46
Riverman, The (2005). *See* Keppel, Bob
Robertson, Pat, 72
Robinson, Brett A. B., 9
Rodger, Elliot, 128–29, 132, 134–35, 136, 138, 139, 142. *See also* incels
Roediger, David, 159
Rolling Stone (magazine), 131
Rosenfield, Lawrence W., 72, 74
Rubin, Kathy Kleiner, 56–57, 67, 102, 112, 117, 145, 147, 150, 163, 165
Rule, Ann, 41, 42, 46, 55, 56, 57, 63, 97, 102, 103, 117, 119, 130, 133, 140, 141, 154, 156, 165
Ryalls, Emily, 129, 130, 134

Sade, Marquis de, 24, 30–31, 32, 83, 92. *See also* sadism; sadistic form
sadism, 6, 7, 8–10, 11, 16, 18, 20, 21, 24–28, 30–36, 40–41, 42, 44, 46, 48, 51–53, 58–59, 65, 67, 68, 71, 72–73, 76, 80, 82–84, 85, 87–88, 89–90, 92–93, 95, 97, 101, 102, 104, 112, 117, 123, 126, 127, 129, 130, 148, 157, 158, 159, 161, 162–63, 166–67; as different from cruelty, 25. *See also* Sade, Marquis de; sadistic form
sadistic form, 24–27, 28, 31, 32–33, 52, 59, 73, 75, 92, 130, 136, 145, 159, 161, 162–63, 166
Saló, or the 120 Days of Sodom (1975), 31, 82, 83
Salt Lake City, Utah. *See* Utah
San Francisco, California, 133, 140
Sartre, Jean-Paul, 92
scapegoating, 40, 127, 141–42, 156–57
Schaefer, Donovan O., 127
Schmid, David, 9, 118, 148
Scorsese, Martin, 86
Sealey, Amber, 8, 57, 150, 157, 158, 163–64, 165, 166. *See also No Man of God* (2021)
Seattle, Washington. *See* Washington
Segarra, Ignacio Moreno, 75
Seltzer, Mark, 9, 48
September 11, 2001 attacks, 9, 106
serial killers and murder, 3, 4, 27–28, 30, 33, 80, 103, 166–67; definition of, 10–11; gender and, 25–27, 31, 39, 47–48, 58, 81, 88, 90, 95; genius and creativity and, 10, 103–4; in public culture, 6, 8–10, 32, 50–51, 67, 148; rhetoric and, 10–11
sexual violence. *See* rape
shame, 38, 75, 79, 96–97, 103, 125–34, 135–37, 139–40, 141, 143, 144, 146, 150, 157
Shattuck, Roger, 83–84
Shaye, Lin, 96
Silva, Kumarini, 32
Simpson, Philip L., 28, 51
Singh, Julietta, 104
slasher films, 39, 106
slavery, 13, 14, 15, 24, 27, 28, 31, 58, 90, 104, 112, 166. *See also* anti-Blackness
Smith, Melissa Anne, 39
Smith, Susan, 47
Snowmass Village, Colorado. *See* Colorado

Solondz, Todd, 40
"Something I Can Never Have" (song), 138–39
"Sometime Around Midnight" (song), 129
Sontag, Susan, 118
Sotos, Peter, 92–93
sovereignty, 26–27, 30, 31, 34–35, 75, 80, 82, 86, 89–90, 112, 117, 126, 142, 144, 153
Speck, Richard, 10
Spillers, Hortense, 81, 86
Squires, Catherine, 79–80
Steffensmeier, Timothy R., 118
Stevenson, Robert Louis. See *Strange Case of Dr. Jekyll and Mr. Hyde, The* (1886)
Stewart, Potter. See *Jacobellis v. Ohio* (1964)
Stone, Oliver. See *Wall Street* (1987)
Strange Case of Dr. Jekyll and Mr. Hyde, The (1886), 37, 46, 49, 55, 68–69, 77
Stranger Beside Me, The (2002), 55, 56, 67, 97, 133, 141, 149
Stranger Beside Me, The (2009). See Rule, Ann
Stratton, Jon, 9
Stuart, Charles, 47
Subirats, Eduardo, 27, 31. See also sadism
suburbia, 40, 44, 64, 126
suicide, 128, 150–51, 154
Sulkowitz, Emma, 104
Sullivan, Kevin M., 91, 131
Superman (1978), 120
Sutcliffe, Peter, 161
Sutherland, Donald, 100
Szpunar, Piotr. See double

tailgates, 65, 115, 118, 119
Tallahassee, Florida, 101, 112, 114–15, 120, 159. See also Florida
Tallahassee Democrat (newspaper), 112–14, 115
Tatar, Maria, 90
Tate, Andrew, 135
Taylor, Diana, 13, 17
Ted Bundy (2002), 3–5, 6, 7, 55, 85, 148, 149–50, 155
Ted Bundy: American Boogeyman (2021), 8, 42, 55, 56, 90–91, 96

Ted Bundy: Falling for a Killer (2020), 8, 44, 45, 56, 68, 102, 147, 158, 163, 165
Ted Bundy: Natural Porn Killer (2006), 77, 96
Ted Bundy Project, The (2014), 159–61
Telfer, Tara, 131
Terrible Place, 39–41, 46, 64, 80, 126
Thatcher, Margaret, 33. See neoliberalism
Theweleit, Klaus, 26, 34–35
Thomas, Cheryl, 112
Thompson, Deanna, 114
Thorsen, Karen, 106
Tithecott, Richard, 67
toga party, 108, 110. See also *National Lampoon's Animal House* (1978)
Tomkins, Silvan, 136
torture, 31, 76, 80, 83, 88, 145, 160. See also sadism
True Detective (2014), 80
Trump, Donald J., 8–9, 23, 161
Tucciarone, Krista M., 110
Turner, Kathleen, 125
twelve-step recovery, 14, 37, 125. See also addiction; Alcoholics Anonymous
2024 US Presidential Election, 161–62

uncanny, 35, 36, 49, 50, 51, 53, 58, 65, 67–68
university, 101–2, 104, 108, 115; and gender, 85, 100–101, 102–5, 106–7, 108–9, 111, 120–21, 122–23; and sexual violence, 99–100, 104–5, 109–10, 112, 119, 120, 122–23; in US cinema, 100, 106
University of California, Santa Barbara, 128
University of Florida, 115, 120
University of Pittsburgh, 100
University of Utah, 59, 103
University of Washington, 14, 101, 103, 130, 132
Utah, 3, 11, 19, 29, 39, 41, 42, 46, 52, 57, 114, 158

Valencia, Sayak, 81
Van Sant, Gus, 86
VanHaitsma, Pamela, 94
Vanity Fair (magazine), 96, 141
vengeance, 127, 128, 130, 134, 135, 139, 140–42, 143, 144, 146, 150
victimhood, 105, 134, 164, 166

Vietnam War, 120
von Trier, Lars, 104, 184n31
voyeurism, 41, 91–92, 128, 129, 130, 133
Vronsky, Peter, 88–89

Wall Street (1987), 34
Wallace, David Foster, 138, 150
Walz, Tim, 161–62
Wanzer-Serrano, Darrel, 35
Ward, Jane, 76, 79, 92, 95
Washington, 5, 11, 44, 46, 49, 59, 101, 139, 140, 158
Washington, DC, 129
Watergate scandal, 120
Weheliye, Alexander G., 81, 86
"welfare queens," 121
West, Fred, 161
Whippman, Ruth, 162
white masculinity, 4–9, 12, 15, 17, 18–19, 28, 39, 45, 47–49, 51, 52, 55–58, 61, 65–68, 73, 95, 97, 120, 126, 127, 128, 130, 132, 134, 136, 138, 142, 144, 145, 148, 153, 154, 155, 157, 159, 161–62, 163, 165, 166; possession and, 9, 14, 16, 26–27, 34–35, 81–82, 89–90, 104, 112, 138, 164, 165, 166; violation of norms and, 8, 80–82, 83; and violence, 23, 27
whiteness, 4, 18, 32, 33, 48, 64, 101–2, 103, 118, 120, 159, 165. *See also* white masculinity
Wilcox, Nancy, 39
Wilderson, Frank B., III, 27, 31, 35
Wildfire, Jessica, 132
Williams, Linda, 76, 94
Wohead, Greg. See *Ted Bundy Project, The* (2014)
Wood, Elijah, 150
Wood, Trish, 163, 165. See also *Ted Bundy: Falling for a Killer* (2020)
World War II, 88–89
Wuornos, Aileen, 9, 10

X, Malcolm, 4, 167

ABOUT THE AUTHOR

Bryan J. McCann lives in Baton Rouge, Louisiana, and is faculty in the Department of Communication Studies at Louisiana State University. His published work has appeared in journals such as *Communication and Critical/Cultural Studies*; *Quarterly Journal of Speech*; *Rhetoric and Public Affairs*; and *Women's Studies in Communication*. He is also author of the book *The Mark of Criminality: Rhetoric, Race, and Gangsta Rap in the War-on-Crime Era* (University of Alabama Press, 2017).

www.ingramcontent.com/pod-product-compliance
Lightning Source LLC
Chambersburg PA
CBHW030106170426
43198CB00009B/517